SWORDS INTO
MARKET SHARES

ALSO BY GLENN E. SCHWEITZER

Experiments in Cooperation:
Assessing U.S.-Russian Programs in Science and Technology

Moscow DMZ: The Story of the International Effort to Convert
Russian Weapons Science to Peaceful Purposes

Superterrorism:
Assassins, Mobsters, and Weapons of Mass Destruction

Techno-Diplomacy:
U.S.-Soviet Confrontations in Science and Technology

Borrowed Earth, Borrowed Time:
Healing America's Chemical Wounds

SWORDS INTO MARKET SHARES

Technology, Economics, and Security in the New Russia

Glenn E. Schweitzer

JOSEPH HENRY PRESS
Washington, D.C.

Joseph Henry Press • 2101 Constitution Avenue, N.W.• Washington, D.C. 20418

The Joseph Henry Press, an imprint of the National Academy of Press, was created with the goal of making books on science, technology, and health more widely available to professionals and the public. Joseph Henry was one of the founders of the National Academy of Sciences and a leader of early American science.

Any opinions, findings, conclusions, or recommendations expressed in this volume are those of the author and do not necessarily reflect the views of the National Academy of Sciences or its affiliated institutions.

Library of Congress Cataloging-in-Publication Data

Schweitzer, Glenn E., 1930-
     Swords into market shares : technology, economics, and security in
the new Russia / by Glenn E. Schweitzer.
          p. cm.
Includes bibliographical references and index.
     ISBN 0-309-06841-X (casebound)
     1. Technological innovations—Economic aspects—Russia (Federation)
2. Capitalism—Russia (Federation) 3. Technology and state—Russia
(Federation) 4. Russia (Federation)—Economic policy—1991- 5. Russia
(Federation)—Economic conditions—1991- I. Title.
     HC340.12.Z9 T478 2000
     338'.064'0947—dc21
                              00-009622

Printed in the United States in America

Contents

ACKNOWLEDGMENTS   ix

PROLOGUE   xi

1   DISMAL ECONOMICS HOLDS BACK
     TECHNOLOGICAL INNOVATION   1
     Implosion of the Economy, 5
     The Economy and Innovation, 9
     Barter Replaces Cash Transactions, 12
     Role of Small Business, 15
     Technology at the Regional Level, 17
     The Long and Uncertain Road to Prosperity, 25
     Notes, 29

2   STRUGGLING TO EMBRACE MODERN
     TECHNOLOGIES   33
     Living with the Soviet Legacy, 37
     Russian Enterprises and Innovation, 41
     Preferential Treatment for Oversized Scientific Centers, 45
     Innovation at the Micro-Level, 48
     New Ways to Turn a Profit, 51

The Future Outlook, 55
Notes, 57

3   PROFITING FROM INVESTMENTS IN
     MILITARY TECHNOLOGY   61
     Declining Market Niche for Russian Armaments, 64
     The Dual-Use Issue, 70
     Realities of Industrial Conversion, 74
     Controlling Leakage of Sensitive Items, 79
     Whither Russian Military Technologies?, 82
     Notes, 84

4   THE MONEY TRAIL: FINDERS KEEPERS   87
     Sources of Finance, 91
     Protecting Income Streams Flowing from the West, 95
     Roofs for Businesses in Russia, 99
     Privatization and the Enterprise Managers, 101
     Bankers and the Flow of Money, 104
     Multiple Challenges, 110
     Notes, 111

5   LONG-TERM PATENT PROTECTION AND
     SHORT-TERM TAX RELIEF   113
     Patents, Copyrights, and Hope for Brighter Days, 117
     International Sharing of Intellectual Property Rights, 123
     The Tax Man Cometh, 126
     Taxation and Technical Assistance from Abroad, 131
     Other Hurdles in Carrying Out International Programs, 133
     A Legal Environment to Facilitate Innovation, 135
     Notes, 136

6   REDIRECTION AND EROSION OF RUSSIAN
     BRAINPOWER   140
     New Income Streams for 60,000 Weaponeers, 144
     Growing Pressure on Weaponeers, 147
     An Aging Manpower Base for Space Exploration, 151

Widespread Decline of the Research and
    Development Workforce, 153
External Brain Drain, 154
Role of Russian Technical Universities, 159
Future of the Russian Manpower Base, 165
Notes, 166

7   SIXTY-FIVE SCIENCE CITIES WITH
     THREE MILLION PEOPLE   169
     Innovating for Profit in Siberia, 172
     Science Cities Encircling Moscow, 176
     Ten Nuclear Cities, 186
     Cities that Supported Biological Defense Activities, 189
     Future of the Science Cities, 191
     Notes, 193

8   THREE NUCLEAR CITIES WITH AN
     ABUNDANCE OF TECHNOLOGIES   195
     An Experimental Science City under Market Conditions:
         Obninsk, 197
     Astride the Transiberian Railway: Zarechny, 205
     Diversification of Research in the Southern Urals:
         Snezhinsk, 211
     Outlook for the Three Cities, 219
     Notes, 220

9   U.S. EFFORTS TO CONTAIN DANGEROUS
     TECHNOLOGIES WHILE PROMOTING
     FOREIGN INVESTMENTS   223
     DOE's Support of Technology Commercialization, 227
     DOD's Programs to Redirect Russian Technologies, 232
     The International Space Station and the
         Aerospace Complex, 234
     Promoting Interests of U.S. Companies, 236
     Whither Cooperation?, 242
     Notes, 245

10　THE REVIVAL OF RUSSIAN TECHNOLOGY　　　249
　　Political and Economic Challenges, 254
　　Implementing a Realistic Technology Policy, 258
　　Showstoppers: Increasing Corruption and
　　　　Declining Health, 264
　　Disproving the Hypotheses, 267
　　Notes, 270

EPILOGUE　　　　　　　　　　　　　　　　272

APPENDIXES

A　Characterization and Sources of Russian
　　Research and Development　　　　　　　277

B　Scientific Organizations with the Status of State
　　Scientific Centers of the Russian Federation　　279

C　Science Cities of Russia　　　　　　　　283

D　Commercialized Technologies at Russian Institutions　　286

E　Technology-Intensive Projects of Priority Interest to the
　　Russian Ministry of Foreign Affairs　　　288

F　Next Steps to the Market Program of the U.S.
　　Civilian Research and Development Foundation　　290

INDEX　　　　　　　　　　　　　　　　293

Acknowledgments

Most of the factual information and many of the ideas presented in this book were provided by Russian colleagues too numerous to name. Leaders of the Russian Academy of Sciences and officials of the Ministry of Atomic Energy and the Ministry of Science and Technology have been particularly patient in responding to my inquiries over many years. Managers of Russian and international science and technology programs, directors of Russian enterprises and institutes, and entrepreneurs of all stripes have almost always been willing to provide insights about the practical problems they are confronting during a difficult period of political and economic transition. And Russian and American analysts have generously shared their data and findings with me.

A research and writing grant from The John D. and Catherine T. MacArthur Foundation provided the financial resources that allowed me to explore activities in depth in several atomic cities, and the Villa Serbelloni of the Rockefeller Foundation provided an ideal setting in Bellagio, Italy, for interactions with Russian and American colleagues interested in technological innovation.

Sandra Hackman was indispensable in turning a tortured text into a document with sign posts that should help the reader follow logical pathways to end points. Chris Findlay provided an important final checkpoint in ensuring that the rules of composition and grammar were not forgotten. Through it all, my friend and wife, Carole Schweitzer, offered words of encouragement and, when needed, pitched in with her magic pencil to put the final touches on the manuscript.

Prologue

Every business participates in technological change as an originator, user, or victim of technological invention and innovation.

U.S. National Academy of Engineering, 1992

"We are very careful in selecting advanced technologies that we support since unlike other Russian entrepreneurs, we are using our own money. And we do not have much money."[1]

With these introductory words, a group of four Russian physicists sitting in their dusty penthouse office atop one of the towers of Moscow State University related to me in 1998 their experiences in mobilizing Russian scientific talent to develop new high-tech products. They were convinced that the care they exercised in shepherding Russian inventions along uncertain paths could lead to viable commodities in western markets that would bring them handsome returns. New automobiles, three-room apartments, and even a jointly-owned dacha would finally be within their reach.

The group had spent five years as technology hunters. Such entrepreneurs exact a price from western firms for putting foreign specialists in touch with hidden Russian scientific talent. But this Russian "gang of four" had tired of working in three-month spurts as short-term agents for western firms only to be relegated to driving gypsy taxicabs until the next contracts materialized. They had shifted course.

The four physicists now concentrated on obtaining legal ownership of promising technical ideas that originated in Russia and on transforming those ideas into commercial successes. They began with a market analysis to identify promising products that could be based on

Russian technologies, to identify western companies that might incorporate the technologies into products, and to figure out ways to reach these companies. When they satisfied themselves that a technology would have a reasonable chance of finding a paying customer, they made sure it had no existing intellectual property claims. Then they organized a group of Russian scientists to perfect it. Since the four provided financing for the work, with the researchers contributing their time and energy, they insisted that the researchers terminate their ties to previous employers so that any breakthrough would be the intellectual property of the four physicists.

Their scheme called for early patent protection within Russia for each technical innovation. Patent filings in other countries might eventually follow. In the interim, the filing for a Russian patent would provide worldwide protection for 22 months, according to their interpretation of recent international conventions.

The goal was to enter into licensing arrangements with western firms which would incorporate the innovations into salable products, with paybacks to the physicists—and cuts for the researchers—for up to 15 years. Techniques for manufacturing a new medical probe for diagnosing chemical changes in the body was their initial breakthrough. They were confident other technologies in the pipeline would also lead to financial bonanzas—sufficient to eliminate their need for second jobs.

Since every expenditure meant dipping into their own pockets, a rare practice in Russia, the physicists had adopted several important operating principles. They handled all overhead operations themselves. No need for an accountant when they could learn how to set up the books, pay taxes and social fund contributions, and generally keep bill collectors at bay. No need for a patent specialist when they could read the patent laws and regulations and figure out the twists and turns in this uncertain terrain. No need for personal security guards to fend off the mafia, at least for the time being, since they would be operating on deferred income. Cash would materialize only in future years when crime and corruption would, they reasoned, be less of a concern. And, as has been noted, no wasting time with technologies which enterprises, institutes, or individual inventors could later lay claim to. With this orientation, they spent most of their energy making contacts with western businessmen, since marketing efforts were the key to success. But they protected all technology secrets until a deal was in hand.

The four readily acknowledged that there were only a limited number of unencumbered technologies in Russia simply waiting to be linked to western customers. Few existing technologies are free of claims of ownership by some Russian entity or individual. Even fewer are ready for market.

However, they quickly pointed to the extensive brain power in Russia to develop new, marketable technologies. Whether developing new types of coatings to protect metal products from corrosion or inventing acoustic devices for finding defects in construction material, the talent is there. An essential step is to provide the physical facilities for teams of Russians to shape items that will be of high enough quality and low enough prices to attract buyers. When given a sense of direction toward the marketplace, Russian scientists can produce new items in record time at bargain costs. So argued the physicists.

I sought their views on the future of the large Russian enterprises that had given birth to the world's most powerful rockets, largest nuclear arsenal, and most far-flung airline system. They still produce cars, refrigerators, and television sets; and the trains run on time, I noted. But the technology gurus argued that these oversized facilities had already lost the race.

They pointed to the ever increasing array of imported products. Aeroflot purchases Boeing and not Tupelov airplanes. Russian banks and hotels hire Turkish construction companies that outperform Russian firms. Russian electronics enterprises and institutes hardly participated in the introduction of computers into the economy. Less than 5 percent of the computers used in Russia are even assembled in the country. In short, the physicists added, the technological achievements that had been the basis for the modern Soviet state were quickly forgotten when customers learned they could obtain more suitable products from abroad.

Then I asked the crucial question of the four entrepreneurs: During the next few years will technological innovation in Russia have a discernible impact on the overall economy? "No," was the reply. They were convinced that they themselves would have a few successes and that other small-scale entrepreneurs would also find customers for new products. They agreed that several large enterprises probably would succeed in building modules for the International Space Station and that two or three Russian oil companies would provide support for the geophysics community to help assess potential production fields.

But they contended that in the larger scheme of a Russian economy in turmoil and political governance in disarray, new Russian technologies will have limited impact on the future of the country. The four physicists would simply figure out ways to make comfortable livings for themselves within a broken economic system without abandoning their passion for scientific discovery; but they did not expect to participate in a technological transformation of Russia.

Few Russians are as bold and confident as these physicists in searching for new ways to continue their scientific careers amidst a crumbled industrial base and prolonged inflation. The economic model taken from western textbooks in the early 1990s didn't work, and a new model is now being born. Will the new model lead to an efficient and equitable economy? Will it provide a framework for nurturing technology that can help Russia reclaim its position as a leading industrial nation? These questions are of key concern to both friends and adversaries of Russia.

Searching for a Russian Economic Model

Most analysts within Russia and in the West agree that such a model—efficient, equitable, market-driven, and technology-friendly—should be the goal for Russia. But there is great uncertainty as to the exact shape of the economic model that should emerge in one or two decades as well as to the near-term steps needed to move toward the still-to-be-defined model. Some argue that the best course in the foreseeable future is for Russia to rely on its exports of oil, gas, minerals, and timber while continuing to import manufactured items. Others contend that only foreign investments will save the day. Still others suggest that Russia unilaterally disarm, thus freeing up resources for economic development. Russian officials obviously reject such subservience to the West.

The purpose of this book is to explore other opportunities for technology-driven progress toward a viable market economy that might be pursued during the next decade. Modern technologies must play a stronger role than at present if Russian products are to move onto the global stage or even compete successfully with imported items. Strategies for expanding technological capabilities so Russia can add value to natural resources prior to export and can reduce reliance on imports are possible approaches. At the same time, some technologies must also be contained within Russia lest their military potential fall into the hands of parties with malevolent intentions.

The next decade of transition will undoubtedly be characterized by advances and retreats toward western concepts of a market economy. As to the technology dimension of the economic model, Russia must work out for itself policies that will strengthen the research and development infrastructure of the country and will encourage innovating for profit. In this effort, western experience can help avoid mistakes.

The United States has a strong vested interest in continuing to be actively engaged in Russia's economic transition process. We have seen that science and technology channels can be among the most informative and influential routes of engagement. Sustained financing of cooperative programs in science and technology that encourage more effective use of Russian technological capabilities on civilian problems deserves high priority, however distasteful Russian actions in Chechnya or elsewhere might be. The alternative is to sit on the sidelines worrying about a possible coup, the next nuclear accident, or the appearance of Russian missile technology in distant lands.

Neither Russia nor the West should allow the pessimism of the four physicists to become an accurate prediction of the importance of technological development for Russia. They are correct, of course, if policies to support an updating of the nation's industrial base are not adopted. In that case, few Russian firms stand a chance of having a major impact on the economy. Deprivation could continue to deepen, leading to greater internal turmoil and perhaps violence in the streets.

The outlook for the rest of the world could be foreboding, as a hungry bear with only a weapons arsenal to barter for honey and other sustenance searches for markets in countries on our blacklist. However, even in the most difficult times innovating for profit has been possible; and throughout this book I encourage steps that will facilitate the expansion and replication of proven innovation efforts.

Many Dimensions of Innovation

To help understand the technology dimensions of an economic model that will work in Russia, this book draws heavily on over 200 visits to Russian institutes and enterprises, presentations by Russian and foreign experts at several dozen conferences and workshops throughout Russia, and private discussions with many Russian colleagues within and outside government. These observations and interactions began in 1985, and their frequency increased in the 1990s. Also, I have relied on the writings of dozens of other western and Russian analysts to help fill in the knowledge gaps as I studied the frustrations and aspirations of the Russian science and technology community and sought to understand complex policy considerations of government officials and the more pragmatic concerns of the Russian people.

Walking through both lighted and unlit laboratories and listening to both disgruntled and optimistic colleagues have provided most of my insights concerning the interactions of technology, economic, and security concerns in the new Russia. A large number of case studies highlight common problems and opportunities facing the science and technology community but also point out many different types of challenges in a variety of settings throughout the country. My impressions and conclusions are clustered under the following topics:

• *The economic environment.* The policies of the International Monetary Fund, the different economies in different regions of Russia, the emergence of barter and other non-cash forms of payments, and the aspirations of small business provide a range of perspectives on the economic setting for innovation. Of special interest is the relevance to

Russia of the economic model that propelled Japan from the ruins of World War II to the status of technological giant.

- *The research and development infrastructure.* Government funding for research and development has dropped 20-fold in a decade, with little sign of recovery despite the importance of government support for innovation efforts. Meanwhile, the highly targeted marketing approaches of individual entrepreneurs housed in innovation incubators and technoparks contrast sharply with the broad search for customers of many profiles by Russia's 57 large State Scientific Centers (sometimes referred to as State Research Centers).

- *Exports of armaments and dual-use technologies.* International sales of lethal items raise a steady stream of security issues. In a related area, the experience to date in converting military industrial capabilities to civilian applications on a large scale has been discouraging; nevertheless, defense-related technologies in selected areas can be important for economic revival.

- *Controlling the finances.* Finding customers with cash for goods and services, avoiding bureaucratic garnishments of promised funds, and protecting money from criminals are large challenges for Russian research and development organizations. At the national level, capital flight deprives Russia of potential investment capital—the lifeblood of innovation—and a corrupt banking system complicates financing of research and development efforts.

- *Patents and taxes.* Enforcement of the laws and regulations governing intellectual property rights and taxation are lightning rods for complaints from both Russian and foreign entrepreneurs. The importance of long-term protection of innovations too often takes a back seat, while immediate tax policies are a constant source of concern.

- *The brain drain.* While international attention focuses on possible proliferation of weapons knowledge by underpaid scientists and engineers, the technical workforce including both weaponeers and non-weaponeers has downsized by 50 percent, with many of the losses being outstanding young specialists attracted by business careers. The technical universities must provide work-study and other programs to help convince students that research and development careers offer both technical challenges and financial rewards.

- *The Science Cities.* The 65 science cities of Russia, with a population of three million, possess 20 percent of the technological prowess of the country. Developing customers for their high-tech products on a regional basis and easing access to the cities by interested business partners could help develop desperately needed new income streams.

- *U.S.-Russian cooperation.* Cooperative programs have a major impact on the containment of dangerous materials and technologies in Russia and on redirection of Russian weapons expertise to civilian problems. As to commercialization of technologies, U.S. government efforts have been less effective; and the U.S. private sector, with a few exceptions, has been reluctant to invest in Russia, preferring to wait until better times when Russian customers have cash to pay for goods and services.

- *Russia's technological future.* A variant of the Marshall Plan concept that would jump-start innovation efforts on a broad scale deserves careful consideration. At the same time, corruption must be held in check, and the health of the Russian youth must be restored if they are to be scientific entrepreneurs in the future.

This book considers innovation in the broad sense, encompassing not only new products that incorporate technical novelty but also new ways to manage technologies developed many years ago. What is novel in Russia may not be novel in other countries. For example, in many regions of Russia, ATM machines, internet connections, and even reliable elevators are innovations.[2]

Also, developing and upgrading production processes are at the core of innovation efforts. Russian tinkering to keep obsolete machinery running is often quite innovative and frequently the only route to achieving a payoff of three, four, or even one ruble for every ruble invested. Such supporting services are in high demand in Russia and sometimes provide income for engineers who otherwise would leave their profession out of financial desperation.

This book does not analyze the role of basic research, the environmental impacts of industrial development, nor the frequent industrial accidents in Russia. These topics are important, but they are not pivotal determinants of near-term steps that could be taken to enhance the role of technology in Russia's future. Such analyses would expand the manuscript significantly and are left for other writers.

Realistic Hopes

The entire Russian population remembers when technology sustained an economy that fed, clothed, and educated the vast Soviet population even after the government had skimmed off the best products to build and operate the world's largest military machine. Politicians rightfully ask why the achievements of decades past cannot be replicated. The Russian resource base remains huge, the population is highly educated and resourceful, and there is now no need to divert such a large portion of production to military purposes.

Russia is different from the Soviet Union. The Soviet economy in many ways resembled a huge technology company, but now USSR, Inc., has been replaced by tens of thousands of independent production units that were not intended to be profitable in the first place. And the world is different. State-owned and private firms from dozens of countries are competing for the same consumer and industrial markets around the globe, including markets in Russia and in the other former Soviet republics.

Russia tried to adjust to these realities, but Russian leaders have learned that the western model of reform that was to facilitate this adjustment has brought them only economic grief.[3] They now hope for a better, Russian model, a model that must correct large levels of inequality among the population and must overcome widespread disillusionment with market economics. A model that enables the country to realize the "economic multiplier" by drawing both on past investments in Soviet technology and on new investments in Russian technology is essential. Progress toward such a model, however, will be apparent not in a few months but in a few years.

The four physicists have demonstrated four principles that, in combination, have overcome even the handicaps of the broken model. Give priority to marketing. Ensure the quality of the product. Protect the right for exclusive use of a successful innovation. Minimize overhead charges. A model that also provides access to investment capital would dramatically increase the interest and capability of many other Russian innovators to follow in their wake.

Such a model, one that responds to technological opportunities and also to social needs, will have been successfully implanted only when "made-in-Russia" no longer engenders fear that military weaponry is on the way to a rogue state nor skepticism that a nuclear plant will function properly. Rather, the label will signify that a new biological preparation will cure and not threaten people and that a television set will receive a clear and uninterrupted signal.

Notes

1.   Visit in Moscow to the company Tetra, June 1998.
2.   For a thorough discussion of modern concepts of innovation, see William G. Howard and Bruce R. Guile (editors), *Profitting from Innovation* (New York: The Free Press, 1992).
3.   For a summary of an important view of the economic debate, see Joseph Stiglitz, "For Economists, No Time to Party," *Newsweek*, Special Issue, November 1999, p. 58.

SWORDS INTO
MARKET SHARES

1

Dismal Economics Holds Back Technological Innovation

It irritates me when IMF delegations of young kids who've seen almost nothing but have read a lot of books start to dictate development plans. We are obliged to act in our own fashion, but also to listen.

Prime Minister Yevgeny Primakov, 1998

A fledgling market goes through several stages: rampant theft, trade and services, and only at the final stage development of production.

Roundtable of six Russian regional governors, 1998

In early 1998, the Russian pharmaceutical company Akrikhin was riding high, with profits having jumped for three years in a row and reaching $8 million in 1997. Despite the company's impressive performance, buyers began cooling on Akrikhin stock, along with all other Russian stocks. Russian government spokesmen blamed the decline of the stock market on the Asian financial crisis and the related drop in worldwide prices for oil which has always been one of Russia's export staples.

The company's expansion plans were put on hold. Then, in the summer of 1998, the economy crashed: the government defaulted on debt payments, inflation spiraled upward, and a number of major banks abruptly closed their doors. Akrikhin suddenly lost its customer base and was close to becoming a basket case. Its new priority was simply to avoid bankruptcy.

As a producer of generic drugs, Akrikhin was hardly in the same technological league as major western pharmaceutical firms. But, in

Russia, it certainly was an innovator. It had converted a rusting chemical production facility into a plant producing drugs that were not only cheaper than the imports flooding the market but were so cheap that impoverished Russians would buy them. To sell its products, the firm had successfully coped with a steady stream of corrupt officials. Needing special attention were those officials demanding favors to put specific drugs on the government's approval lists. Purchasers of these drugs would be reimbursed for the costs if they figured out how to qualify for elusive health insurance payments.

Before the economy collapsed, the company planned to retool outmoded facilities. It needed to expand its product lines of pills and ointments so as to benefit from economies of scale. Also, it planned to include in its product offerings a variety of injected solutions that were not available in Russia. But it was short of operating cash to buy raw materials from abroad that would ensure uninterrupted operation of its lines.

Even the most solvent Russian banks had never warmed to the idea of providing loans for more than a few months to any firm, and Akrikhin itself could not absorb the costs of factory renovation. Thus, the only source of financing was western investors. As the fiscal turmoil within the Russian government intensified, western organizations were not only stopping their investments, they were frantically pulling out as much money as they could from Russian financial institutions. In short, if a potential depositor inquired of any Russian as to whom he should see concerning a new account at a Russian bank, he would be told "a psychiatrist."

Despite difficulties in attracting investment capital, Akrikhin was in better shape than most Russian companies that relied on modern technologies. It had operated on a cash and not a barter basis, thereby avoiding acrimonious entanglements with other Russian firms. It had a good accounting system so as to avoid problems with the tax police. Most importantly, it had a highly motivated management team that was determined to find solutions to the latest series of setbacks.[1]

Will Akrikhin survive? Probably, but not as the independent technological leader that its management had envisaged as 1997 came to a close. By 1998, the U.S. Agency for International Development

(USAID) had provided Bristol-Myers Squibb with grants totalling $4.9 million to train Akrikhin personnel in improved plant operations and to provide advice on better marketing and management practices. When the Russian economy crashed, this western partner decided to continue its close relationship with Akrikhin, which had become a customer for some of the new materials it provided. Both USAID and Bristol-Myers Squibb believe that Akrikhin will be able to claim a small market share in the years ahead.

Given the huge demands for generic drugs in the country, there will always be some room for Russian pharmaceutical companies. In 1998, two-thirds of the drugs on the Russian market came from a variety of foreign countries. An even larger percentage of pharmaceutical manufacturing equipment was imported, primarily from western Europe. The Russian companies most likely to succeed in providing domestic substitutes for these imports in the near term are those that establish alliances with western partners that provide cash for retooling and upgrading. Should Russia drift towards a more controlled economy, however, then those Russian firms chosen by the government for support will obviously have an advantage.

Russian government support for existing or new domestic firms capable of producing a significant share of drugs or other imported items—support through preferential government purchasing of products of these firms or through higher import duties—is a concept that attracts Russian politicians not enamored with technological dependency on the West. But advocacy of such impediments to international trade in order to spur technological growth is a policy that sends shock waves through western governments determined to push Russia into an open trading nation.

Beyond pharmaceuticals, every sector of the economy was rocked by the financial meltdown of 1998. Many technological aspirations of both large enterprises and individual entrepreneurs were shelved. The government faced an immediate need to reschedule its foreign debts, since unpaid creditors were knocking on the door. This knocking is likely to intensify in the future, even if international prices for Russian oil exports continue their upward spiral of 1999. The only place for Russia to turn for debt rescheduling is the International Monetary

Fund (IMF) which in the past has paid little heed to preserving Russia's technological base. A review of IMF policies at the time of the 1998 collapse is instructive in anticipating future pressures from abroad for economic reform with clear implications for technology-based companies in Russia.

Three dimensions of economic developments also shape the challenges of innovation. First, barter and other non-cash payment schemes pervade business transactions to the detriment of the innovator who has not yet developed useful products to barter but needs cash to purchase specialized equipment and materials. Second, a growing number of small businesses are beginning to find high-tech market niches, and a special focus on problems confronting the small business sector is warranted. Third, each region of Russia has unique geographic characteristics and its own political and economic history, leading to highly diversified approaches to technological innovation.

Whatever the perspective, the economic road ahead will be rocky and uncertain. The western prescription so eagerly adopted by Russian reformers in the early-1990s has been repeatedly discredited. The emphasis on free international trade and readily exchanged currency, deep cuts in government spending for social programs, and rapid privatization of industry simply did not produce the results predicted. Free to choose quickly became free to lose. Of particular importance for innovation, the emergence of capital markets which would allow newly privatized industries to borrow cheaply and rebuild never took root.[2]

Among the many warning signs about undesirable byproducts of western intervention in Russian economic policy has been the behavior of Anatoly Chubais, for years the symbol in Moscow of the western economic model, both as an intellectual and as deputy prime minister. In 1998, Chubais admitted that while representing the Russian government, he had deliberately covered up the weakness of the Russian economy in his efforts to obtain IMF credits. If Chubais is not reliable, who can western economists trust?[3]

Implosion of the Economy

When Akrikhin reached the pinnacle of profit-making at the beginning of 1998, western economists were hailing the unprecedented performance of the Russian stock market as a sign that macroeconomic policies imported from the West had been a huge success. During the previous six years, according to the IMF, Russia had made remarkable progress toward a free market economy. The IMF outlook emphasized that Russia had become a democracy. A large and increasing share of Russian economic activity was being channeled through market mechanisms. A professional central bank had made impressive movement toward price stability. Output had begun to grow, and inflation had been reduced to near single-digit levels.[4] Still western economists were calling for more reforms of the economy as a condition for assistance. Among these demands of early 1998 that still remain on the front burners of western financial institutions are a tax code that is enforced, faster and more transparent privatization, and an efficient banking system.[5]

In 1998, with the IMF clearly able to jerk the most sensitive purse strings, it seemed that Russia would pay attention and take decisive steps to improve the economy. Yet, despite the IMF optimism and its prescription for further growth, in May of 1998 the IMF was confronted with a Russian economy about to implode without an immediate infusion of large sums of western funds. In staying its course of optimism, the IMF apparently was relying on the long shot that the prime minister would be successful in encouraging the Russian Duma to immediately adopt his anti-crisis package. This package included additional reform elements—shifting the tax burden from oil producers and refiners to consuming industries, leasing federal property on a competitive basis, cutting the public work force by 20 percent, and accelerating bankruptcies.[6]

Even in June 1998, as investors fled the Russian market, the IMF insisted that, contrary to what the market was experiencing, there was no financial crisis. In July, the IMF delivered to Moscow payments and commitments totaling $20 billion. It drew on its own financial coffers and on the resources of other western lending organizations. But this financial bailout was not without controversy.

Opponents of the IMF policy were abhorrent of the idea of sending money to a country whose major economic achievement was development of techniques for companies to escape debts by declarations of bankruptcy. They protested that the continuing infusion of western capital was simply delaying the inevitable day when all activity would stop in Russia and paychecks would simply become historical remembrances. Russia should put its financial house in order and pay its bills before receiving additional western resources. In short, they added, bailing out a sick economy had turned into abetting it.[7]

The U.S. government put its full weight behind the IMF to buy time for yet another wave of government reformers to take promised steps that would shore up the Russian economy. As Russia's experts continued to plead that the country was a victim of the global economic crisis, the IMF was willing to trade loans for actions to reform the economy. However, as reflected in Box 1.1, skeptics have long considered the IMF policy as simply a series of politically inspired bribes to keep the Russian government, with its nuclear arsenal, quiet and non-threatening.

Box 1.1
The IMF Policy of More Reform for More Cash

For the past six years our governments have been living from one International Monetary Fund infusion to the next. . . . The Russian authorities have learned the craft of pulling the wool over the eyes of the West, and the West has learned to pretend not to notice it. . . . The West does not believe that any economic reforms are underway in Russia, and so it simply aims at producing the appearance of decency with the help of IMF missions and negotiations. . . . We want to get new credits, but in fact we are not planning to reform anything.

Source: Boris Fyodorov (former Minister of Finance), "Loans to Russia? A Russian 'Nyet,'" *The Washington Post*, July 27, 1999, p. A19.

One month later, the economy did implode. Russia's external debt was approaching $140 billion, including $100 billion of liabilities inherited from the Soviet Union. The government's internal debt added another $100 billion. Interest payments were absorbing any government funds that were not protected by the most powerful Russian interest groups.[8] While the debt burden was low by international standards, it was too much for Russia to handle. When financial relief from the IMF and other foreign sources arrived, the dollar infusions were used to buy up mountains of rubles that were threatening to trash the ruble/dollar exchange rate, which had been at a near-steady state for almost two years.

Soon the value of the ruble had fallen dramatically, while speculators pocketed much of the money that had come in from abroad. By fall, the only discernible trace of the tranche of foreign money was increased debt. The results were disastrous.[9] Even the financial giant Agrobank closed its doors; and one of its former customers, the Russian Ministry of Foreign Affairs, was in a quandry trying to figure out how to pay its diplomats. Indeed, the ministry informed me they could not even process a cash deposit into their frozen bank account so they could authorize my multiple entry visa into the country. (Finally, they waived the fee.)[10]

As the country struggled to climb out of the rubble of devalued rubles, the explanations of Russia's economic troubles were as varied as the commentators. For example, in searching for an instant economic miracle, Russia went too far in attempting to adopt western principles of a market economy. Alternatively, in trying to avoid confrontations with the Russian robber barons who systematically plundered Russian financial reserves, industrial assets, and natural resources, the government was too timid in enforcing privatization regulations that were essential for decentralization of economic power. Other theories blamed the communists in the Duma who tied the hands of government officials, decried inept procedures for controlling capital flight from the country, bemoaned inherent inefficiencies in operating defense plants as producers of civilian goods, and ridiculed reliance on obsolete manufacturing equipment and an aging workforce.[11] Finally, cold warriors have been accused of recklessly manipulating western aid so they could socially engineer a "pure" private property market to replace evil communist institutions.[12] There is no single explanation of what went wrong. All of these theories contain elements of the underlying causes. Reluctant to accept responsibility for the economic mess, Russian politicians have repeatedly singled out two American institutions as major contributors to the collapse of their economy.

The now discredited Harvard Institute for International Development—and particularly its Director Jeffrey Sachs—have been portrayed as designers of misguided economic reform packages. According to critics, their scheme allowed ousted Soviet political leaders to become economic czars presiding over massive industrial assets through a poorly conceived privatization process. Sachs defended his role in the Russian newspaper, *Novoye Vremya,* in December 1997. In an article entitled "The Immaculate Conception of Capitalism in Russia," Sachs regreted that his name was linked to Russian reform. He argued that reform was impossible in view of the widespread corruption within the Russian government that had no analog in the last 50 years of the world's history. This theme is often repeated by other western reformers, who just a few years earlier urged that Russia move ever faster in changing its economic system despite well known corruption problems.[13] Skeptics of the approach of the Sachs' team believe they were trying to apply cookie cutter solutions developed in Latin America and Poland to a Russia that was quite different in geography, history, and mentality. Neither the Russian government nor the Russian people were prepared to adopt his formula for shock therapy.[14]

Another American villain identified as contributing to Russia's 1998 economic problems, in the view of at least a few leading Russian economists, was the New York City-based investment firm Goldman Sachs and Company. With ex-President George Bush in their entourage, the American financiers announced in Moscow in the spring of 1998 their plan for financial "deals" to generate badly needed money. After an initial success in brokering Eurobonds for the Russian government, the firm reportedly designed the scheme for Russia to sell short-term treasury bills, or GKOs, that earned high near-term interest rates in exchange for paybacks of the principal over a long-term period of many years. But this and related efforts to raise cash for the near-term were not sufficient. The Russian government stopped debt payments—whether they be principal or interest—leaving the holders of the GKOs with nearly worthless paper. At the same time, according to press reports, Goldman Sachs turned a healthy profit on each of its deals.[15]

The story is undoubtedly far more complex. Still, many Russian officials resent the firm's speed in quickly selling securities it had bought and had advocated for other investors. These critics doubt that the company was concerned about the long-term interests of its client, namely the Russian Federation.

The Russian government cannot escape its share of blame. It clung to shortsighted western advice that reform means reform at the macro level—get the government's policies right and good things will happen. Not enough attention has been paid to microeconomics. Broad policies, however perfect by western standards, cannot have the desired effect within a society that does not behave according to western rules, rules that recognize the legitimacy of financial gains from risk taking and that are based on enforcement of regulations. For innovation, economic incentives also matter at the micro level (the level of the firm and the institute which provide the environment for innovation) and at the microscopic level (the level of the individual researcher and the entrepreneur who promote innovation). Make no mistake, government actions to encourage an appropriate macroeconomic framework are important. They simply are not adequate, particularly if nurturing technologies with economic payoff is a goal.

The Economy and Innovation

Against such a discouraging background mosaic, what can be said about the relationship between the state of the economy and opportunities to profit from introducing improved and cheaper products into the marketplace? Clearly, the healthier an economy the more likely that funds will be spent by government and industry on developing products of the future. A healthier economy means more cash is available to companies that are interested in product or process improvement, to banks that desire to expand their loan operations, and to entrepreneurs who need new equipment to upgrade their activities. Also, a healthy economy is more likely to attract risk takers from home and abroad who are looking for ways to use technology to increase personal wealth.

But the relationship is not so jigsaw puzzle neat. For example, in the early 1990s the Russian oil companies had large sums of money to invest. Historically, the state had supported widespread oil exploration activities. When the privatized companies took over, it was reasonable to expect they would invest in the sustainability of their activities as the older oil fields began to run dry. However, such reasoning made little sense to the financial magnates who controlled the companies.

It seemed far more profitable for the companies to invest available funds into Russian bank accounts that paid 50 percent interest than to take a chance that oil exploration would in a few years lead to large returns. It was even more profitable for the companies to establish their own banks for their funds—and they did. Is it any wonder that new fields were not ready to come on line as production began to slip? By 1995, oil production had dropped to one-half the levels in the late 1980s, underscoring predictions of communist politicians in the oil-producing regions that new capitalistic approaches would lead to economic disaster.[16]

Thus, it is not only the state of the economy as reflected in macroeconomic indicators that is important in providing an environment for innovation. It is also how those individuals who control financial resources perceive the utility of innovation in enhancing their personal futures. Surely if a large oil company cannot appreciate the importance of opening new fields, less well endowed industrial enterprises will lean toward options other than research and development for investing funds in ways that maximize returns. While innovation has earned its place in the West as an important vehicle for enhancing profits, in Russia—where financial outlooks are usually measured in weeks and not years—the economic framework simply has not been conducive for research and development investments.

Even more basic, as a result of the economic crisis, most scientists and engineers receive minimum wage, if they are paid at all; and their firms and institutes have outdated equipment and limited supplies needed for productive work. Why should they press forward to solve technical problems of interest to nonpaying customers? Also, they have little enthusiasm to search for technological solutions to problems they cannot solve without upgraded laboratories. As researchers have repeatedly demonstrated during recent years, under such conditions they prefer to spend their time looking for ways to put food on their tables tomorrow—driving taxis, refurbishing apartments, and tending their gardens.

Because of the weak economy, most manufacturing plants are stagnant; and few companies are interested in financing new product development activities. As to government support for research, the Ministry of Finance, with little tax revenue, places research near the bottom of its priority list even if proposed technological innovations appear to be certain winners. Finally, the economy is perceived internationally to be foundering on rough shoals, and few foreign investors will risk funds against a distant hope that they will provide the impetus for new customer spending patterns. As we have seen, even well-endowed Bristol-Myers Squibb required cost sharing by the U.S. government before investing in Akrikhin.

In short, technological innovation is never without costs. Someone must put up the funds in advance to allow it to take place. With Russian companies unable to meet their payrolls and with foreign investors hesitant, industry interest in funding innovation—however cost-effective in the long run—has waned; and linkages between manufacturers and researchers have atrophied badly. Also, few rich Russian angels are willing to take a chance on backing a new idea when there are more certain investments to multiply profits from other activities.

With reduced tax collections and a mounting foreign debt, the Russian government has very limited funds to fill the void and support technology innovation. The Ministry of Science and Technology tries to ensure that its modest funds will mean the difference between a few research results languishing in the laboratory and these results reflected in commercial products. However, the state of the economy clearly reduces the success rate for projects financed by the ministry.[17]

That said, what can a Russian company with no excess cash do when it needs technical help to maintain even its current technological levels? It usually draws on the skills of its own personnel who are on the job, with or without paychecks, and with or without appropriate technical credentials for the needed fixes. Alternatively, it searches for outside specialists who will accept some of the company's products as pay for services. For some companies, barter is the only route for obtaining technical support.

Barter Replaces Cash Transactions

The degree of non-cash transactions among Russian firms and institutes reached a startling level in 1998. Transactions based on barter, use of promissory notes, trading debt for goods, and debt swaps represented between one-half and two-thirds of inter-enterprise commerce. Bicycles for diesel fuel, trucks for electricity, cranes for rolled steel, and of course vodka for spare parts are but several examples of the way of life of Russian industry.

The stories of employees being paid in the goods that they produce edge toward a state of ridiculousness. Somehow, employees at a brassiere factory are expected to accept brassieres as compensation and then develop a distribution system for selling a commodity that can no longer compete with western brassieres. A dozen employees at an automobile plant have the opportunity to accept joint ownership in a new car as their paychecks, with the only alternative being personal faith that the company will someday pay them in devalued rubles. A television plant ensures that employees are provided with an abundant supply of new television sets that technologically are at least one generation behind the Sony models most Russians covet. Even in the army, units in the north are paid in licenses for hunting reindeer. They can then sell the antlers and eat the meat.[18]

One widespread practice of local authorities is the issuing of promissory notes to be used by enterprises in a specific region for facilitating non-cash trade. Under this scheme, when an enterprise cannot find a customer who has items of interest as payment for goods of the enterprise, the enterprise can accept promissory notes for its products and then try to use them for acquiring useful items produced by other enterprises of the region. While early in 1998 Moscow authorities had been hopeful that this practice could be phased out to protect the integrity of the ruble, the subsequent collapse of the ruble convinced many regional leaders that reliance on their promissory notes is far safer than reliance on the ruble. Meanwhile, the tax service attempts to gain control of its rightful cut of the value of transactions. But it has not yet been interested in brassieres; and it is having trouble finding cash.

In 1997, a Russian commission investigated payment of taxes and released the "Karpov Report" on the extent of trade in goods and promissory notes of over 200 of the largest firms. In the case of the Berezovsky coal mine, the report pointed out that in 1997 the mine had gross revenues of 551 billion rubles—335 billion were in promissory notes, 215 billion in barter, and only one billion in cash. This was an extreme case of operating outside the cash economy. However, only 16 percent of the surveyed companies received more than one-half of their revenues in cash.[19]

As to tax obligations and required contributions to the pension fund, the companies paid about 7 percent in cash. The remainder were settled either through offsets against unpaid debts by government agencies for their purchases or through provision of goods or services. For example, the Gorky Automobile Plant, which employs about 100,000 workers, actually overpaid its federal taxes in 1997, but not in cash. It wrote off the entire payment against debts owed to the plant by government agencies which received its vehicles. What did the government do with those thousands of automobiles?[20] As to local taxes, a similar pattern of payment of taxes through offsets against goods and services provided to city departments is revealed in data from the city of Zarechny in the Urals, with cash revenues flowing to the city limited to 7 percent of the city's income.[21] In short, if you do not have cash to pay your local taxes, volunteer to repair the roof of the schoolhouse and deduct the value of your labor.

The Karpov report indicates that the true value of the promissory notes is much less than the declared value—in some cases only 20 percent. This overvaluing by enterprises of payments made to each other and to the government has led to the description of the Russian economy as a virtual economy. The economy simply does not exist in the size that it is portrayed in the statistics of the Russian government.[22] Despite this distorted portrayal of the economy, non-cash payments have been essential in keeping enterprises operational.[23]

Meanwhile, most research institutes have innovations from years past and from research efforts in progress that they hope will eventually lead to commercial successes. Moving these innovations to market requires some level of financial support—for adapting technologies to specific customer needs, for pilot runs, and even for marketing expenses. But the institutes have few tangible items to offer employees or suppliers as alternatives to cash, and the emergence of a barter economy has hampered their operations considerably.

A lonely non-cash success story in settling debts of research institutes is the provision of technical services by a few institutes to utility companies in exchange for electricity, gas, telephone service, heat, water, or waste disposal. The Kurchatov Institute for Atomic Energy, for example, has set up an arrangement with the gas monopoly, Gazprom, whereby the institute has paid its $15 million annual gas bill by providing technical services that will enhance the operating efficiencies of Gazprom.[24] And the Research and Engineering Institute for Water Supply, Sewage Systems, Hydraulic Engineering Structures, and Engineering Hydrogeology, located in Moscow, has a well-heeled customer in the city administration that is struggling to maintain the functioning of its water and sewage treatment facilities. The institute is able to trade a variety of advisory and repair services in exchange for many types of communal services provided by the city's departments.[25]

Do such technical services contribute to an institute's innovation capability? Probably not very much, but many research institutes have no choice but to become low-tech service centers in exchange for payments to them in other types of services that they can use (e.g., power and heat). Until economic recovery leads to greater reliance on cash transactions throughout the country, such service activities will continue to displace innovation as focal points within research institutes.

Of even greater significance for many research institutes, the budgets at all levels of government are being starved by the lack of cash payments to the tax collectors. This means there is less state money to support research, or any other activity that is traditionally the responsibility of government. In the words of the Karpov report:

> The negligible amount of cash paid to the budget raises the question: How does the budget receive any cash at all? The answer: From customs duties, personal income taxes, privatization revenues, taxes on retail and wholesale trade and banking—but not from industrial enterprises *which are traditionally regarded as the main taxpayers* (emphasis in report).[26]

The widespread practice of non-cash payments declined in 1999 as devalued rubles became more available. But it will not end soon—nor should it end abruptly lest more production activities come to a halt.

One intriguing exit strategy from this morass is the "gas ruble" proposed by Gazprom for the fuel and electricity industries. Under this scheme, Gazprom would issue gas commodity bonds (or gas rubles) which the Ministry of Finance purchases from Gazprom with loans from abroad. The ministry would distribute the gas rubles to state-funded enterprises. The enterprises would then use the gas rubles to repay their debts to Gazprom; and Gazprom would use its own "real money" to pay back taxes, thus enabling the ministry to pay off its original loans while reducing the level of unpaid debts throughout the industry. Variations on this scheme have also been discussed for the agricultural sector.[27]

But, until the level of cash payments for goods and services and for taxes increases dramatically, research institutes will continue to be at a disadvantage in participating in economic activity.

Role of Small Business

Since the early 1990s, the Ministry of Science and Technology has advocated greater attention to small technology-oriented businesses that can be started and sustained by individuals with modest investment capabilities. The important role of small businesses in the West as suppliers of goods and services to large and medium high-tech companies has intrigued Russian officials. While the role of small firms that are dedicated to technological innovation will be discussed in subsequent chapters, small businesses as providers of low-tech goods and services have been pathfinders for important economic reforms on a broad front and deserve special attention in considering economic trends.

The number of small firms registered in Russia in 1998 was about 900,000, reportedly employing 12 million people. Of course, many individual entrepreneurs do not register with the authorities, often to avoid taxes; and the total number of persons earning a portion of their income from loosely defined small business activities is estimated at 20 million. Some businesses thrive. Others barely function. Some registered businesses are transient, lasting but a few months before disappearing even though they may remain on the official records of the government. While extremely important for a decade in a number of fields, such as restaurants, transportation, and retailing, small business activity in the industrial sector is still many years away from maturity.[28]

In 1993, I came to respect Russian business instincts during an encounter with a small businessman who owned a brew pub. His first and probably most important decision was to locate his establishment behind well-guarded walls in an exclusive housing area of Moscow. I joined the owner at a well-appointed table in his upscale restaurant next to the brewery, where his beeping Japanese cell phone was always at the ready. The heavy security inside and outside the restaurant surely meant that this 22 year-old entrepreneur was tightly linked to some branch of the Russian mafia.

Nevertheless, his business strategy was impressive. First, he established and aggressively promoted his core business of brewing beer, using the most modern brewing equipment available. The vats and piping from New Jersey, with a glistening, antiseptic appearance, produced a high quality product at reasonable cost. The silvery equipment had an equally important byproduct—excellent photo opportunities for advertising a cutting edge business.

He spread additional financial resources over five small companies rather than building one large company—expanding and contracting each one as the market or changing government regulations dictated. Given Russian labor laws, shifting personnel between companies was easier than trying to reorganize a large company. If price regulations made bakery products in state stores more competitive than his cakes and breads, he would simply expand activities at his sawmill. If rich Russians stopped building wooden dachas, he would increase candy production. His workforce was sufficiently flexible that layoffs were unknown, and the need to provide surge capabilities at any particular facility was easily handled. He could always count on beer sales to keep his empire solvent.[29]

Even if a Russian businessman has a marketable product, such as beer, there are formidable barriers to sustaining a profitable undertaking. Purchase of land where facilities can be built is not yet an established practice. Seldom are there desirable buildings simply waiting for buyers. Thus, rental of space is usually essential; and squabbles among claimants have become legendary in Russia. The tax system has been in a state of flux for years, both in revisions of the code and in enforcement of what appear to be the regulations at any given moment. On a daily basis, droves of inspectors from health, fire, sanitary, architectural, and other government agencies visit small businesses and for a fee provide stamped papers necessary for conducting business. Crime and corruption haunt any activity that involves the handling of money, particularly small businesses that cannot hire large security forces or provide heavy bribes to ensure that no one hassles them every day.

Despite Russia's economic difficulties, small entrepreneurs—whether they're interested in producing beer, construction materials, or computer software—have before them many yet to be realized opportunities for providing a multitude of goods and services that are currently imported. Indeed, if the small business sector is to become a vital part of the Russian industrial economy, the government should, as a start, strictly enforce import duties already required on a wide range of items that are within the grasp of individual Russian entrepreneurs.[30]

Technology at the Regional Level

Regional and local leaders are taking an increasingly aggressive role in attempting to promote development of new technologies within their jurisdictions, particularly as the secrecy wraps begin to come off hundreds of previously closed enterprises and institutes throughout the country. Some governors and mayors have obtained a measure of control of activities at federal research facilities on their territories. Others have gained various types of federal tax exemptions as a basis for attracting investments. Still others have established regional facilities that conduct innovative activities at the behest of regional leaders.

While most governors want the maximum amount of autonomy, whether dealing with small businesses or large enterprises, they inevitably seek financial support of all types from Moscow. But, with a sputtering economy such support is slow in coming. Thus, the regions have become accustomed to fending for themselves with a gradual weakening of the role of the central government. With four different prime ministers in Moscow in the span of 12 months during 1998 and 1999, the governors were seldom challenged as they exerted greater leadership for their regions.

The outlook for spinning out of economic decline seems brightest in regions rich in natural resources, particularly with a greater emphasis on processing resources prior to export. One "region" with no natural resources, however, stands out as perhaps the biggest success story—namely the city of Moscow. The Far East economic region and the Samara region provide other perspectives on the need for diverse and pragmatic approaches to technology development throughout the sprawling country.

City of Moscow

Moscow's economic revival has been the result of a money-oriented effort led by a mayor who has been good both for the city and for dozens of research and educational institutions within. The impressive accomplishments of Mayor Yuri Luzhkov have little to do with neo-liberal market theories. They simply reflect pragmatic urban corporatism as a realistic alternative to abstract economic principles.[31]

In 1992, potholes in the streets of the capital were so large that entire cars sank into deep pools of water during heavy downpours. Not a flower could be found in the parks; babushkas had scavenged them and were selling them on street corners. Metal handrails along crumbling concrete stairways leading to metro stations were peeling from rust, and uncollected garbage was burning everywhere in overstuffed bins. These and other ugly scenes made lasting impressions on foreign visitors.[32]

By 1996, Moscow had become a new city. The roads were newly paved. The parks had begun to sparkle. Fresh paint was in evidence everywhere, and modern glass buildings were dotting the landscape. The revitalization of an ailing metropolis of 10 million people stood in stark contrast to conditions in other cities.

Luzhkov won an important early battle with the federal government, insisting that privatization in Moscow be in the hands of local authorities. Consequently, the city could assess assets of Moscow's enterprises at a high level. Luzhkov and his associates adopted their own brand of privatization—demanding high prices for the sale of city assets. They boasted they earned more money from privatization than did the federal government throughout the entire country.[33] At the same time, the city has retained title to much property within the city limits, with the right to grant long-term leases of up to 49 years.

Still, most of the city's early revenue came from taxes on corporations. Due to a quirk in Russian law, corporations paid federal taxes through the local government of the city where their headquarters were located. Thus, the gas and oil companies paid taxes through and to Moscow until 1997, when the federal government began a campaign to stop this practice. But by then, Moscow had benefited from billions of tax dollars flowing into its coffers.

To ensure that the wealth is not spread too thin, Moscow has retained the Soviet system of residential permits (propiska). The permits, ostensibly based on birthplace, marriage commitments, and employment location, help keep undesirable residents out. At the same time, city officials welcome those who enrich the city's revenues.[34]

A large portion of the working population of the city—perhaps one-half—are directly or indirectly on the municipal payroll. One example of a mega-employer, under the direct patronage of the mayor, is the holding company AFK Sistema, with assets of $2.6 billion and a payroll of 50,000. This company is the owner of the Moscow city telephone company, Moscow newspapers, a TV station, major department stores, automobile plants, oil companies, and other enterprises.[35]

An often overlooked tactic of a mayor with an insatiable appetite for capital renovation has been his habit of borrowing from the West. Now the city is saddled with repayment of more than $1 billion in loans.[36] Nevertheless, it has so many assets, geographic advantages, and friends in the federal government that this debt burden will not seriously challenge its economic leadership among the cities of Russia.

The bustling laboratories of the firm Radon, financed by the city to clean up radioactive waste sites in Moscow and also hired by other cities in the Moscow region, provide convincing evidence that science is not forgotten by the city administration. I had known about the radioactive hospital waste deposited decades ago in the lot adjacent to what is now the American School. But the dozens of other spots in the city glowing on the maps of Radon raised apprehension about every vacant lot and each pile of rubble.

Just prior to my visit to Radon, I had walked through the dormant radiation chemistry laboratories at two leading research institutes of the Academy of Sciences and the Ministry of Atomic Energy, both closed because of lack of funds to pay electricity bills. This was not the case at Radon, where research was booming and achievements were reported in the best scientific journals. With access to resources of the city, these scientists were secure in their professional futures. They were not only providing services in cleaning up wastes, they were carrying out important research that would improve capabilities of the company.

As to state-owned research facilities and universities located in Moscow, the city government has taken many initiatives to supplement their meager budgets. The mayor has a special affinity for biotechnology. Also, ecological research projects are especially popular with the mayor and his constituency and are generously supported.

Far East Region

Many time zones to the east of Moscow, the cities of Yuzhno-Sakhalinsk, Vladivostok, and Khabarovsk are largely on their own in dealing with the economic crisis. Aside from the presence of units of the Russian army, navy, and air force, the links with Moscow are often hard to find. The cities are three of the administrative centers in a loosely defined territory, the Far East economic region.

Some geographers extend this territory westward to include over one-third of the country. However defined, it is sparsely populated, with even the broadest geographic boundaries encompassing a population of less than two-thirds the number of inhabitants of Moscow. It is punctuated with a handful of small cities. It has vast reserves of land-based natural resources and a coastline that should provide easy access to rich marine resources. However, the downturn in the economy during the past decade has devastated the population and has brought a near halt to most efforts to modernize the technological base of the territory.

A bright star on the horizon is the discovery of oil off the cost of Sakhalin Island and the influx onto the island of hundreds of specialists from Marathon, Arco, Shell, and a dozen other western companies poised to help recover the oil. With them come sophisticated drilling and pumping technologies and the latest techniques for survival in extremely harsh climates. Already the local government has been the beneficiary of millions of dollars in taxes that help strengthen the infrastructure for the 600,000 residents of the island.[37]

Another favorable development has been the increase of timber and processed food exports from the area near Khaborovsk following the fall of the ruble in August 1998. However, the outlook remains blcak in this arca as the Ministry of Defense does not pay for the ships and planes that are built. Also, "butterfly" companies quickly register, conduct their business, and then fly away before tax payments become due.

Fisheries are at the top of the list of important industries in the Far East economic region, and there has been growth in the catches after dramatic declines through the mid-1990s. In recent years, the stocks of salmon and other fish have become a poacher's mecca, with illegal catches said to rival legal catches in value. One report from the Kamchatka Penisula indicates that fishermen may be earning more than $20,000 per year and that one of every five residents has a car.

At the same time, there often is no heat or light in some areas of Kamchatka. Authorities cannot afford the costs of providing these services. The shipyards have lost much of their repair business to Korean competitors due to the heavy Russian tax burden, and the municipality has lost tax income from the shipyards, from its workers, and from the poachers.[38]

Overall, the situation in the Far East region is grim, as illustrated in a report from the village of Dappi 200 miles north of Khabarovsk, where 400 people have no work and no place to go. Since no one pays wages, logging has been abandoned, and the tractors that dragged logs out of the woods have departed. The single remaining priority is keeping children clothed and fed. The only growth industry in the entire district is employment of young women abroad—as prostitutes. While the word is out that a free ticket to Japan means bondage, desperate young women feel that somehow they will be able to escape from this fate and are willing to risk going abroad in preference to facing another miserable winter in villages like Dappi.[39]

Many Far Eastern enterprises, cut off from their historical partners in other parts of the country, have been faced with the choice of either closing their doors or finding profitable markets in neighboring countries of the Asia-Pacific rim. In a few cases, enterprises have developed limited export opportunities in the fishing, mining, forestry, and machine building sectors. They are hardly of sufficient scope, however, to restore the standard of living to a tolerable level.

At the same time, Russian enterprises in the Moscow region and in the Urals that had supplied goods to the Far Eastern region—metals, oil products, and consumer items, for example—have been forced to look elsewhere for customers, often with little success. It has become cheaper for Far Eastern enterprises to buy oil from the Persian Gulf, oil products from the United States and Korea, and even gasoline from Japan than to pay for deliveries from Russian suppliers thousands of miles away.

Also contributing to the increased isolation of the region has been an 8,000-fold increase in the prices of rail and air travel since 1991. Graduates from universities in the western part of the country seldom go east. If they do, they will be unable to return home on holidays or possibly ever.

The economic woes have greatly weakened a research base that had been heavily financed from Moscow. The decline in production, capital investment, and population in the region will continue to bode ill for researchers. Some have left their laboratories, others are content in providing testing and repair services, and still others continue their research despite the lack of regular paychecks.

Two frequent complaints from researchers have been that market demand calls for mundane engineering services, not scientific endeavors, and that privatization of government research institutes has placed technical assets in the hands of entrepreneurs interested only in immediate returns.[40] Clearly, research for the sake of science must give way to research for economic development, although a payoff period that is too short may drive the best researchers from their laboratories. Also, unless Moscow devotes greater resources to supporting the transportation and communication infrastructure of the region, which are important for both researchers and commercial interests, much of the region's potential will remain very distant from the marketplace.

Samara Region

Located in the heartland of Russia about 1,000 miles southeast of Moscow is Samara, the capital city of a region with a long heritage of carefully guarded military production. The region is rich in natural gas and is a major oil producing and refining area. Samara is home to several important aerospace enterprises, and the city is an important transportation hub of the lower Volga River basin. The region has attracted investments from the likes of General Motors, IBM, Corning, and Bayer.

Russia's largest automobile manufacturer, Avtovaz, is the leading employer in the region, reporting increased sales during 1999. Avtovaz claims important strides in moving to cash rather than barter transactions. Also, the company contends it is reducing the crime and corruption that have plagued the sales force of every automobile manufacturer in the country; but machine gun-toting guards are still in evidence near outlet facilities.

Following the devaluation of the ruble at the end of 1998, a number of companies in the Samara region took advantage of opportunities to expand sales on the Russian market as imported products became prohibitively expensive. For example, Nestle promptly increased its investment in the country's largest chocolate factory, Rossiya, and expanded production lines. As one simple example of cost control so often neglected in Russia, the company shifted from increasingly expensive imported sugar to less expensive Russian sugar.

Overall, the region is doing much better than most areas of the country, with salaries perhaps double the national average. At the same time, despite a few bright spots, the industrial base is on the decline. Most companies did not take advantage of the window for expanding the customer base in Russia as foreign products became more expensive following the financial crisis of 1998. The urgent need to upgrade outdated production lines is reflected even at Avtovaz, with unreliable electrical systems and corrosion plaguing many owners of the cars it produces.

Small firms, which currently account for 10 percent of the region's production and should be wellsprings of technology, are on the rise. However, only 2 percent are seriously involved in innovative activities, with most seeking immediate profits through trading and public catering. Credit lines for activities that will not turn profits for more than a few months are simply difficult to find regardless of the long-term potential of the proposed investment.

The higher education system is well established in Samara, with a number of strong universities that have long been attuned to the region's reliance on well-trained engineers. Most engineering graduates find employment locally, with Avtovaz among the highest paying companies and offering new graduates $120 per month. Although most graduates find jobs, there is substantial unemployment and underemployment for technical support personnel, as the engineers provide their own supporting services in order to keep busy.

Still, the market demand for high-tech products or services is very weak. A startling example of desperate efforts to market high-tech products came to light in 1999. A former defense factory attempting to convert to civilian products began producing titanium shovels, virtually giving them away. While the women who shovel snow rave about the light weight of these shovels, this can hardly be categorized as a conversion success story.[41]

The Long and Uncertain Road to Prosperity

There are similarities in Russia between the economic situations in 1999 and in 1992, when the specter of financial instability—and particularly rampant inflation and delayed paychecks—also clouded all proposed policies. But there are particularly disturbing trends in the contemporary scene. The population is numbed by its inability to buy goods that fill the shops, reconciled to sustained widespread unemployment, and disenchanted with repeated promises of a brighter future. A swollen international debt and a substantial internal debt demand larger repayments. A virtual economy provides the government with less budgetary resources than advertised. All the while, stubborn financial kingpins will not easily give up resources they have stolen and those they plan to add to their treasuries.

In October 1999, the highly respected McKinsey Global Institute brought a surprising degree of optimism to predictions over the industrial future of Russia. In a detailed analysis of 10 industrial sectors, McKinsey economists and consultants concluded that about three-quarters of the country's industrial assets are still usable. They added that from a microeconomic point of view there should be no insurmountable constraints that would prevent Russia from quickly joining the ranks of the advanced economies.[42]

However, this optimism must be tempered with the harsh realities of life in Russia in 1999. Almost 40 percent of the population had crossed below the poverty level of incomes of less than $34 per month, and the purchasing power of average salaries had declined by a third from 1998 to 1999.[43] While reliance on barter may be slowly declining, production levels gradually increasing, and tax revenues also rising, many years of economic growth will be needed to provide an acceptable standard of living for most Russians.

Can current policies be fine tuned to improve economic efficiency? At present, there are so many distortions in the economy that frequently less efficient producers of commodities win out in competitions with more efficient producers. These distortions include unequal taxation, different energy payment requirements for different consumers, privileged access to government procurements and land allocation, arbitrary red tape requirements, and tolerance of stealing trademarks and false advertising. Such distortions are often traced to policies and practices at the regional and municipal levels. Better overarching laws and enforcement at the federal level are the obvious responses, but the distortions are deeply ingrained and will be difficult to uproot.[44]

What about a major upsurge in foreign investment as the eventual salvation? Should the Russian government sell the rights to a small portion of Russian natural resources—say 5 percent—with trillions of dollars eventually flowing into the country and thereby saving the day?[45] As indicated on Sakhalin Island, small steps are being taken in the oil sector. But a massive sale of Russian resources seems out of the question for political reasons alone.[46]

Finally, why should Russia be expected to carry the debt burden of the former Soviet Union? Western creditors eased the burden for Poland's repayment of its old debts. Russia is unable to collect the $140 billion owed to it by North Korea, Cuba, Afghanistan, and other Soviet debtors. Nevertheless, western institutions will resist letting Russia off the hook, noting that it acquired not only the Soviet debt but also most of the Soviet military assets, its overseas bank accounts and embassies, and other riches. Still, these acquisitions are dwarfed in current value by the debt. A degree of relief of the debt that is hobbling the economy could be important in the evolution of a prosperous Russia as an alternative to a struggling Russia with a nuclear arsenal.

Looking at broader solutions, in the early 1990s, only Japanese experts stood up among the foreign advisers to warn that government protection from imports and/or government subsidies would be necessary to sustain Russian industrial economic growth. They argued that stability depended on equitable wealth-sharing among the Russian people, which meant jobs in the manufacturing sector. They predicted that if only a few hundred thousand people are busy and rich while tens of millions are idle and poor, political turmoil will soon destroy economic policies.[47]

Japanese specialists have had great difficulty watching the evolution of an economy that seems to encompass all the undesirable developments in Latin America. Latin American experiences of high inflation, a heavy debt burden, negative economic growth, low levels of foreign investment, depressed industrial research and development, weak electronics industries, deteriorating higher education, and growing disparities in income distribution certainly have a familiar ring in Russia.

The Japanese reflect on the advantages of an Asian model that enabled Japan to leapfrog into the new technological age and then concentrate on the transition to a less centrally driven economy. They acknowledge that Japan had a relatively reliable civil service to carry out policies, that capitalism already had a history in Japan, and that the country was aided by an unexpected market demand associated with the Korean War. However, they point to the advantages of the huge technical workforce in Russia and the underexploited markets in most of the countries of the former Soviet Union.[48]

The marriage of government and industry interests that transformed Japan after World War II also attracts interest among Russian financial magnates who control many industrial purse strings. Of course, they twist the approach to serve their personal interests. They have called for an Industrial Policy Board akin to Japan's Ministry for International Trade and Industry, apparently believing that they could serve on such a board and then direct the Russian economy. European governments too seem increasingly interested in a heavier governmental hand, one that could ensure economic stability. However, they underscore the importance of concurrently attacking graft and theft and insisting on the rule of law, even if the law is not the western model.[49]

There will be violent criticism, particularly in Washington, of policies that divert from Russia's original path to reform. The free marketeers will argue that any move toward central planning and control—including the Japanese model—will lead to government confiscation and misuse of assets, simply providing opportunities for another wave of corrupt officials to steal even more. But it is not at all clear that the level of corruption inside the government would be any worse than the current degree of corruption led by forces outside the government in failed efforts to separate private and public sector activities.[50]

In general, potential innovators believe they would see more of their ideas incorporated into manufacturing activities if the government played a more effective role in supporting and promoting their research activities. The technological achievements of the Soviet Union cannot be denied. Much of the Soviet philosophy remains dogma among many inventive people of the country—a philosophy that emphasizes that, once technologies are demonstrated, they will somehow find their way into the manufacturing sector *if the government helps.* A partial return to this philosophy, at least on an interim basis, seems essential to reverse the current course of technological decay of state assets and provide the country with new capabilities for economic growth. But coupled with such a move should be insistence on transparency of financial dealings, early bankruptcy procedures when even subsidized activities are not viable, and mechanisms for enforcing contracts.

The Russian research community has cause to be apprehensive about receiving its due within a free market economy. An example of a no-win situation is the development in the Urals of a process to leach gold from underground ore deposits. Using technologies developed to mine uranium, a Russian research institute in Zarechny has succeeded in leaching gold valued at $1 million dollars from veins located on municipal property and stockpiling it on the surface, with many times that amount of gold readily available underground. The city has enacted legislation that provides for one-half the revenues from the gold mine to be devoted to support of research activities. But the banks cannot buy the gold because they have no money, and the notion of exporting the gold has raised grave governmental concerns. All the scientists want is some of the money so they can get on with the job of extracting more gold and can use some of the income to restore the research and development base of the region.[51]

In sum, both Russian and international policy officials should adopt a long-term perspective of at least 10 years in designing economic and industrial policies and programs intended to energize the Russian economy rather than the three-year formulas of the past. They should recognize that, at least for this transition period, the economic model will differ substantially from western approaches. The Japanese post-war model may be the most relevant experience in attempting to jump start the manufacturing sector. However, as emphasized in Chapter 10, anti-corruption measures must be built into the model.

The eventual goal should be a technology-driven market economy that enables Russia to be an important participant in the global trading system. The alternative is a Russian economy increasingly dependent on exports of arms and natural resources and imports of equipment and consumer goods that stymie employment opportunities and delay indefinitely an increased standard of living in Russia.[52] The challenge is to design an approach that harnesses the creativity of the owners of Akrikhin, of investors in breweries, and of the gold miners of Zarechny in pushing toward the goal of a market economy. But the push must be responsive to the immediate needs of the population while restoring the technological base of the country on a step-by-step basis as quickly as possible.

Notes

1.   Sharon LaFraniere, "Russian Crisis Saps Companies' Hopes," *The Washington Post*, August 29, 1998, p. A13. For difficulties faced by U.S. companies see David Lynch,"U.S. Companies in Russia," *USA Today*, September 8, 1998, p. 11b.

2.   Katy Daigle and Matt Bivens, "The Way Out," *The Moscow Times*, September 8, 1998. For different viewpoints see Vladimir Milovidov, "Solving the Russian Economic Puzzle," *Investing in Russia,* Moscow, January 1998, pp. 16-19, and Lawrence H. Summers, "Russia in 1998: Building a Pluralist Market Economy," Presentation to US-Russia Business Council, Washington, April 1, 1998.

3.   Richard C. Paddock, "Russia Lied To Get Loans, Says Aide to Yeltsin," *Los Angeles Times*, September 9, 1998, p. 4.

4.   Stanley Fischer, "The Russian Economy at the Start of 1998," *The Potential of Russia*, vol. 1, no. 1, Moscow, 1998, p. 39. Also, Michel Camdessus, "Russia and the IMF," Presentation to the U.S.-Russia Business Council, April 1, 1998.

5.   *Ibid.*

6. "What's in Kiriyenko's Anti-Crisis Package," *Russia Review*, vol. 5, no. 13, July 17, 1998.

7. *Ibid.*

8. Michael R. Gordon and David E. Sanger, "IMF Comes Through. Now, Will Russia?" *Russia Review*, vol. 5, no. 15, August 14, 1998, pp. 12-14.

9. See for example "Russia: Is There a Solution?" *Business Week*, September 7, 1998, pp. 28-29. Also see Neela Banerjee, "The Bottom Falls Out in Moscow," *U.S. News and World Report*, September 7, 1998, pp. 10-12.

10. This situation came to light when I applied for a multiple-entry visa.

11. See for example "Special Crisis Report, What Went Wrong?" *Russia Review*, vol. 5, no. 17, September 25, 1998, pp. 12-35.

12. John Lloyd, "The Russian Devolution," *The New York Times Magazine*, August 15, 1999, p. 38.

13. Jeffery Sachs, "The Immaculate Conception of Capitalism in Russia," *Novoye Vremya*, no. 49/97, December 14, 1997, p. 14.

14. See also D.W. Miller, "An Anthropologist Faults Academics for Offering 'Misguided' Assistance to Former Soviet-Bloc Nations," *The Chronicle of Higher Education*, November 27, 1998, p A16. This article summarizes relevant parts of a book by Janine Werdel, *Collision and Collusion: The Strange Case of Western Aid to Eastern Europe 1989-1998* (New York: St. Martin's Press, 1998). My personal interactions with members of the Harvard team also confirm this observation.

15. Joseph Kahn and Timothy L. O'Brien, "How Goldman Sachs & Co. Aided Russia's Collapse...and Got Rich," *The St. Petersburg Times*, November 3, 1998, pp. VI-VII.

16. Discussions in Tyumen and Moscow with Russian specialists, June 1997.

17. Discussions in Moscow with officials of the Ministry of Science and Technology, June 1999.

18. Discussion in Moscow with Russian specialists who follow the Russian press, April 1998.

19. "On the Causes of the Low Collection of Taxes, General Reasons for the Nonpayment Crisis, and Possibilities for Payments by Russian Enterprises," Interagency Commission under the Chairmanship of P.A. Karpov (Karpov Commission), Moscow, December, 1997.

20. *Ibid.*

21. Discussions with a participant in the activities of the Zarechny city council and a review of that city's budget documents.

22. Clifford G. Gaddy and Barry W. Ickes, "Russia's Virtual Economy," *Foreign Affairs*, vol. 77, no. 5, September/October 1998, pp. 53-68.

23. Stephen S. Moody, "The Virtual Monetary Fund and Russia's Current Industrial Expansion," Foreign Policy Research Institute, Philadelphia, distributed by e-mail, August 20, 1999.

24. Discussion at Kurchatov Institute in Moscow, April 1998.

25. Discussion at the Ministry of Science and Technology in Moscow, July 1998.

26. Karpov Commission, "Russian Enterprises."

27. "Gazprom Lobbies for Gas Ruble," *The Russia Journal*, May 31-June 6, 1999, p. 15.

28. For background on small businesses see, for example, Irina Khakamach, "In Search of the Middle Class," *The Potential of Russia,* Moscow, vol. 1, no. 1, 1998, pp. 46-48. Also see "Troubles of Small Business," *Argumenti i Fakti*, No. 46, November 1999, p. 8.

29. For a more detailed description, see Carole D. Schweitzer, *Russian Lessons* (Arlington, VA: Cameron Publications, 1997).

30. Discussions in Moscow with Russian economists, November 1998. For a typical and overly optimistic assessment of developments in the regions by governors, see "Investment: Expectations Boom, A Roundtable with Six Regional Governors," *The Potential of Russia,* Moscow, vol. 1, no. 1, 1998, pp. 13-22.

31. Blair Ruble, "The Rise of Moscow, Inc.," *Wilson Quarterly*, Spring, 1998, pp. 81-87.

32. For an expanded description of these impressions see Schweitzer, *Russian Lessons,* pp. 149-152.

33. Judith Matloff, "A Russian Leader on Porridge, Czars, and Real Estate," *The Christian Science Monitor*, February 25, 1999, p. 11.

34. Ruble, "Moscow, Inc."

35. Paul Klebnikov, "The Slick City Boss or the Rough Edged Populist General," *Forbes*, November 16, 1998; "The Meteoric Rise of Luzhkov's System," *The Russian Business Review*, February 1999, pp. 10-13.

36. David Hoffman, "Economic Crisis Reaches Moscow, City Must Restructure Debt," *The Washington Post*, May 9, 1999, p. A18.

37. "Commercial Overview of the Russian Far East," *BISNIS*, U.S. Department of Commerce, October 1998.

38. Yulia Latynina, "When a Rich Land Has No Heat or Light," *The Moscow Times*, August 25, 1999, p. 8.

39. "Black Winter in Russia's Far East," *Russia Review*, January 1999; Comments by experts from American University during seminars in Washington, D.C., and Boston, February, 1999. Also see Gillian Caldwell, Steve Galster, Jyothi Kanics, and Nadia Steinzor, "Capitalizing on Transition Economies: The Role of the Russian Mafia in Trafficking Women for Forced Prostitution," *Transnational Organized Crime*, vol. 32, no. 4, Winter 1997, pp 45-46.

40. Yaroslav N. Semenikhin, "Economic Change in the Far East and the Role of Science and Technology Institutes," *Russian Science and Industrial Policy, Moscow and the Regions, A Conference Report*, Georgetown University, Washington, D.C., March 24-25, 1997, pp. 205-217.

41. Joan Agerholm, "Samara Region: In the Vanguard of Change," USAID, Moscow, September 1999; "Sweetly Flows the Volga," *Economist*, June 5, 1999, p. 38; Comments concerning the shovel were made by Vladimir Shorin at a conference at the National Academy of Sciences, November 1999.

42. *Unlocking Economic Growth in Russia*, McKinsey Global Institute, Moscow, October 1999, Chapter 4.

43. Comments by Clifford Gaddy at a conference at the National Academy of Sciences, November 1999.

44.   McKinsey Global Institute, *Growth in Russia.*

45.   V.I. Vidyapin, "Russia's Choice, a Socially Oriented Market Economy," Management of Technology, Russian-American Workshop, Russian Academy of Engineering, Moscow, 1996, pp. 79-85.

46.   Jim Hoagland, "Russia on the Brink," *The Washington Post*, September 10, 1998, op-ed page.

47.   Seminikhin, *op. cit.*; William Odum, "Losing It! Our Russian Illusions, Crushed by Reality," *The Washington Post*, September 6, 1998, p. C1.

48.   Alexander A. Dynkin and Natalia N. Ivanova, "The Russian Innovation System: Painful Adjustments in the Process of Economic Transition," *Russian Science and Industrial Policy: Moscow and the Regions, A Conference Report*, Georgetown University, Washington, D.C., March 24-25, 1997, pp. 45-59; "The Strange Rage of Boris Yeltsin," *The Economist*, March 28, 1998, p. 15.

49.   Daigle and Bivens, *op. cit.*

50.   Gerald Hough, Presentation at Woodrow Wilson Center, Washington, D.C., October 18, 1999. He argued that corruption within government may be preferable to corruption outside government.

51.   Discussions in Bellagio, Italy, with specialists from Zarechny, Russia, September, 1998.

52.   Discussions in Moscow with directors and deputy directors of three Russian economic research institutes, November 1998.

2

Struggling to Embrace
Modern Technologies

*Both Russians and foreigners are prejudiced against anything that bears
the label "Made in Russia."*

The Economist, 1997

We will pay salaries as usual: little and rarely.

Ministry of Finance, 1999

More than 90 percent of Russian scientists simply wait for someone to
give them money. They are not interested in searching for research contracts or grants. They believe the government owes them the financial
support needed to conduct research. And they don't pay attention to
whether anyone will use the products of their research. They assume
that introducing research results into practice is someone else's responsibility. I had difficulties changing my attitude. I hope other scientists will
also change their outlook.[1]

With these words, Gennady prepared to return to Moscow after a
brief visit to the United States amidst the economic chaos in Russia in
August 1998. There, his small environmental technology firm would
have to find new ways to fulfill its obligations pursuant to ruble-based
contracts that he had painstakingly developed and had then trium-
phantly signed in 1997. Inflation would slash his real income from
these contracts by two-thirds. But Gennady had survived financial
shocks in the past. As he boarded the Aeroflot plane at Dulles Airport,
he was reconciled to simply working harder to find new contracts.

Gennady and his team of a dozen scientists specialize in designing and operating systems for monitoring environmental pollution. Strapped for financial resources, the team has to make up in ingenuity what it lacks in sophisticated equipment so commonplace in the West. Originally, they developed computer models for estimating air and water contamination levels, using sparse data from monitoring devices already maintained by local government agencies rather than building more advanced monitoring stations. However, they soon realized that without better data, their estimates of pollution patterns would be highly uncertain. They gradually accumulated a financial base for designing and installing new stations that could provide better data, particularly measurements of exposure of children to dangerous levels of toxic chemicals in urban areas.

The story of how Gennady began his company in the early 1990s parallels histories of a number of other technology entrepreneurs in Russia. He was working in an institute of the Russian Academy of Sciences, where pay was uncertain and interest in his research on electronic control systems was minimal. He brought together several computer programmers and successfully competed for a grant to the institute of $65,000 from the European Union. European specialists were not only concerned over Russian pollutants drifting westward, but they were also intrigued by the ability of his group to model complicated pollution pathways on small computers. At about the same time, he landed several smaller contracts with cities in central Russia to assist in assessing local pollution problems. With income for his team guaranteed for two years, Gennady then searched for additional customers.

He quickly realized, however, that a large portion of the funds coming into the institute was absorbed by management. His first response was to include the leaders of the institute as members of his team. For a while his funds were well protected. As the institute fell on more difficult times and needed additional money to sustain its large staff, Gennady witnessed more and more raids on his limited budget.

He established a small independent firm to serve as the vehicle for business arrangements—paying the institute a fee for space rental. The team members working for the firm also kept their formal status as employees of the institute. They received little pay from the institute, but as institute employees they retained use of the health clinic of the academy and eventually would qualify for state pensions, however small.

With bulldog tenacity, Gennady obtained additional contracts from municipal and regional environmental agencies as he spent many weeks traveling throughout Russia in search of those few local agencies that were prepared to devote funds to environmental assessments. Then, in 1997, he found a new customer. He was awarded a three-year contract with Gazprom to monitor air pollution levels along gas pipelines and near chemical refineries. This contract with the gas industry giant would ensure that paychecks for him and his employees arrived on time well into the future.

As his firm grew, it was refreshing to hear Gennady speak at a governmental forum in Moscow in 1997, organized in response to demands by environmentalists for a voice in national policy. He was one of 25 speakers at the session on environmental monitoring. While other speakers complained about shortages of governmental funds for supporting their work, Gennady's pitch was different. He just wanted the opportunity to compete fairly for the occasional government contracts that were being signed in Moscow and throughout the country. If he lost a competition, so be it. In his view, the government had a responsibility not only to finance environmental assessments to the extent they could but also to select the most efficient firms to carry out the required monitoring.

Business was thriving until the August 1998 financial crisis. Not only did the value of the firm's ruble-based contracts plummet, but financial reserves were lost as the company's bank closed its doors. In September, the firm again set off on the slow road to financial viability. Within a year, they had discovered additional monitoring opportunities near the Caspian Sea, as Gazprom and Russian and foreign oil companies expanded their interests in the lucrative energy resources of that region.

In Russia, 42,000 small firms such as Gennady's, each with less than 60 employees, are classified as innovative. (In the United States, two million firms fall into such a classification.) By 1999, about 10,000 of these had found profitable market niches, although only 1,000-2,000 were performing serious research and development. In a particularly lucrative field, western businessmen had become interested in the computer software activities of 1,000 or more of these small businesses, and they were trying to establish partnerships that would help compensate for the shortage of computer specialists in the United States and Europe.[2]

Collectively, the 10,000 firms represent about 5 percent of the nation's innovation potential, but their capabilities are slowly increasing.[3] They are particularly important in pioneering roads around the three-pronged albatross of outdated equipment, outmoded management techniques, and outrageous financial manipulations. A few government officials recognize the significance of small-scale technological entrepreneurship and try to encourage embryonic businesses by providing safe working space and communication services for them.

As to governmental financing of the early research and development stages of innovation, through budget allocations the Russian government supports about 50 percent of the nation's research and development effort spread over many institutions. The remainder is financed by special government contracts, by the commercial sector, by the research institutes' internal funds, and by foreign sources. In recent years, this government investment has been less than 10 percent of the U.S. government's support of research and development (see Appendix A).

Research and development is distributed among 4,000 enterprises, research institutes, and universities. Much of the funding provides salaries at nearly dormant facilities. Indeed, leaving aside the 10,000 small innovative firms such as Gennady's, almost all research and development effort likely to lead to new products and processes with paying customers is concentrated in about 1,000 organizations.[4]

The government gives priority funding and also tax advantages to 57 State Scientific Centers. While most centers are oversized and not very efficient, they nevertheless are repositories of important technologies. In Soviet times, when the government assured full-cycle funding from research through production, the predecessor organizations of many centers were tightly linked to industrial activities. The enterprises which had been the customers of the predecessors retain much of the nation's capabilities for realizing near-term benefits of technological innovation, but few are now interested in paying the centers or anyone else for research and development programs with uncertain returns. Thus, the centers are scrambling to find new partners, accepting contracts from whatever sources are willing to provide them.

About 15 percent of the large Russian manufacturing enterprises are performing well despite the economic crisis. Some use modern technologies and effective management and marketing techniques to improve their positions at home and abroad, and a small percentage sponsor research and development activities. But they are the exceptions. Managers of many Soviet-era enterprises continue to believe that raw technical talent at their facilities is the key to financial viability. They have yet to adopt contemporary marketing approaches and effective financial controls so essential to bringing new technologies into the mainstream of business at home or abroad.[5]

Living with the Soviet Legacy

Funding shortfalls within industry and research and development institutions are usually cited as the principal reason for the stagnation of Russian technology. In addition, however, the Soviet industrial legacy inhibits effective use of financial resources that are available. Box 2.1 identifies barnacles of the past that still retard technological development—from an emphasis on quantity rather than quality of products to poor mechanisms for diffusing innovations throughout the industrial base to inflexible research institutions. Also, remnants of the research and development command system limit opportunities for personal initiative and waste resources. Such a system is ineffective in an open market economy, where competitiveness and timeliness are critical to commercial success.[6]

Organizationally, the best Soviet researchers were concentrated within the enterprises and institutes comprising the defense complex and within the institutes of the Academy of Sciences. These specialists received high salaries and had access to modern facilities and equipment and to foreign scientific journals. Trips abroad for academy scientists and extended holidays for defense specialists were common. In most cases, they had better housing, higher quality medical and child

---

Box 2.1
A Lingering Soviet Legacy that Retards
Technological Development

• Central planning guaranteed that all output would be "purchased," and there was little incentive to improve the quality of products already in use.

• There were few incentives for personal initiative—few opportunities to penetrate a rigid economy with new approaches.

• Research and development efforts were spread across every conceivable discipline with no sense of prioritization.

• Technological development was organized on a "departmental" basis, as each ministry supported its own needs with little regard to duplication or to spin-off technologies of interest to others.

• Research and development expenditures supporting the military effort had limited applicability to civilian problems.

• Research and development programs frequently relied on labor-intensive approaches that are no longer competitive in quickly producing high-quality results.

• Gargantuan research institutions were extraordinarily slow in taking advantage of new technological opportunities.

• Research and development programs were not tightly coupled to the educational system, with many entrants into science and engineering poorly prepared for innovative work.

Sources: Boris G. Saltykov, "Russian Science on the Threshold of a New Stage of Reform," *Russian Science and Industrial Policy: Moscow and the Regions*, Conference Report, March 24-25, 1997, Center for Eurasian, Russian, and East European Studies, Georgetown University, pp. 1-9; Leonid Gokhberg, Merton J. Peck, and James Goes (editors), *Russian Applied Research and Development: Its Problems and Its Promises*, International Institute for Applied Systems Analysis, Vienna, April 1997, pp. 12, 18.

---

care facilities, and easier access to foodstuffs and consumer products than their colleagues in other sectors. This practice of favoritism created a significant social stratification within the science and technology community.[7] With the defense complex having concentrated on military applications and the academy concerned primarily with basic research, the neglected civilian-oriented applied research base that should have led the technological efforts to spur the economic transition during the 1990s simply languished even further.

Technology gurus who honed their skills in the Soviet defense complex and in the Academy of Sciences want to participate in the emerging market economy. But some have had difficulty understanding that they must both limit their spending habits and find new sources of money if they are to survive the rapid decline of government budgets. Like Gennady, 10 percent or so have been successful in finding new income streams for innovative activities—from foreign governments and international organizations and from other Russian entities still able to pay for research and development support.

A second group has relied on a reorientation of most research activities to technical services hoping that some funds will then be available to also support research and development. To earn immediate income, their institutes install electrical systems in office buildings, produce specialized items for home use from machine shops, modify computers, provide security systems, test the quality of building materials, and analyze chemical compositions of interest to large companies, for example. Also, those with large facilities rent space—to banks, to automobile dealers, to clothing outlets, and to grocery stores. These strategies have provided income, but at the expense of sacrificing innovation capabilities.

Russian survival instincts mesh with any strategy that helps ensure a payroll. Few research institutes have closed. Indeed, only in 1998 was I able to confirm the total abandonment of a single institute. The animal research institute that trained dogs, pigs, and monkeys for the space flights of the 1960s finally closed its doors 35 years after the Soviet Union switched from orbiting animals to cosmonauts.

Meanwhile, the number of active researchers has plummeted from one million Soviet researchers located in Russia in 1991 to less than 500,000 in 1998. Most departees have simply given up their careers in science and engineering. Those reluctant to change professions have remained in their jobs hoping the financial situation will change. A few have uncovered opportunities to participate in international projects that pay well and provide opportunities for further professional development. Those who have set up private technology-oriented firms have had mixed results, as we have seen.[8]

Russian statistics show that a few manufacturing enterprises have been formally closed; but only when you visit an enterprise can you determine what happened. Tours of a rusting animal feed plant in Kirov far to the northeast of Moscow, an abandoned aluminum plant in the heart of the capital city, and a closed paper products plant in Podolsk on the southern edge of the city, for example, provided glimpses of reality. The old facilities were still there. They remained legal entities. Both maintenance crews and nominal managers refused to face reality and expressed confidence that some day the production lines and the associated research and development units would be revived. It is not clear whether these enterprises show up on the official statistics as operating as usual, transformed, or closed. Probably, most are listed as operating as usual.

If recent trends persist, the outlook for technological innovation on a national scale is not good. In short, the financial and administrative barriers to profiting from innovation that are encountered in any market economy, as depicted in Figure 2.1, are compounded by the lingering Soviet legacy. In comparison with other industrialized economies, few customers look toward Russian firms for new products; and few angels are willing to put up venture capital. Meanwhile, greedy officials and criminals seek to siphon off funds that might be available for research and development or other purposes.

The Ministry of Science and Technology constantly decries the neglect of technological innovation, a necessity in moving from Soviet production, largely isolated from the world, to Russian production that is competitive at home or abroad. In 1997, less than 3 percent of the limited capital investment in industry involved innovation. Less than 5 percent of industry sales had some relevance to innovation. Only 6 percent of exports were in any way new products. These numbers are five times lower than the norm for modern economies.[9]

Directly linked to the decline of Russia's technological position, the vast majority of new industrial equipment is now imported. Much equipment needed by Russian manufacturers simply is not produced in Russia. Russian-made equipment often is not capable of meeting

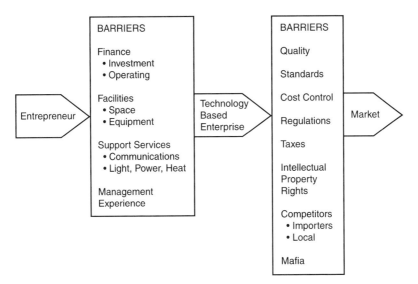

FIGURE 2.1 Hurdles to profiting from innovation in Russia. SOURCE: Adapted from Rustam Lalkaka, *Technology Transfer Seminar*. The World Bank, February 1999.

standards required for producing exports for western markets or is so wasteful of energy and raw materials that the products are too expensive to sell. The label, "Made-in-Russia," signals questionable quality in the eyes of customers of civilian products in Russia as well as abroad.[10]

Russian Enterprises and Innovation

The large Soviet research and manufacturing organizations, usually employing tens of thousands of scientists, engineers, and production workers, were made to order for central planners promoting development and use of the latest technologies. New designs reflected instructions from Moscow. Money and materials were available, and shining new equipment was produced. Usually, someone was prepared to use the latest innovations.

Now, however, these large organizations are on their own in finding customers ready to pay for products. They have so many employees demanding pieces of ever-shrinking payrolls that few directors can divert resources to explore risky new technologies with uncertain futures. When the directors succeed in winning contracts of any sort, employees throughout the organizations clamor to share the proceeds. Nevertheless, a handful of enterprises recognize the need to support research and development efforts if their products are to remain of interest to old or new customers, and they earmark funds for research.

Gennady has learned that the largest supporter of research and development activities, aside from government ministries, is Gazprom. The gas company's network includes a number of Russian technology-oriented organizations: three research institutes, three applied geophysics and engineering institutes, a design institute, and more than 15 equipment factories and construction organizations. Also, Gazprom supports a few consulting firms and individual scientists with needed skills.[11]

Gazprom officials contend they spend several hundred million dollars annually supporting research and development—an eye-opening figure in contemporary Russia. A large portion of these expenditures is not directed to research and development, however, but covers technical services rather than systematic searches for new innovations. Nevertheless, Gazprom sometimes supports innovation—such as adaptation of aircraft turbine engines for use in gas-fired power plants— and their research and development funds dwarf research expenditures of other enterprises for maintaining a technical base within the country. Of course, no other enterprise is in the favorable financial position of Gazprom and has the technical capability to effectively use scientists and engineers from outside the company.[12]

After a decade of neglect of research and development, a few Russian oil companies realize that applied research can often lead to cost savings. In the late 1990s, they spent tens of millions of dollars annually in improving operating efficiencies. Contracts with western firms help maintain and upgrade field and refinery operations. Significant funds also have gone to Russian institutions and to individual Russian specialists interested in both geophysics and petroleum engineering. However, in 1997 as earnings declined due to the depression in world oil prices, research support began to shrink; but if oil prices continue the upward trend of 1999, research support should again increase. Meanwhile, the state research institutes established decades ago to support the Soviet oil program search for funds from the new companies—arguing for mandatory research and development taxes on sales of oil.[13]

In another sector, a few aerospace firms are struggling to remain on the frontiers of technology. Most enterprises suffer as the Russian air force scales back its operations, Russian airlines increasingly look to American and European firms as their suppliers of replacement equipment, and the export market for Russian civilian aircraft evaporates. But in space activities, several international business alliances provide for high-tech activities at major Russian facilities. One example is the anticipated purchase by Lockheed Martin of 101 rocket engines, at a cost of one billion dollars, from a joint venture between Pratt & Whitney and Energomash, which is producing the engines in the town of Khimky on the outskirts of Moscow.[14] Several such international alliances are discussed in Chapter 9.

Engineering innovation characterizes large numbers of construction projects. Moscow, of course, is a showcase for the building industry—from an underground shopping mall in the very center of the city to several glass towers built for the tax service. Marble has become a building material synonmous with wealth and is being used in unusual ways, particularly by banks. The Russian Nuclear Safety Institute made the mistake of constructing a marble facade on an otherwise rundown building and quickly became a target of widespread interest among a mafia that equates marble with wealth.[15]

A less glitzy, but important, example of the continuing need for good construction technology is highway construction in a country subjected to the harshest of climates. The road network of the country is not well developed; and even in the hardest of economic times, asphalt will be in wide demand. Few of the 2,000 asphalt firms in the country are interested in improving their product, however. They simply want to be paid for producing the same old asphalt, even if the quality of the tar has gone downhill as firms cut corners during acquisition of raw materials and during mixing of asphalt.

One exception is Rosasfalt, a giant of the asphalt industry, which works with the German firm, Wirtgen, to improve road durability of its material and to reduce pollution during mixing and spreading. Not unexpectedly, Rosasfalt is campaigning heavily for establishment of new road improvement funds throughout the country. These funds would guarantee money for construction activities, with a little left over for improving the technology.[16]

The conventional wisdom that Russia now lacks capacity for innovation is sometimes challenged by Russian engineering companies when they put their works on public display. For example, at the 1997 Russian Industrial Exhibition in St. Petersburg, the holding company Energomashstroitelnaya displayed modern power generation equipment produced by eight firms in its conglomerate, firms with domestic and international sales of about $2 billion annually. Discussions with officials of the companies revealed that the companies have considerable capacity to innovate. But while sales provided stability for maintaining workforces, sales have had limited impact in advancing the companies' manufacturing capabilities. The customers have no stake in reducing production costs of their suppliers, and therefore their contracts do not allow for the suppliers to install and use improved engineering approaches that are available.[17]

Progressive management policies that foster innovation can be found in the machine tool sector. The joint stock company, Sverdlov, in St. Petersburg, for example, has an efficient work force of about 500 compared to the bloated force of 4,000 of its Soviet-era predecessor. It has shifted to the model of a small American machine-tool company, customizing products for individual Russian machine-tool manufacturers with orders for exports or licenses. Thus, it works out innovative approaches, designs new equipment, and provides automation systems tailored to specific needs. In providing support for its clients, it does not shrink from spending money to overhaul its own machinery to improve performance.[18]

Overall, expenditures for innovation by Russian enterprises are minimal for a country with a large industrial complex—less than 2 percent the expenditures by U.S. companies. Privatized firms have little incentive to support research. The state firms also use their resources to meet immediate needs.

Preferential Treatment for Oversized Scientific Centers

Immediately upon disintegration of the Soviet Union in 1991, western science policy experts began advocating a downsizing of the large and bloated science and technology infrastructure of enterprise laboratories, design institutes, and research and educational institutions established in the Russian part of the USSR over several decades. Then, at an international conference in Moscow in 1993, western delegates finally heard the words they had waited for. After these delegates had railed at Russian officials for three days over the need to reduce the infrastructure by 50 percent, the Russian Minister of Science and Technology announced he was taking a step in their direction.

His plan was to create a network of State Scientific Centers modeled after the group of a dozen national laboratories of the U.S. Department of Energy. The ministry would pick the very best research institutes, designate them as centers, provide them with ample funding, and let other research institutes gradually shrink as their funding levels dropped. With this initiative setting the pace, the research establishment would eventually become one-half its size in Soviet times. So promised the minister.[19]

Neither the minister nor the delegates were interested in my rejoinder that the proposal for State Scientific Centers was not a good idea. Focusing resources on the best Russian institutions and letting other facilities fend for themselves made a lot of sense. But defining a center of excellence as an entire institute made far less sense. Russian research and development institutes often employ more than a thousand scientists and engineers, and supporting an entire institute of such enormous proportions—housing both productive and poorly performing specialists—is contrary to the goal of excellence.

My alternative was to support outstanding laboratories of not more than one or two hundred employees each and then let the less effective laboratories whither on the vine. But Russians were accustomed to thinking on large scales and entrusting the fate of institutes to directors. The idea of discriminating good from poor within a single institute did not even make it onto the decision screen.

The concept of a system of State Scientific Centers had been born in 1991 when the internationally known physicist Yevgeny Velikhov decided to seek autonomy and stature for the institute where he was the director, the Kurchatov Institute for Atomic Energy. His institute was to be the first independent research center. The analogous laboratories of the U.S. Department of Energy, like the Kurchatov Institute, each employ thousands of specialists and support personnel, although under drastically different economic conditions and management practices than those encountered in Russia.

Velikhov convinced the Ministry of Atomic Energy to cut his institute loose from its jurisdiction. Then the research grants and contracts from the West began rolling in. This new "independent" research powerhouse in Russia reflected western views that decentralization of research, production, and other activities was essential in destroying the communist tradition of central planning and control.

At the time of the conference, the Kurchatov Institute was riding high. The Ministry of Atomic Energy had not fully terminated its support of the breakaway institute. Foreign contracts focused on the institute's capabilities in the national security arena, such as technologies for enhancing the protection from theft of weapons-grade nuclear materials and for detecting nuclear items being smuggled across international borders. However, many institutes that were candidates for status as State Scientific Centers had few active links to national security concerns and were therefore of less interest to western governments.

With only my negative voice at the conference, the Russian government promptly established the system of State Scientific Centers. While I continue to believe that small centers of excellence would be preferable to the large centers, the system that has evolved is certainly a step forward in preserving the most important technological resources. Initially, the government was flooded with over 400 applications from institutes seeking designations as centers. Forty were selected.

By 1999 the list had been expanded to 57 centers (see Appendix B). They have many technical profiles. All are large, with some employing thousands of workers and the others hundreds. The government provides funding for each center, although much less than promised. The centers also are entitled to preferential electricity, water, and telephone rates—at least on paper, and they have a few exemptions from taxes and customs duties.[20] In return, the government has the authority to review and approve research programs of the centers and to participate in the selection of center directors.

In mid-1998, the executive director of the association that serves as a voice in Moscow for the State Scientific Centers brought me up to date on their activities. He proudly reported that his staff had succeeded in helping one of the centers climb out of debt, although the other 56 were still operating in the red. How did his staff achieve this turnaround?[21]

Each center has contracts with various government agencies covering specific research projects and support services. But, when time for payments arrives, the agencies usually do not pay their bills. The centers in turn have no money to pay their own bills. The heat and electricity are sometimes turned off, the staff works on the basis of promises of future salary payments, and the tax authorities keep hovering at the doors.

The highest priority of the staff of the association has been to persuade government and quasi-government creditors—such as the tax inspectorate or the electric company—to write off debts of the centers in exchange for cancellation by the centers of debts of government customers for their services. These debt swaps are frought with arguments and accusations over the details of contractual arrangements and payments that had been made. Nevertheless, debt swapping is a primary activity of the association. The first success clearly boosted the morale of the staff.

The outlook for the future of the State Scientific Centers has not been bright. This outlook became even gloomier following the financial crisis in the summer of 1998. By that time the centers depended for one-third of their budgets on the Ministry of Science and Technology. But the funds were soon in jeopardy. The ministry, and hence the

centers, are constantly short changed, as the Ministry of Finance re-
fuses to release funds for science and technology allocated by the
Duma. Also, all centers suffer from the increased costs of electricity.
Despite their claims for reduced rates, regional authorities and local
electric companies are not interested in "special interest" decisions in
Moscow. Finally, the intake of young specialists into the centers has
almost stopped. The only incentive for young scientists left is for the
government to exempt young specialists who work in State Scientific
Centers from the military draft, but obtaining such exemptions is not
easy.[22]

Despite their oversized staffs and the steady obsolescence of their
equipment, the State Scientific Centers should play an important role
in promoting innovation. In Soviet times, they housed an estimated 30
percent of the nation's technological capability, including unique international know-how. Much of this prowess remains in place.[23] As currently configured, the centers may not be the best models for the future of Russia; but they have both staff and alumni in influential
positions in many regions of Russia who will resist change.

Innovation at the Micro-Level

Since the early 1990s, a handful of officials of the Russian Ministry
of Science and Technology have also promoted much smaller innovating organizations. The ministry's objective is to encourage low-cost efforts of individual scientists and engineers interested in using their talents to build technology-based businesses. The officials have correctly
concluded that whatever the macroeconomic framework, the microeconomic framework will be decisive in encouraging or discouraging
initiative by potential innovators. They want to accelerate progress toward economic revival by gradual multiplication of small commercial
successes rather than trying to upgrade technologies throughout all of
industry with new decrees from Moscow. They know that some innovative scientists and engineers, such as Gennady, have already started
their own businesses, and they are convinced that others will follow if
given limited support.[24]

Technoparks, incubators, and innovation centers have been identified as important pathways to modern technology in Russia. Such institutions are temporary homes for small innovative businesses. In 1997, small traders were responsible for most of the 4 percent reduction in imports for the retail sector, while paying 40 percent of the taxes in the most stable regions of Russia. Couldn't small technology innovators who emerged from these temporary homes do as well?[25]

What are the distinctions among the three innovation concepts? Technoparks are usually located on the grounds of universities. With government funding, the university provides space, utilities, and communication services at reduced rates for entrepreneurs trying to grow technology-oriented businesses, often from scratch. Incubators are also sites—often in rented space of research institutes—where such support is provided at reduced rates. However, the small business occupants already have a greater semblance of a customer base and at least a limited track record in providing commercial products. Innovation centers are more ambitious undertakings that bring together educational institutions, research institutes, and small entrepreneurs to develop advanced-technology businesses that can eventually survive without governmental support. In practice, these three concepts often become mixed. The best approach is "whatever works."

Two dimensions of support for embryonic technology-oriented businesses are important. Advisory services by resident Russian staffs concerning marketing, intellectual property rights, and contract preparation are usually in high demand. Also, access to low-interest loans or equity investment capital is often critical—for operational costs, for modest equipment purchases, for market testing, and for initial production runs. As we shall see, several Russian funds have been established to provide loan and equity support for projects, usually in the range of $50-100,000 but sometimes up to several hundred thousand dollars.[26]

There are hundreds of success stories associated with the small offices and laboratories that populate the technoparks, incubators, and innovation centers. Two widely advertised successes are international sales of Russian-English translation software and CD-ROMs containing the art history of Russia based on the collections of the Hermitage in St. Petersburg. Less well known is software that enables hundreds of Moscow seamstresses to rapidly turn out all types of clothing carefully designed to cling to customers with a variety of body proportions. If you would like a photograph etched on your tombstone, a firm will scan the photo into a computer and chip the marble to very exact specifications, provided you are ready to wait in line for six months. Another firm provides plastic vacuum wrap for food products, having discovered that other Russian wrap is of low quality and imported wrap is expensive. Finally, if you want to make long-distance phone calls to remote areas that are poorly served by the telephone system, a telecommunications service provider is ready. He has an arrangement with a Moscow TV station to send digitized voice transmissions over portions of the satellite band that carries television programs to remote areas.

Unfortunately, technoparks sometimes fall under the control of middlemen determined to extract as much money as possible from both the government and the small entrepreneurs. For example, in 1993 Moscow State University offered interested companies the opportunity to occupy a new building in the adjacent technopark. The rental rates were reasonable. The location was excellent. The university would guarantee all needed support for an acceptable fixed price. The catch was that the building was set back from the main roadway, and the middleman responsible for the financial aspects of the technopark insisted that the occupant build an entire road network for the technopark. He had already received university funds for road construction, but they somehow vanished. Three years later, the building was still empty.

Criminal elements usually lurk in the shadows around embryonic business centers. In response to this threat, the incubator at the Electrotechnical Institute in Moscow is behind towering concrete walls with no external signs of occupancy. The visitor must choose the correct entrance and then pass through three security doors. While not customer friendly, according to the manager it is safe from criminals with extortion in mind. The occupants confirmed that the favorable security conditions were a primary reason they decided to move into the incubator.[27]

A third consideration is the exaggerated promises of the government for supporting small innovative businesses. The innovation center in Obninsk, 60 miles south of Moscow, has impressive plans for stimulating industrial growth in the city and the surrounding region through supporting expansion of high tech organizations already at the starting line. Every senior science and technology official of the Russian government, from the president's office on down, and leaders of the Duma and Federal Council have been to Obninsk to participate in the opening of a new era of innovation. The governor of the region and the entire city council declared the innovation center a new beacon of hope during dismal days. But little money followed the words of encouragement—not even enough to pay all the center's staff let alone stimulate innovative activities.[28]

Most innovative firms that obtain infrastructure support from the government have a few common characteristics: small-scale production with a lack of access to capital for major expansion; optimistic management, but with management experience limited to low-volume sales; and products and services geared almost exclusively to the Russian market (except for computer software, which often reaches international markets). In time, some will overcome such handicaps and launch operations on a larger scale, some will be absorbed by larger companies, and others will simply continue their modest activities or else go out of business. The outlook for small innovative firms is quite promising since they reflect a pragmatic way to cope with challenges facing technological innovation in Russia in the immediate future.

New Ways to Turn a Profit

Russian managers have many master plans for reversing the decline of their institutes—inevitably long on ideas but short of cash. Some plans may seem like blue-sky dreams to western visitors. To Russian patriots, however, they reflect an unwavering confidence in the future of their technological ingenuity. On occasion this confidence is rewarded.

One of the most imaginative institute directors is the previously mentioned Yevgeny Velikhov. In the fall of 1998, he briefed specialists from a leading western oil exploration company on his proposal for finding and extracting off-shore oil and gas under the Arctic ice. Donning his second hat as president of the Russian company, Rosshelf, which was founded by his institute in cooperation with Gazprom and the Russian navy, Velikhov planned to mount a drilling platform between two nuclear submarines that would place it on the seafloor. With adequate power from the submarine reactors, drilling into the seafloor would proceed until subsurface oil and gas deposits were located and well characterized. Then, pumps and well heads would be placed on the seafloor, with the oil and gas brought to port by submarine tankers. Although skeptical and not prepared to invest their own funds, the western experts mused that the project might just work. Perhaps increases in oil prices in 1999 will provide capital to move beyond theoretical studies of the concept.

Seven years earlier, Velikhov had unveiled another plan to a skeptical audience from Russia and abroad that turned into a success story. He established Relcom, a 50-50 venture of the Russian Commodities Exchange and the Kurchatov Institute as the first Russian internet service provider. By 1994 Relcom had enlisted 70,000 subscribers throughout the country. Relcom used the Russian telephone lines for internal communications. In addition, with the help of western private foundations, Velikhov obtained a dedicated telephone line from Moscow to Helsinki. Once e-mail messages were in Finland, they were into the world-wide Internet system.

By reinvesting all profits, Relcom managed to double in size each year until 1997, when capital needs outstripped available resources. It then joined forces with the former telecommunications monopoly, Rostelcom, with the Kurchatov Institute retaining only a 5 percent ownership in the new company, called Business Network. Still, there are many professional opportunities for underemployed institute specialists. Also, the new company supports a variety of research and education activities at the institute.[29]

Fifty miles south of Moscow, the Institute of Immunological Engineering for many years was heavily dependent on contracts from the military-industrial complex. This support has disappeared, and Russian funding for public health-oriented research is very small. On the wall of the director's office is a photo of one very important asset—a large land area in a pleasant setting not far from Moscow. The map shows that eight new buildings were scheduled for construction in the undeveloped part of the territory.

But times changed. Four foreign companies were interested in renting space in the undeveloped territory. A French company was already manufacturing irons and frying pans in 1999. Another French company was producing yogurt. Alcoa was producing plastic cups for soft drinks. Finally, Bristol-Myers Squibb was considering production of generic drugs. With a slimmed down staff and a guaranteed source of income from its rental activities, the institute was in a reasonably good position to maintain its core research competences: molecular immunology, cell biology, physiology, and immunobiotechnology.[30]

Also related to the interests of the pharmaceutical industry, but located 2,000 miles to the east of Moscow, is the State Scientific Center for Virology and Applied Biotechnology, called Vector. The Soviet military establishment set up this institute in the 1970s to investigate the most dangerous viruses, such as smallpox and ebola. As Russia disclaimed interest in biological weapons in the early 1990s, the center struggled to find new ways to utilize its capabilities, with an emphasis on serving the nation's public health needs.

By 1999, Vector had reduced its workforce by more than 30 percent, with 2,000 employees still in place. Also, there had been a dramatic transformation of the institute from one of total secrecy to one that was on the agenda of hundreds of foreign scientists visiting Russia during that year. It was featured in documentaries on American TV networks about the history of biological weapons and the new threat of bioterrorism. In 1998, the institute leadership proudly proclaimed that it had opened all formerly locked doors for specialists from the West to witness the transformation to an exclusively civilian institution. Indeed, a number of western experts have visited some of the most tightly guarded buildings of the past.

With no support from the Russian military establishment, how was the institute surviving? As a State Scientific Center, it received some funds from the Ministry of Science and Technology. But most of the institute's income was from commercial activities—sales of the following products within Russia and the former Soviet republics:

- Test systems for diagnosis of infectious diseases
- Vaccines for hepatitis A and measles
- Recombinant cytokines including interferon
- Medicinal and veterinary drugs
- Nutrient media for cultivating viruses and cells
- Sera of calves, cattle, pigs, and sheep
- Enzymes and reagents

The U.S. government has provided research grants to encourage researchers to redirect their expertise to public health problems—encephalitis, liver fluke, hanta virus, and other infections of concern. Other countries as well, including China and South Korea, have invested in drawing on the technical capabilities at Vector.[31]

A sterling example of commercial success in taking research results to the market can be reported from Nizhny Novgorod. In this case, the activity moved out of a cloistered research institute to a more appropriate location in the center of this major Russian city.

The story began in June 1994 with my visit to the formerly secret city of Sarov, also known by its post office designation as Arzamas-16. This atomic city was the birthplace of the Russian nuclear weapons program and was not accustomed to receiving foreign visitors at that time. My task was to interest researchers in working on western-funded civilian projects in order to reduce temptations to look to rogue countries for financial support, but with the provision that their efforts would be subject to scrutiny by specialists from the West. Prior to my visit, Lyudmila Nesterenko, a talented mathematician, was among those designated by the institute as project leaders. While only one female in a group of 20 project leaders may seem unfair, the fact that even one woman was permitted to rise to such a senior position in this masculine environment was noteworthy.

Within five years, Nesterenko had successfully directed several western-funded software development projects at Sarov. Then, with a contract from Intel in hand, and realizing that government support may well be short-lived, she decided to move 65 miles north to Nizhny Novgorod and establish her own firm. She would be free from reliance on uncertain funding from either the Russian or western governments.

Such a move was remarkable. The security services allowed her to move to an open city with intensive contact with foreigners. She was willing to take a chance on her untested entrepreneurial skills. She even succeeded in finding an apartment.

Nestorenko chose Nizhny Novgorod over Moscow and St. Petersburg because good schools and a bad economy in that Volga city gave her a buyers market in recruiting personnel. Also, she believed that the work ethic in the provincial capital was higher than in the larger cities. Finally, industrial security problems were less intense, which was important in protecting software.

She obtained contracts with Philips, Motorola, Toshiba, Gazprom, and several smaller firms and assembled a staff of 40, including several colleagues from Arzamas-16. Soon, in a smart move, she turned over the reins of running the company to a physicist with more business experience while she concentrated on the technical aspects of software development. By 1999, her firm had grown to 160 employees, with Intel contracts being her principal source of support. The American Embassy in Moscow, reflecting on the initial U.S. government grant five years earlier, described her activity as a textbook example of how to successfully incubate small, high-tech companies from Russia's closed research establishment.[32]

The foregoing examples of capitalizing on modern technologies to penetrate the marketplace are encouraging. They are the exception rather than the rule, however, and the size of the activities is not always great. They give some hope, nevertheless, that clever people can continue to bring technological achievements into the economy, looking to the day when, in the aggregate, their efforts will have a significant impact on economic growth.

The Future Outlook

There are rays of hope for technological revival on the horizon as a few large enterprises press ahead with modern manufacturing lines and small innovative entrepreneurs increasingly find their market niches. When foreign companies left Russia in 1998 and imports into the country became prohibitively expensive, both large and small firms suddenly had unprecedented market opportunities on their doorsteps. As one example of the response, a converted defense facility in Kazan quickly became home for more than 40 small innovative enterprises, with almost all turning a profit.

Even without this impetus, the Russian science and technology community has been incredibly resilient. Despite the absence of economic incentives, excellent specialists throughout the country are prepared to devote their careers to research and development. The story of Viktor Vyshinskiy, who learned his trade in the fluid dynamics department of an institute engaged in testing missile systems, sends a message that the game is far from over. He tried his hand at designing pollution control devices, but had no success in attracting customers. He tried to improve timber drying, with the same outcome. And he turned to flood prediction, which no one would support. Then, with characteristic doggedness, he had better luck in stimulating the interest of the Boeing Company and other aviation firms in new techniques for predicting turbulence created by airplanes at commercial airports.[33]

Vyshinskiy and others pick themselves up off the floor of despair every day and plunge again and again into the uncertain world of innovation. After the economic crisis of 1998, the veterinarian responsible for the avarium at the Shemyakin Institute of Bioorganic Chemistry in Pushchino told me that he had used his meager personal paycheck to buy feed for the carefully bred mice under his care. I knew that research was far from dead in Russia.[34]

But scientists and engineers, however determined, cannot succeed on a significant scale without help from the government. Substantial funding by the government to support introduction of new technologies into industrial processes when there is a clear demand for such technologies is necessary if Russia is to have a sustainable economic recovery. Contracts and grants that are carefully targeted and controlled to avoid misuse of funds are not only appropriate but essential, despite the obsession of free marketeers for opposing any program that smacks of corporate welfare.

Skeptical reformers often have difficulty with concentrating more research and development funds in a central bureaucracy for supporting their favorite projects. But they should look carefully at government incentives for technology development in western countries. Western practices include, for example, defense contracts and associated funding of overhead costs that support dual-use technologies with clear civilian applications. Government research programs are designed to enhance the technical capabilities of small businesses, and government research and development funds are provided to even the largest multinational companies on a project-by-project basis to improve their global competitiveness.

The Soviet Union's industrial might was built on government subventions. Old-line managers and researchers—now saddled with both overhead costs that are difficult to shed and outdated equipment—will operate effectively only when they have some level of government support. Industry simply will not revive in the foreseeable future without help from the government.

Hopefully, in one or two decades, Russia will have a new type of economy requiring few government subsidies. In the interim, the remnants of the old Soviet industrial complex, the reoriented State Scientific Centers, and the growing number of small innovative firms will be the flagships of technological change. They all need help. Government research grants with matching contributions from the intended industrial users of new innovations is one attractive option. Re-equipping laboratories to perform research and development of priority interest to the government is another. Guaranteed purchases by the government of innovative products is a third.

Those Russian technology entrepreneurs who can make it on their own do not welcome such suggestions. Government grants could give competitors an edge. But, in the larger scheme, the choice is governmental support of Russian technologies or continued industrial stagnation.

Notes

1.   Author interview in Washington, D.C., August 1998, as well as previous interviews in Moscow. The Russian scientist is Professor Gennady Yarigin, who had a distinguished career as a control systems specialist in the military-industrial complex, as a professor, and as a senior researcher at several institutions before

turning to the problems of environmental monitoring after the collapse of the Soviet Union.

2.   Author interviews in Moscow of Russian experts involved in support of small innovative firms, November 1999. The estimates are consistent with general writings on the topic, particularly writings in the Russian press and in Russian reports.

3.   Ibid. Also see Nikolay Rogalev, *Technology Commercialization in Russia: Challenges and Barriers* (Austin, TX: University of Texas IC2 Institute, 1998); and S.G. Polyakov and M.V. Rychev, *Incubators for Business: Russian Experience* (Moscow: U.S. Agency for International Development, 1996).

4.   Author interview in Moscow with experts in the Russian Ministry for Science and Technology, September 1999.

5.   Presentation at the National Academy of Sciences in Washington, D.C. by Boris Milner, Deputy Director of Russian Institute of Economics, November 1999. For more general background see *Russian Science: Conditions and Problems of Its Development*, Second All-Russian Seminar, State Committee for Science and Technology, Moscow, February 11-12, 1997.

6.   Boris G. Saltykov, "Russian Science on the Threshold of a New Stage of Reform," *Russian Science and Industrial Policy: Moscow and the Regions*, Conference Report, March 24-25, 1997, Center for Eurasia, Russian, and East European Studies, Georgetown University, pp. 1-9.

7.   Leonid Gokhberg, Merton J. Peck, and James Goes (editors), *Russian Applied Research and Development: Its Problems and Its Promises*, International Institute for Applied Systems Analysis, Vienna, April 1997, p. 12.

8.   L.G. Zubova, *Values and Motivation of Scientic Work*, Center for Science Research and Statistics, Moscow, 1998, p. 52.

9.   *Report of Activity during 1998*, Fund for Development of Small Firms in the Science and Technology Sphere, Moscow, 1999. This report is based on data provided by the Center for Science Research and Statistics of the Ministry of Science and Technology, Moscow.

10.   N. Gaponenko, "Innovation and Innovation Policy during Transition to a New Technological Order," *Voprosi Ekonomiki*, No. 9, 1997, pp. 84-92.

11.   Speech at the St. Petersburg State Mining Institute by R.I. Vyakhirev, President of Gazprom, "Conditions and Perspectives for the Gas Industry of Russia," November 3, 1998.

12.   Ibid.

13.   Author interviews in Moscow with Russian oil company executives and energy research specialists, April 1996 and November 1998.

14.   "Lockheed Martin To Buy 101 RD-180 Rocket Engines from Russian-American Joint Venture," Press Release, Lockheed Martin Company, June 17, 1997.

15.   Author interview in Moscow at the Nuclear Safety Research Institute, April 1998.

16.   "It Is Not Necessary to Chrome Plate the Roads," *Passport Express*, No. 8, 1998, p. 20.

17.   "The Russian Industrial Exhibition," Studies on Russian Economic

Development, Vol. 9, No. 2, 1998, pp. 207-8; "On the Energy Front," *Russia Review*, March 27, 1998, p. 44.

18. "The Russian Industrial Exhibition," pp. 207-8.

19. Discussions in Moscow during OECD-sponsored conference on Russian Science and Technology Policy, May, 1993.

20. Leonid Gokhberg and Levan Mindeli, *Research and Development in Russia, Trends of the 1990s*, Center for Science Research and Statistics, Moscow, 1997, pp. 9-10.

21. Author interview in Moscow, July 1998.

22. V.B. Kozlov, "State Scientific Centers in the System of Scientific-Technical Progress," *Russian Science: Conditions and Problems of Development*, Second All-Russian Seminar, Moscow, February 11-12, 1997, State Committee for Science and Technology, 1997, pp. 90-103.

23. *Ibid.*; Gokhberg and Mindeli, *Research and Development in Russia*, pp. 9-10.

24. Author interviews in Moscow, April 1998. See also brochure of the Fund for Development of Small Firms in the Science and Technology Sphere, available in Moscow since April 1998; I.M. Bortnik, "Experience of the Fund for Development of Small Firms in the Science and Technical Sphere in Engineering Innovation Management," *Technology Development and Commercialization: Russian and Global Experience*, Proceedings of International Conference, TechnoCon 97, St. Petersburg, July 7-10, 1997, (sponsored by the State Committee for Science and Technology), pp. 19-20.

25. *Ibid.*

26. *Ibid.*

27. Author visit to incubator and interviews with entrepreneurs in Moscow, April 1998.

28. Author interviews in Obninsk, July 1998; Author interviews with specialists from Obninsk in Bellagio, Italy, September 1998. Also see I.V. Gonnov, O.P. Luksha, A.P. Sorokin, "The Business Innovation Center as Infrastructure for Small Innovation Business Development in Obninsk and International Cooperation in the Sphere of Technology Transfer," *Technology Development and Commercialization: Russian and Global Experience*, Proceedings of International Conference, TechnoCon 97, St. Petersburg, July 7-10, 1997, (sponsored by the State Committee for Science and Technology), pp. 214-216.

29. Author interviews with Yevgeny Velikhov, July 1992, August 1995, and November 1998.

30. For a description of the institute's research activities see the brochure of the Institute of Immunology, available in Lyubchany, Russia, November 1998.

31. Author interviews at Vector in Koltsovo, Russia, November 1998 and September 1999.

32. Author interview in Moscow with U.S. Embassy official who had visited Nesterenko in Nizhny Novgorod, July 1998; Additional, updated interview in Moscow with Russian specialist knowledgable about her activities, November 1999.

33.   David Hoffman, "Why It's Wrong To Write Off Russia Now," *The Washington Post*, September 9, 1999, p. B-2.

34.   Author interview in Pushchino, Russia, November 1998. For an optimistic assessment of future projects see Leonid Gokhberg and Irina Kuznetsova, *Technological Innovation in Russia*, Center for Science Research and Statistics, Moscow, 1998, p. 10.

3

Profiting from Investments in Military Technology

The SU-27 fighter aircraft, based on five generations of advanced technologies, has become a global best seller.

Air Fleet magazine, Moscow, 1999

Titanium is not like other metals—the added value on rolled products is huge. If you can get $10,000 a ton for a titanium ingot from Russia, you'll get $15,000 a ton for rolled products.

Russia Review, 1998

As a Chinese delegation negotiated with officials of the Sukhoi aircraft company over purchase of Sukhoi SU-30 fighter bombers at the 1998 air show in Zhuhai, China, Americans attending the show worried about possible consequences in Taiwan. Americans and Chinese alike recognized that China's military technology effort was in such an underdeveloped state that there was no chance the country would soon threaten U.S. military power in Asia. But Taiwanese sensitivities are razor sharp when it comes to Chinese military capabilities. Such sales also reverberate in Japan, Korea, and India, with government leaders challenged by their opponents to respond politically and militarily.[1]

China provides the second most lucrative market after India for exports of Russian armaments. For decades the Soviet Union and now Russia have been apprehensive that the expanding Chinese population might spill over China's northern border in a quest for additional territory. Moscow's strategic doctrine has always included military responses to repel such a northern surge. But today, immediate opportunities for sales of Russian products take precedence over more distant threats to the sanctity of the border. Among the top sellers to China are:

- Sukhoi SU-27 fighters: long-range and capable of carrying 10 air-to-air missiles.
- S-300 air defense missiles: launched from the ground and capable of shooting down both aircraft and missile warheads.
- KILO-Class submarines: diesel powered with sophisticated search and attack sonars.
- T-72/T-80/T-90 battle tanks: reliable, maneuverable, and heavily armored.[2]
- Sunburn anti-ship missiles: speed of twice the velocity of sound skimming along the ocean's surface.[3]

Russia is not, however, transferring its most advanced military technologies to China. What's more, in 1997 Russian trade with Beijing was only 7 percent of U.S.-China trade, and just one-fourth of Russia's total trade with China, or $1 billion per year, involved sales of military hardware. Nevertheless, for Russia—and particularly for its defense enterprises—this modest income is important. For the West, such sales raise anxieties over Russian-Chinese military alliances.[4]

The transactions meet a short-term economic need in Russia. But related transfers to China of manufacturing technologies to produce modern weapons threaten the long-term viability of Russia's arms exports. In particular, under a licensing agreement concluded in 1995, China is scheduled to begin production of SU-27 jet fighters by the year 2000. Russian analysts have called this arrangement "an act of outrageous stupidity," since the deal will reduce China's purchases of aircraft from Russia. Also, China may be able to avoid licensing restrictions by introducing its own technological modifications and then competing with Russia for future sales on the Asian market.[5]

Given the size of the Russian military complex and the enormous investment in science and technology that it represents, Russia will undoubtedly continue to press for arms sales throughout the world.

While the importance of these sales to provide immediate economic relief and also help sustain a modern industrial base in Russia is clear, western governments focus on security implications and seek to constrain Russia's exports. Western exports of armaments far exceed Russia's sales, but the U.S. and European governments do not acknowledge unfairness in their opposition to any Russian sales. For its part, Russia does not agree that its arms transfers cause security unrest in distant parts of the world.

Closely related to Russia's arms transfers are international sales of military-related technologies that can be adapted to serve civilian purposes—nuclear power plants, rockets for launching satellites, jet engines, electronic control systems, ship propulsion systems, and laser targeting devices, for example. This is the dual-use issue. Analogous to exports of weapons, Russia has a responsibility to show constraint in selecting its customers while western governments need to recognize Russia's right to compete in the growing civilian markets for dual-use technologies.

In both the military technology and dual-use technology areas, Russia has joined with the leading western nations in adhering to a number of international agreements that set forth ground rules for international trade in dangerous items. But these ground rules give individual governments considerable discretion in selling specific items that are on international watch lists of sensitive technologies. This discretionary uncertainty often leads to diplomatic disputes over the appropriateness of Russian transfers of military technologies.

Another aspect of Russia's effort to capitalize on Soviet defense investments is its widely publicized industrial conversion programs. Most of these programs were established in 1991 and 1992 to help redirect military production lines to civilian activities. Few successes stand out among the many frustrating failures, and the concept of conversion as an easily achievable key to economic revival is fading fast. Converting a factory, together with its existing workforce, from production of hardware that meets military specifications regardless of cost to a plant producing equipment that is cost-competitive as well as quality-competitive is not an easy task. Still, the Russian mindset to

preserve all assets of perceived value seldom permits abandonment of
any facility, however inappropriate in the new business environment.

Declining Market Niche for Russian Armaments

Russia ranks third in the world in arms exports after the United
States and England. Russia, like its competitors, justifies these exports
as meeting both strategic and economic needs. But the government is
reluctant to release detailed data on sales of military equipment. Perhaps they want to avoid international criticism of specific items. Also,
it is difficult for any single office to obtain reliable and detailed information for incorporation in reports on just what the various ministries,
trade organizations, and enterprises are doing.

In rationalizing Russia's dramatic loss of customers for its armaments, Russian politicians point out that worldwide annual arms sales
by all countries slipped from $46 billion in 1992 to $21 billion in 1998.
As indicated in Figure 3.1, the decline of Soviet/Russian exports was
very sudden as the Warsaw Pact collapsed and Soviet armament lost
popularity in Eastern Europe. Beginning in 1992, sales became relatively stable at 10 percent of the level of sales during the late 1980s.
While acknowledging that Russian revenues for arms exports slipped
even further to $2.3 billion in 1998, ever optimistic politicians predict
increased annual sales up to $7 billion in a few years. They foresee a
revival of demand from important customers in countries that were
ravaged by the 1998 Asian financial crisis.[6]

During the late 1990s, Russia sold military hardware to more than
50 countries, with the principal big ticket items being jet aircraft, combat infantry vehicles, multiple rocket launch systems, helicopters, and
air defense systems. The relatively new market of China and the long-
standing Indian market absorbed two-thirds of the exports. In the
Middle East, Syria is the most reliable customer, although Russian
equipment can be seen in a number of other military inventories of the
region as well. Russia has achieved some success in selling equipment
in Latin America and other Asian countries. Also, Greek Cypriots are
a potential customer, infuriating Turkey, which has reconsidered plans
to purchase helicopters from Russia.[7]

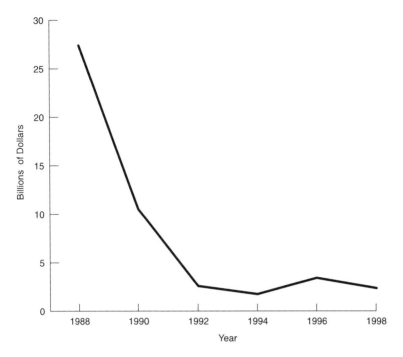

FIGURE 3.1 Exports of Soviet/Russian military equipment (in billions of dollars). SOURCE: Igor Khripunov, "Russia's Weapons Trade," *Problems of Post-Communism*. Vol 46, No. 2. Mar/Apr 1999, pp. 39-48. Data for 1998 from "Stable Arms Sales Seen," *Moscow Times*, April 1, 1999, p. 11.

At the 1999 arms bazaar in Abu Dabai in the Persian Gulf region, potential buyers from nearby states, Africa, and Southeast Asia were prepared to spend tens of billions of dollars in modernizing their armaments. The extent to which they will empty their pocketbooks is not clear as negotiations initiated at Abu Dabai continue around the world. At the bazaar, Russian manufacturers displayed a well-laden tray of offerings of possible interest to both rich and poor states, as indicated in Box 3.1.[8]

A small but important aspect of the Russian arms trade is the emergence of weapons-for-cocaine deals in Latin America that have been arranged through organized crime groups. The extent to which Russian small arms and even hand-held rocket launchers are finding their

Box 3.1
**Russian Military Hardware Advertised at Abu Dabai
Arms Bazaar (March 1999)**

Tula Instrument Design Bureau
• Combat module of cannons, missile launchers, and automated firing control system for armored vehicles
• Arkan guided missiles for upgrading armored vehicles already in the region
• High precision missile-artillery complex for coast guard and patrol vessels

Ulyanovsk Mechanics Plant
• Anti-aircraft system (Buk M1-2) for destroying short-range ballistic missiles
• Self-propelled artillery system

Kurgan Machine Building Plant
• BMP-3 infantry battle vehicle

Splav State Research and Production Organization
• Volley fire installations

Central Research Institute of Precision Engineering
• Machine guns, underwater automatic rifles, guns with silencers

Almaz Central Design Bureau
• Air defense systems (analogous to Patriot system)

Uralvagonzavod
• Modern battle tanks

Rubin Central Design Bureau of Marine Equipment
• Submarines

Source: "Russia Shows Off Arms at Abu Dabai Expo," *The Russia Journal*, March 29-April 4, 1999, p. 11.

way into this trade remains clouded in secrecy. But from time to time, traders are caught. Recent trials in Miami document that such trade is a work in progress. This trade has serious repercussions in Washington on U.S. relations with Russia, where linkages between government officials and organized crime are a constant worry.[9]

For many years, the Soviet and then Russian military trading firm, Rosvooruzhenye, was the sole organization authorized to export military equipment. By 1999, however, the *primary* authority for foreign sales had been divided among three organizations: Rosvooruzhenye continues to sell modern weapons systems, Promexport handles older equipment and spare parts, and Russian Technologies handles exports of technologies, particularly dual-use technologies, while recruiting experts needed to demonstrate equipment. A deputy prime minister oversees all military-related exports.[10]

In combination, these steps were intended to dilute the monopolistic powers of Rosvooruzhenye. The firm never divulges the details of how it uses its annual profits, estimated at $50 million. Also, it was cordoned off from penetration by the tax authorities and other government agencies as it became a government within a government.[11]

Of even more importance, by 1999 the government had given 16 manufacturers quasi-independent status to make their own export deals, further cutting into the previous power of Rosvooruzheniye. While these manufacturers are required to comply with government regulations concerning exports of armaments and dual-use technologies, the devolution of export authority has led to sales that have triggered international controversy over appropriate recipients of sophisticated weapons. Enterprise directors, desperate for income, arrange their own export deals, assuring customers that they comply with all government regulations, regulations which they may not understand or may choose to ignore. The details of one famous case attributed to overzealous directors were uncovered in 1998.

During the mid-1990s, as the process of devolution of export authority to enterprises was under way, Iraq went shopping for missile components and technologies in Russia. Iraq's initial interest was to upgrade the performance of their notoriously inaccurate Scud missiles with ranges of 150 to 500 miles and then to develop the technological base for a new longer-range missile with a flight path of 4,000 miles. In 1998, aggressive Russian journalists reported that Iraqi buyers enticed officials at the Research and Testing Institute of Chemical and Construction Equipment, at a missile dismantlement facility, and at yet another defense facility to sell them guidance instruments. On the list were gyroscopes, potentiometers, and tachometers that could be modified for use on the Scuds the Iraqis already possessed. A limited number of these items were shipped to Baghdad.[12]

A second deal was far more ambitious, involving at least eight Russian design and manufacturing organizations. The extent to which the Russian government was a party to this deal is clouded. The firms undoubtedly pushed any uncertainties as to their authority to the limit—and perhaps beyond. Negotiations were conducted at production facilities, in offices, and in apartments, underscoring the secretive nature of the dealings. According to press accounts, Russian institutions would supply missile engines, designs, training, and technology. Also, they would provide manufacturing and testing equipment for engines, airframes, and guidance systems.

One particularly significant deal was for the Mars Rotor company, a Russian machine building complex, to provide equipment for manufacturing guidance systems along with Russian experts to certify the operation of the equipment and to supervise training. The space technology giant, Energomash, was to provide a complete rocket engine of four-ton thrust, as well as design calculations, final design, and five complete samples of a propulsion system for a "communication satellite." The size of the satellite was said to match the payload specifications for an intermediate range Scud-type missile.[13]

The third, and most ambitious, deal provided for Iraqi purchases of gyroscopes and accelerometers from submarine-based missiles being dismantled in accordance with international arms control agreements. The first batch of gyroscopes and accelerometers was sent to Baghdad via Jordan. Shortly thereafter, Saddam Hussein's son-in-law defected to Jordan and revealed the plot. The Iraqis immediately dumped the loot into the Tigris River, where it was subsequently discovered by United Nations inspectors. A second batch of similar items was then intercepted in Jordan en route to Iraq, and the entire nefarious network was exposed.[14]

These particular shipments probably had little impact on Iraqi capabilities. But they may have paved the way for more meaningful deals that have not yet come to light.

On the domestic front, the Russian armed forces have had few funds in recent years to modernize their weapons inventories. They have a difficult time making the case that they need new weapons in Chechnya and elsewhere when their warehouses and marshalling yards are full of excess rockets, tanks, guns, and support equipment of all varieties. Still, an ambitious plan of the Ministry of Defense picked up support in the Duma in 1999, calling for production of a new class of long-range land-based missiles, the Topol-M missiles. Russian military leaders justify such expenditures, even during the dreariest of economic times, as follows:

- The most advanced rocketry is essential if Russia is to retain its seat at the table of powerful nations.
- Arms control agreements in various stages of development limit the number of warheads on a missile, thus requiring destruction of existing multi-warhead missiles. A newly designed single-warhead missile must be introduced into the Russian strategic arsenal.
- There will eventually be an important international market for weapons with the capability of the Topol-M missile.

A misfiring during one of the tests of the Topol-M raised questions over reliability, but the Ministry of Defense seems determined to meet a deployment target of between 10 and 20 well-functioning missiles per year beginning in 2002. Of course, they would like to have double that level but will probably be satisfied with the reduced number. The manufacturing plants will gladly accept whatever orders—large or small—they are able to attract.[15]

From the end of World War II until the disintegration of the USSR, the development and production of weapons were the core of the nation's technological effort. While this effort has stagnated in recent years, the accomplishments of past decades remain the primary reason the world still considers Russia an advanced industrial nation. As Russia seeks to derive profit from its inheritance of all types of military technologies, other countries envisage scenarios that lead to explosive conflicts in some of the most sensitive regions of the world. The effort of Russia to gain lucrative shares of international technology markets without endangering the security of other countries is one of the most daunting challenges facing not only Russia but the entire world.

The Dual-Use Issue

Around the globe, dual-use technologies have become indispensable for modern economies—from computers, to new metal alloys and plastics, to electronic control systems. Broad dissemination of these and hundreds of other technologies that could be misused for military purposes, even though they may be intended for peaceful uses, is not only inevitable but is often desirable. From the perspective of advisers to the U.S. Congress,

> The dissemination of technologies that have at least some relevance to producing weapons of mass destruction needs to be encouraged if populations in developing nations are to improve their health, environment, and standard of living.[16]

This report means that chemical, biological, nuclear, and aerospace technologies with civilian applications should find their way into many areas of the world. Therefore, even countries that the U.S. government considers highly unreliable and potential threats to international security are legitimate claimants to dangerous technologies that will help in their respective development efforts. Of particular interest in developing countries are biotechnologies that support agriculture and public health programs, chemicals that control pests in the cities and the countryside, and aircraft systems that bring remote areas closer to the mainstream of a nation's development.

As a principal repository of dual-use technologies, Russia searches for markets for its high-tech products, raising never-ending international concerns. In some cases, Russia competes with western countries in capturing customers. Moscow often views efforts by the West to constrain its international deals simply as attempts to reduce international competition. It only grudgingly accepts the notion that there are legitimate security concerns over dissemination of dual-use technologies that might contribute to a spread of weapons of mass destruction. Of course, Russia has its greatest competitive advantage for marketing its products in precisely those countries that the United States considers the least reliable nations—Cuba, North Korea, and Syria, for example.

A major focal point of contention is Iran. For years Iran has been searching for ways to upgrade its nuclear capabilities. Western analysts are convinced that one of their motivations is development of nuclear weapons. Thus, when Russia announces its intention to expand its cooperation in peaceful nuclear activities with Iran, intelligence officials in Washington raise objections.

Beginning in 1995, the U.S. government tried repeatedly to prevent Russia from selling components for a nuclear power plant to Iran. Despite Russian pronouncements that only civilian nuclear power would be supported and that the specific items and expertise being provided had little relevance to the production of highly enriched uranium or plutonium that could be used in nuclear weapons, the United States has been dead set against this transaction. Iranian assurances that the reactor will be open for inspection by the International Atomic Energy Agency and Russian reminders that, in the 1970s, the United States had been involved in supporting the evolution of a nuclear power capability in Iran have little impact. The U.S. government simply has not wavered in its opposition.[17]

The essence of the U.S. argument is as follows. Even if the Russian Ministry of Atomic Energy supports only a civilian program in Iran, that program can mask a hidden weapons program in the background. Also, training of an Iranian cadre of nuclear engineers who help install and operate the power plant is not a good idea since these same engineers can adapt their skills to support a weapons program. Adding to U.S. suspicions about the deal, the written agreement between Russia and Iran calls for Russian assistance in developing a uranium mining capability and in installing a centrifuge with capability of enriching natural uranium to the point that the uranium could be used in a nuclear explosive device. This specter of a growing Iranian capability that extends well beyond nuclear power helps buttress the American case.[18]

As of 1999, the Russians had succumbed to western pressure and had agreed to cancel the sale of the centrifuge. They were, however, moving ahead full steam in supporting the civilian nuclear reactor complex. Then, when Iranian scientists and engineers began visiting Russian facilities as part of the reactor arrangement, suspicious American officials hypothesized that side conversations were undoubtedly being directed to military applications of Russia's nuclear capabilities.[19]

Even when Russian nuclear scientists from civilian institutions show up in countries such as Brazil or Mexico to attend conferences or to participate in academic exchange programs, some American officials suspect nefarious purposes.[20] It is surely true that there are overlaps between civilian and military nuclear technologies. It is also true that not everything nuclear poses a military threat.

Even more challenging overlaps of military and civilian technologies exist in programs for use of outer space. Some components of missile systems also have direct civilian applications. Russian enterprises are attempting to expand space-based navigation, communication, and remote sensing systems that may be intended for civilian uses but can be adapted for military purposes. As Iraq and other countries seek to upgrade their military capabilities with advanced rocketry and improved guidance capabilities, western governments increase diplomatic pressure on Russia to curtail proliferation of aerospace as well as nuclear technologies to countries that pose a threat to neighbors.

As one example, such pressure to check Russia's cooperation with North Korea in the development of space technology capabilities played out in 1994. Russian rocket designers who had been cooperating with North Korean counterparts, allegedly to develop satellite communication systems, appeared in my office in Moscow in search of funds for civilian projects at their home institute in the Urals. At that particular time, the Russian Foreign Ministry was responding to western approaches to stay away from Korean military-related developments and had cancelled the scheduled trip to Korea by those specialists even as they waited to board their airplane to Pyongyang. This group thereupon decided to shift interests in international cooperation to a western civilian program which would also provide guaranteed paychecks. They succeeded in attracting the interest of a U.S. aerospace firm and began work on improving navigation systems for commercial airplanes.

The Korean technology that was eventually employed in rocket flight tests in 1998 was undoubtedly a spinoff from many years of close technical cooperation with Russia. The Russian scientists who were rerouted in 1994 could have been helpful, and the western pressures to keep them home worked. At the same time, they were not critical to continued progress, as the North Korean program demonstrated.[21]

The seriousness of protection of critical information leaking from Russia's aerospace complex to rogue states should not be underestimated. The complex has huge underemployment problems, involving many tens of thousands of highly trained scientists and engineers. They remain on the payrolls of enterprises, although they receive little pay and have almost nothing to do. A few Russian enterprises are participating in international space activities, including construction of the International Space Station and building rocket systems for launching satellites that link the world's telecommunications networks. But the scope of these international alliances is far short of the overall challenge of finding alternative outlets for the innovation capacity of specialists accustomed to responding to military requirements.

Dual-use issues often surround research projects in Russian laboratories. For example, nuclear bomb designers are interested in many aspects of physics research, but it is the military applications that raise near-term anxieties. What is the boundary between fundamental research that advances the frontiers of science for the benefit of all societies and applied military research that directs brainpower and resources to bomb making?

One test of the civilian legitimacy of research has been whether the results will be published in the open scientific literature. However, this test is controversial. Much research in the United States and elsewhere, with no military applications, remains cloaked in industrial secrecy since it may eventually lead to commercial products. Russian authorities in turn argue that they will not release research information which compromises their intellectual property rights even though it is distant from military interests. In short, there is no easy definition of the boundary of defense-related research that should be carefully controlled.

Russian laboratories and enterprises will continue to attempt to capitalize on past investments in some of the most sophisticated and dangerous dual-use technologies that have been developed anywhere. They frequently are uncertain as to the eventual market for the items incorporating these technologies. They know that the military products work, they have seen related civilian items for sale by other countries, and they are convinced that commercial markets will emerge for their products. Financial support from the West can encourage the pursuit of civilian applications of such technologies. But regardless of intentions as to applications, the technologies will retain their inherent military usefulness.

Realities of Industrial Conversion

Most of the 2,000 plants and 1,000 research institutes that comprised the heart of the Soviet military-industrial complex have attempted to adapt cutting edge technologies—totaling in the thousands—to the civilian marketplace at home and abroad. Laser techniques that guided missile intercepts now improve medical diagnostic capabilities, and infrared-enhanced night vision has become popular with deer hunters, for example. Older military technologies, such as powerful diesel-driven engines, while not at the forefront of technical achievements, also are relevant to needs of countries on the path to modernization. However, after a decade of effort, the success rate in finding large civilian markets for products of the former Soviet military-industrial complex has not been high.

This is not to say that some military enterprises and institutes have not found new customers. A visit to the Institute for Light Weight Alloys (VILS) in 1995 was particularly memorable. At the time, the institute was negotiating with a Japanese firm over the production of titanium golf clubs. With only one under-used golf course in Moscow, the institute's management was skeptical that such an idea made much sense but was willing to transfer technology to golf-mad Japan if the Japanese paid the bill—which they did.

Titanium technology was shared by a number of Soviet enterprises, and the story of titanium golf clubs did not originate at VILS. Already in 1992, the Russian firm, Metal Park—a spinoff company of ten metallurgists from the Strela aviation plant just north of Moscow—was in business in an empty vocational school. First, the company rejected proposals to produce titanium bicycles as too expensive. Then, Metal Park responded to an approach by a South Korean businessman and began making golf clubs for sale in Seoul. Next, Metal Park landed contracts in the United States with Taylor Made (subsequently a unit of Adidas) and the Callaway golf company. Finally, in 1995, after investing its limited earnings in new manufacturing and testing equipment worth $250,000 that would ensure quality of the clubs, Metal Park renewed these contracts. Monthly sales approached $2 million in 1998. Metal Park has been quick to point out that there are 25 million golfers who spend $1 billion annually on golf clubs.[22] Indeed, by 1999 "titanium shaft" became a phrase that signalled to golfing pros and hackers around the world that the club is lighter and stronger than older brands.

Another dimension of the titanium prowess of the former Soviet Union has been playing out in the Urals where, on the site of an old aircraft plant, the Verkhne Saldinsky Manufacturing Production Organization (VSMPO) is again producing titanium ingots, but this time for export. Previously a supplier of titanium panels for MIG 25 and Ilyushin 76 military aircraft, VSMPO lost its Russian supplier of titanium sponge when the Soviet Union disintegrated, since the supplier obtained the raw material, ilmenite concentrate, from Ukrainian sources that disappeared. In 1998, with a stable alliance with reliable suppliers who have access to international sources of sponge, the company is clawing its way back into titanium production. It has plans to emphasize production of rolled products, which command a significant markup (50 percent) over low-tech ingots. With 14,000 people on the payroll, VSMPO is betting on predictions that worldwide demand for titanium metal will continue to rapidly increase.[23]

There are other success stories. But for every commercial success there are failures. As noted previously, Russian scientists and engineers often perceive success to mean development of interesting technologies—not sustained sales. For example, in Perm, a city that was largely committed to the Soviet military effort, unique technologies were developed with potential applications in glass-plastic pipes for water filtration and borehole casings, in bullet proof vests and windows, and in light and strong stretchers and crutches. But producing these items is a far cry from selling them. Few are selling, and former military plants of the city have difficulty finding income for their employees.[24]

A brief flashback to the early 1990s, when conversion became a popular theme in Russia, helps explain current skepticism over future economic contributions of military facilities. From the beginning, considerable confusion has surrounded the term "conversion." In 1992, the Russian government defined conversion as "the creation of high technologies for products which are competitive on foreign markets," and made a commitment to provide financial support to achieve this goal. This commitment was initially fulfilled in a very modest way. More recently, special funds to facilitate conversion have been scarce; and simply finding new markets for old weapons is, in the view of many Russians, the fastest road to profit.

The emphasis of early Russian conversion efforts was clearly on exports. Russian officials were convinced that Russian technologies could compete internationally with little difficulty. But they were wrong.

They should have kept in mind the types of civilian production lines that punctuated Soviet military plants. Military enterprises produced 86 percent of Soviet streets cars, 60 percent of the cranes, 32 percent of oil and gas equipment, and 86 percent of the freight cars. These plants also produced almost 100 percent of Soviet TVs, radios, VCRs, tape recorders, cameras, and sewing machines.[25] One particularly pessimistic conversion expert went to the extreme in describing non-military goods that were produced in large quantities as "...compressors and pumps using 1930s technology, harrows and cultivators that had not changed since Russia's collectivization of agriculture, and obsolete electric winches and cranes."[26] Were these really the types of high-tech exports the government had in mind?

Secondly, the enterprises and institutes had neither the marketing nor business skills to penetrate international markets in the face of stiff competition from foreign competitors more attuned to the latest world-wide technological developments. While a few Russian organizations have been able to develop international alliances with western companies to this end, most have not. Had the Russian government emphasized conversion to products that would sell on the internal Russian market, Russian dependence on all types of imported products from Germany, Japan, Poland, Turkey, China, and other countries might not have developed so quickly. Still, a few dormant technologies should be able to penetrate foreign markets with appropriate management savvy, and a larger number have potential under a more aggressive import substitution strategy.

From a different perspective, western governments considering steps to facilitate downsizing of the Russian military establishment have argued that conversion should mean abandoning military activities at a given facility in favor of civilian production lest there be re-conversion back to mothballed production lines. To these governments, producing civilian products without closing adjacent military production lines is simply diversification, a legitimate business practice but not one that should be supported by western funds lest they help sustain a military capability. Neither the Russian government nor plant managers have accepted the concept that they should totally destroy military production lines. They prefer to use as their working definition of conversion "finding new sources of income to meet payrolls and cover expenses— exporting arms, selling high-tech or low-tech products to anyone that is interested, renting space, providing services, and doing whatever is needed to raise money."[27]

Westerners have difficulty comprehending the practical difficulties in producing marketable industrial or consumer items in enterprises that supported the Soviet armed forces. For example, the extraordinarily large plants often have on-site facilities for component manufacturing that in the West would be subcontracted to smaller companies. These facilities and workforces need some level of financial support whether or not they are operating. Also, while defense enterprises have gradually shed responsibilities for supporting schools, transportation systems, and cultural activities, costs persist as incumbent staffs from the enterprises refuse to leave. Finally, most defense conglomerates have limited experience fending for themselves. And, with financial patrons in Moscow having disappeared, they have neither the administrative infrastructure nor the experience for developing new income streams. The following comment from an aircraft plant manager sums up the attitude of many Russian engineers:

> Making fighters is what we know how to do. We can make a lot of them and make them well. Making civilian planes means scrounging around for money and dealing with foreign inspectors and certification requirements—it's a bit alien to us.[28]

Reflecting this outlook, six leading engineers who had designed the MIG 29 and MIG 31 fighters resigned from their enterprise in 1999 in protest over having been reassigned to work on the design of a new civilian airliner.[29]

That said, is it any wonder that more than one-half of the defense enterprises—with huge bank debts, atrophied sources of raw materials, and few customers—are barely surviving?[30] In more concrete terms, a microeconomics study of Soviet defense firms highlighted contrasting adjustment strategies of two electronics firms located on the Finnish border, each employing about 5,000 workers.

One enterprise director chose to engage in transactions that would produce liquid assets so top management could maintain high salaries and employees could receive at least minimal wages. No effort was made to invest in enterprise restructuring. The enterprise established shell firms to organize rental of company real estate to wealthy foreign and domestic customers and to trade in ferrous metals. As to manufacturing activities, the director concentrated on electronic games and other simple consumer items to justify credit from the government. After paying wages, the enterprise invested all proceeds in financial markets which, at the time, promised high returns. In effect, the interest of the firm's management was focused on activities outside the manufacturing facility, and equipment quickly deteriorated and skilled labor departed due to low wages.

The director of the other enterprise set the target of eventually exporting low-cost microscopes with electronic control systems for certain market niches, such as educational institutions. He too focused on generating liquid assets through rental of property and sales of items that were on hand so as to buy breathing time to adapt technologies to the new market. In order to stem labor separations that could lead to instability within the remaining workforce, the management acquired sewing machines, and many female employees made intermediate items for Finnish clothing firms. Others found odd jobs at the factory while others simply left. In time, the company concentrated on manufacturing electrical components for automobiles, emphasizing quality despite high costs since the key was to develop satisfied customers. By investing any funds that could be corralled in processes that would ensure quality, the firm convinced foreign investors it could operate effectively despite economic chaos in Russia. A Swiss partner then joined in the production and export of microscopes, which eventually accounted for more than one-half of the company's revenues.

Both directors took advantage of opportunities to develop new income streams. The difference was in how the managers searched for income opportunities. With the collapse of Russian financial institutions in 1998, it is not clear which strategy will pay off in the long run. Perhaps reinvesting funds in a company's assets simply postpones the day of reckoning when such oversized firms must permanently shut their doors. Perhaps a longer-term approach will allow the innovative electronics firm to be a pacesetter on Russia's northern border.[31]

Controlling Leakage of Sensitive Items

As already suggested, the Russian government is committed to compliance with international norms when considering sales of sensitive technologies abroad. Contraints on exports in fulfilling this commitment are important if western governments are to embrace Russia as a trading partner. To be effective, however, the commitment must extend beyond the government and be shared by enterprises seeking markets for either armaments or dual-use technologies.

Of course, the Soviet Union transferred enormous stocks of military equipment to allies in Europe, Asia, Africa, and Cuba. The government kept close tabs on every transfer of militarily significant items, designs, and technical information. Also, with few exceptions, the most advanced achievements were kept behind closed doors in Russia and denied even to other Soviet republics, which were considered unreliable by leaders of Russian ethnic lineage.

Unauthorized shipments and leakages of designs and operating characteristics of sensitive items were seldom a problem. Those privvy to technological secrets were well paid and highly respected in Soviet society. They had little to gain from risking violations of government restrictions on military technologies.

Then, with economic survival an abiding concern throughout the population, the scramble to profit from past technological achievements became an obsession of the government and of many individuals during the early 1990s. One way to reward personal contributions toward developing military technology was to sell sophisticated weapon systems and dual-use items and then distribute the proceeds to managers and designers, with a few rubles left over for the workforce. However, Soviet-era regulations concerning exports were still in place. While far from perfect for a more open economy, requirements for government approval of exports were a deterrent to many unwise transactions.

At the same time, western countries became more concerned about proliferation of sensitive technologies from north to south than transfers of advanced technologies from west to east, as had been the orientation during the cold war. They strengthened international legal regimes to limit the flow of militarily relevant technologies to "rogue states"—Iran, Iraq, North Korea, and Libya, in particular—and to other countries and organizations that might have hostile intentions. An array of international regimes is in place which in some instances requires and in other cases encourages industrialized countries to show restraint in exporting military hardware and nuclear, biological, chemical, and missile technologies. Russia is a member of most of the international agreements establishing these regimes. It also has agreed to abide by international guidelines limiting exports of chemical and biological substances and equipment to produce those substances.

Domestically, a law establishing a new export control system was enacted in 1992 with subsequent elaborations. The central idea of Soviet times remains intact: all proposals for exports of items on specified lists must be reviewed by appropriate government authorities. The law and implementing regulations call for a system similar to interagency review and approval procedures of western countries.[32]

Some powerful Russian managers view export control as preventing profitable sales. Regulatory entities—export control officials, the customs service, and the procurator's office—are not always sufficiently committed to their responsibilities to enforce complete compliance with regulations when confronted by these managers, thereby adding to the potential for illicit leakage of sensitive items from Russia.

In 1994, Russia began cooperating with U.S. government agencies with experience in operating export control systems in a market economy. This program helped familiarize Russian officials with the requirements of international export control regimes and with electronic-based approaches to expeditious but thorough processing of applications for exports. This cooperation probably has assisted the Russian government in keeping entrepreneurial zealots in check.

As to motivating enterprise directors and their key personnel to comply with export regulations, there is no better signal that end runs around export controls will not be tolerated than several high-profile prosecutions of offenders who ignore regulations.[33] Occasionally, public revelations about seizures by Russian security forces of illegal exports remind the directors to be careful. For example, in April 1999 Russian border guards in Central Asia uncovered 40 tons of tank components hidden among scrap metal on a train headed for China. Whether anyone was punished for attempting to evade regulations may never be publicly known.[34]

In sum, the international regimes prescribe the process for reaching export decisions and placing limitations on exports. In many sensitive cases, however, each government decides for itself whether an export should be permitted. The Russian government can approve exports the U.S. government would not approve, such as a nuclear reactor for Iran.

The recourse in such cases is for the United States to apply diplomatic pressure or, in extreme cases, unilateral sanctions that restrict cooperative programs or limit trade. During 1999, sanctions were applied on three occasions on Russian institutions in response to exports of missile-related technologies to Iran, exports of nuclear technology to Iran, and exports of advanced conventional arms to Syria.[35] But such measures may jeopardize U.S. security interests by terminating U.S. involvement among Russian institutions, where cooperation in peaceful endeavors introduces transparency as to previously cloaked activities and encourages movement away from dangerous military activities.

Whither Russian Military Technologies?

The technological base that made the Soviet Union a military superpower will not bring the country the status of an economic superpower. On the other hand, unless appropriately controlled, this technological capability will bestow on Russia the status of an international renegade to be penalized politically and economically by the West. However unfair it may seem, the U.S. and other governments will apply a double standard—defending the legitimacy of all their exports of armaments and dual-use technologies while attacking some of Russia's offerings, even though such offerings do not violate international agreeements.

At the same time, Russia's technology base is a good starting point for achieving profitable businesses in some high-tech areas. As has been mentioned, prime examples are machine tools, aerospace, and computer software. It is also important in areas requiring modern low-tech technologies, such as oil drilling equipment, electrical systems, communication networks, and even household appliances.

Finally, many myths about the defense industry—such as those cited below—have been debunked; and efforts can be directed to more realistic approaches to replace unfounded hopes of the past.[36]

- *Russia can continue to be a major international supplier of armaments.* Russia may sweeten its deals by facilitating recruitment of Russian mercenaries to fly advanced aircraft or operate sophisticated ground systems in combat zones. But competitors for international contracts almost always have substantial political clout and better systems of warranties and spare parts to ensure proper functioning of their systems. Russian arms sales are more likely to decrease than increase during the next decade.

• *Military technologies can easily be adapted to civilian needs.* This might be true if cost is not a consideration; but why pay $10,000 for a welder's face shield using military technology when a satisfactory device using western technology can be purchased for $500?[37] And there are hundreds of other examples of how scientists from the defense complex have priced themselves out of the market, at least for the time being.

• *Defense plants are ready for international competition if only provided with capital and marketing expertise.* Many plants are far from ready for such competition—poorly maintained, equipped with obsolete technologies, and endowed with skill levels and work ethics of aging workforces that have gone downhill. Some have come back, given incentives of potential sales; and a few others could follow.

• *Large-scale conversion programs have been under way throughout the country.* Despite a few highly visible activities that have turned a profit, most assets of the defense industry have been simply standing idle.

The era of defense conversion is over. New approaches are needed. Only determined efforts—perhaps draconian—from the Russian government will salvage a significant portion of past investments in military technology. Those technologies that have a realistic chance in civilian markets must be given priority and other technologies that simply occupy space and time must be jettisoned. Hundreds of thousands of workers may be displaced, but most will have already lost the bulk of their incomes. Obviously social safety nets and public works employment will be essential. Western governments may well be prepared to provide relief for a few years in exchange for permanent abandonment of military production facilities.

As each defense enterprise and institute tries to find its own way, a few will on their own uncover new opportunities for their workforces and facilities. Some will have small programs with western organizations more interested in downsizing the defense complex and in preventing the outflow of technological secrets than in contributing to economic revival. The challenge for the Russian government is to buttress such efforts with targeted programs of financial support that draw on inherent strengths well suited to market opportunities, primarily in Russia and gradually on the international marketplace.

Notes

1. John Pomfret, "Weapons Sales Rekindle China-Russia Relations," *International Herald Tribune*, November 21-22, 1998, p. 1. For additional background on aircraft sales see the Russian magazine *Air Fleet*, No. 6, 1999, Moscow, pp. 4-27.

2. *Jane's International Defense Markets*, Jane's Information Group, 1996; *World Military Expenditures and Arms Transfers*, U.S. Arms Control and Disarmament Agency, 1996.

3. Pomfret, "Weapons Sales Rekindle China-Russia Relations," p. 1.

4. Jane's Information Group, *International Defense Markets*; U.S. Arms Control and Disarmament Agency, *World Military Expenditures*.

5. Igor Khripunov, "Have Guns, Will Travel," *Bulletin of the Atomic Scientists*, May/June 1997, pp. 47-51.

6. *Ibid.*; Leonid Bershidsky, "Maslyukov Happy Being New Top Arms Exporter," *St. Petersburg Times*, October 30, 1998, p. 5.

7. Dmitry Polikarpov, "Russia To Decrease Arms Exports," *The Moscow Tribune*, November 4, 1998, p. 6.

8. "Russia Shows Off Arms at Abu Dabai Expo," *The Russia Journal*, March 29-April 4, 1999, p. 11.

9. Glenn E. Schweitzer, *Superterrorism: Assassins, Mobsters, and Weapons of Mass Destruction* (New York: Plenum Press, 1998), p. 41.

10. Bershidsky, "Maslyukov Happy Being New Top Arms Exporter," p. 5; Khripunov, "Have Guns, Will Travel," pp. 47-51.

11. Bershidsky, "Maslyukov Happy Being New Top Arms Exporter," p. 5.

12. Vladimir Orlov and William C. Potter, "The Mystery of the Sunken Gyros," *Bulletin of the Atomic Scientists*, November/December 1998; CNN Special Report, December 10, 1998.

13. *Ibid.*

14. *Ibid.*

15. "Why a New Topol-M System," *Argumenti i Fakti*, November 6-12, p. 3; David Hoffman, "Russia Set to Deploy Topol-M Missile," *The Washington Post*, December 27, 1998, p. A23.

16. Glenn E. Schweitzer, *Moscow DMZ: The Story of the International Effort to Convert Russian Weapon Science to Peaceful Purposes* (Armonk, NY: M.E.

Sharpe, 1996), p. 69. See also Gregory L. Vistica and Melinda Liu, "The Showdown Ahead," *Newsweek*, September 28, 1998, p. 50.

17.   For the text of the 1995 Protocol between the Russian Ministry of Atomic Energy and the Iranian Atomic Energy Authority see Rensselaer W. Lee, III, *Smuggling Armageddon: The Nuclear Black Market in the Former Soviet Union and Europe* (New York: St. Martin's Press, 1998), pp. 155-157. The Protocol includes, inter alia, provisions for the nuclear power reactor at Bushehr, a light water 30-50 megawatt research reactor, uranium mining assistance by Russia, natural uranium from Russia, a centrifuge from Russia, and training of Iranian specialists in Russia.

18.   *Ibid.*

19.   "U.S. Warns Russia To Halt Nuclear Aid to Iran," *The New York Times*, December 17, 1998, p. A-21.

20.   Discussions in Moscow at the U.S. Embassy, June 1998.

21.   Schweitzer, *Moscow DMZ*, p. 132.

22.   Patricia Kranz, "How Do You Say Fore in Russian?" *Business Week*, October 6, 1997, p. 162.

23.   "Betting on Titanium as the Metal of Choice," *Russia Review*, February 13, 1998, p. 44.

24.   N.I. Pshelkovsky, "The Commercialization of the Military Industrial Complex," *Technology Development and Commercialization: Russian and Global Experience*, TechnoCon 97, Proceedings, St. Petersburg, July 7-10, 1997, Ministry of Science and Technology, pp. 83-87.

25.   Andrei Kokoshin, "Defense Industry Conversion in the Russian Federation," *Russian Security After the Cold War* (Washington, D.C.: Brassey's, 1994), pp. 43-74.

26.   Viktor Rassadin, "Myths about Defense Industry Hinder Conversion," *Business World Weekly*, Moscow, No. 44/89, 1994, p. 10.

27.   Provided by a cynical official of the Ministry of Science and Technology in Moscow, April 1999.

28.   Brian Humphrey, "Converting the Weapons of War," *Russia Review*, February 13, 1998, p. 15.

29.   "MIG Maker: Walkout Won't Affect Work," *The Russia Journal*, December 6-12, 1999, p. 20.

30.   Franklin J. Carvalho (editor), *Russian Defense Business Directory* (St. Petersburg and Leningrad Oblast: Department of Commerce, 1996), pp. 4-1 to 4-10.

31.   Yevgeny Kuznetsov, "Learning To Learn: Emerging Patterns of Enterprise Behavior in the Russian Defense Sector," unpublished manuscript (Washington, D.C.: Brookings Institution, 1996).

32.   For a comprehensive discussion of Russian export control procedures see Gary K. Bertsch and Suzette R. Grillot (editors), *Arms on the Market* (New York, London: Routledge, 1998).

33.   *Proliferation Concerns: Assessing U.S. Efforts To Help Contain Nuclear and Other Dangerous Materials and Technologies in the Former Soviet Union* (Washington, D.C.: National Academy Press, 1997), pp. 85-117.

34.   "Tanks Held at Border," *The Moscow Times*, April 2, 1999, p. 4.

35.   *Proliferation Concerns*, pp. 85-117.

36.   For a discussion of myths see Rassadin, "Myths about Defense Industry Hinder Conversion," p. 10. See also Kevin Whitelow and Richard J. Newman, "The Russians Are Coming," *U.S. News and World Report*, March 15, 1999, p. 40.

37.   Schweitzer, *Moscow DMZ*, p. 218.

The Money Trail:
Finders Keepers

The banker occupies the pilot's cabin of the capitalist system. The banker is easily in position to know all, see all, hear all.

Description of U.S. economy circa 1900, *The Robber Barons*, 1934

The penal code should be amended so that it is a criminal offense if a manager fails to disclose financial information to all stockholders.

Russian Federal Securities Commission, 1999

We do contract work for foreign companies. But we could not just pay our employees from the proceeds of the contracts. We would lose most of the money to taxes. We set up a firm in Cyprus to handle financial transactions—a shell. We make sure that all of our employees have credit cards. Our firm in Cyprus is paid by the foreign companies for work performed under contracts, and we pay our employees by having the firm deposit money in each employee's credit card account. Our company in Russia gets just enough money to pay expenses.[1]

This report from the director of an applied research institute in St. Petersburg shows how scientists are attempting to replicate offshore payment schemes pioneered for more than a decade by well-endowed Russian enterprises that export natural resources. While often distasteful and sometimes precarious, tax avoidance has become ingrained in the Russian approach to business. There is little hope of the government retrieving its fair share of Russian income through taxes in the foreseeable future.

Poor tax collection clearly has a braking effect on progress toward economic reform, reform that requires the government to have funds to do its job. Tax avoidance cannot be condoned. Nevertheless, why should Russian scientists be excluded from the national pastime of taking end runs around the tax authorities? In this case, as well as with other evasive approaches, the participants may in fact believe they are complying with ambiguous Russian laws.

The director has learned that the first responsibility of any research and development manager is to ensure that he or she has a program to manage. This means having income sources that enable the staff to practice their trade. For the St. Petersburg institute, foreign organizations were the only sources of income. Husbanding every dollar that these organizations were willing to pay was the director's top priority. He then faced crucial decisions as to how to divide a financial pie large enough to adequately feed only 20 percent of his staff. His response was to reward those who worked on foreign contracts with credit cards while distributing a small portion of the income among other employees. He claimed that he and his top managers did not receive excessive returns.

Russian organizations attempting to commercialize technology usually receive their funds in small droplets through many spigots. Overall, the largest income streams continue to flow from the federal government. Government support of research and development, however, has declined twenty-fold during the past decade. Also, there was a five-year hiatus of paychecks delayed for months or years.

Small payments for staffs of research and development organizations traditionally supported by the government began arriving on time in 1999. While not all researchers could report an end to delays, most could at least temporarily. This change has been attributed to the personal role of former Prime Minister Yevgeny Primakov who, after the financial crisis of August 1998, insisted on reliable salary payments—however small—to employees of all stripes who depended on governmental funds. Also, as we have seen, some firms found cash-paying customers for modern technological achievements following the devaluation of the ruble in 1998.

In addition to simply allocating financial resources to state institutions on the basis of numbers of employees, the government has established a few special funds to support technological innovation activities. The money from these funds is distributed in various ways: on the basis of habit, on the basis of personal friendships, and sometimes on the basis of merit in competitions for funds. But the allocations are always at a low level.

The dreams of a large portion of the research and development community are pegged to success in obtaining grants and contracts from abroad. Innovators could then live from year to year rather than month to month, and they could boost their incomes from $50 per month up to $100 or even $500 per month. They are not particular as to their tasks, although they would like to participate in some level of innovation—whether modifying fighter aircraft for sales abroad, providing designs to enhance the safety of nuclear power plants in Russia, or developing stronger plastics, as is the case at the St. Petersburg institute.

In practice, few have such challenging jobs. Many accept assignments to provide rudimentary support of utility services or to maintain old and unreliable industrial equipment. While these tasks offer few technical challenges, they provide income to ride out the economic crisis, with the hope that in the future researchers can again become bona fide innovators.

For a decade, western governments have predicted that the only realistic sources of funds to revitalize Russian technological development would be from foreign, private-sector investments. Foreign equity investments will be important. But this narrow vision of Russia's future can contribute to a neglect of development of internal Russian financial capabilities.

Of course, foreign signatories of contracts and grants are very sensitive to attempts to misuse their funds. They would like to pay for goods and services they have ordered when they take delivery and not worry about losing money in the interim. Russian organizations often argue, however, that they need up-front money to be able to carry out agreed-upon tasks. Thus, foreign organizations have developed a variety of approaches to help ensure that neither criminal elements, greedy managers, nor the tax police become beneficiaries of their funds and thereby prevent Russian workers from completing their tasks.

Most ruble transactions, and many transactions involving foreign currency, wind their way through the Russian banking system. After a foreign contract involving an enterprise or institute is signed and money is deposited by the foreign entity, government authorities and financial institutions are eager to take their percentages before rubles arrive at the workplace. Thus, the number of rubles that are available to the enterprise or institute is hard to predict. The reasons given for reduced payments to the institutes—tax obligations, transfer fees, or other charges—are seldom, if ever, subject to appeal.

The reach of organized crime—into the banks, into the enterprises, and even into the pockets of the researchers—is omnipresent. Researchers themselves occasionally join the ranks of the corrupted, where they too can participate in siphoning off funds for their own use in preference to waiting for the eventual payoff from marketing of technology. For most entrepreneurs, protection against criminal activities has become a normal cost of doing business, a cost that technology innovators with dry income streams have difficulty absorbing.

One defensive approach taken by Russian organizations trying to innovate for profit through hard work is to build financial fire walls around their activities—referred to in Russia as "roofs." Then they attempt to operate as normal business endeavors. Also, as noted, a few institutes have mastered the intricacies of safeguarding their funds in foreign subsidiaries in Cyprus and other remote havens. The remainder have grappled with less sophisticated schemes to minimize risks of losing their funds before they themselves can use them.

Despite the uncertainty of sources of funding and the many hands reaching for any money that appears on the scene, innovating for profit has sometimes been possible in Russia. A number of Russian scientists and engineers, having honed their skills in the Soviet military-industrial complex are determined to turn their technologies that produced high-tech swords into lucrative market shares. More recent entrants into the world of technology innovation increasingly look to the West for new ideas that Russian talent can develop and sell at home and abroad.

Sources of Finance

As suggested above, there are many hazards in seeking a profit from almost any legitimate activity in Russia. It would seem that only the foolhardy would risk long-term investments in innovative technologies with uncertain payoffs even in the best of times. But the Russian government is willing to assume at least some of the risk.

For decades, the Soviet and then the Russian Ministry of Science and Technology have provided funds to support enterprises and research institutes in developing technologies with industrial potential. In recent years, the scope of such efforts has declined. At the same time, no longer do manufacturers have funds in reserve to apply the latest developments. Today, Russian companies—state-owned and privatized alike—must be convinced that they will find almost instantaneous payoff if they are to incorporate new products or processes into existing production lines. Nevertheless, the ministry is accustomed to providing funds for pushing technologies that it considers promising. And old habits change slowly.

The money available to the ministry is pitifully small by any measure. The research and development kitty has declined precipitously during the past decade from hundreds of millions to tens of millions of dollars annually for nationwide efforts. Still, ministry support sometimes demonstrates small-scale positive returns from investments in technology projects.

A centerpiece of the ministry's effort is the Fund for Development of Small Firms in the Scientific and Technical Sphere. The fund, established in the mid-1990s by a dynamic and effective Russian director, has combined technological and financial acumen in support of hundreds of Russian firms. The fund has played an important role in finding relatively safe workplaces for its clients in technoparks and innovation centers in Moscow, St. Petersburg, and Nizhny Novgorod—even in an abandoned defense complex in Kazan—away from the grips of the mafia.

With a budget of $6 million in 1999, the fund emphasizes support of technology-oriented firms that already have small market niches and are attempting to develop broader customer bases. The fund usually provides interest-free loans of up to $200,000 for 12-18 months. In 1999, the repayment rate was over 50 percent. There have been several keys to the success of the fund. Proposed projects are carefully screened, taking into account "all" aspects of doing business in Russia—from uncertainties regarding suppliers to changing government regulations to difficulties in collecting payments from customers. The fund operates in a transparent fashion. It recognizes the importance of publishing detailed annual reports about its activities so as to dampen suspicions over the possibility of corrupt practices. Finally, the staff of the fund is in tune with what is happening in the country at the micro level, particularly with regard to handling financial assets and dealing with organized crime. The staff gives special attention to the integrity of the financial systems that support projects chosen for financing.[2]

In 1992, the ministry established another fund, the Russian Fund for Technological Development, to support larger projects proposed by researchers in strategic industries formerly associated with the military-industrial complex. This fund emphasizes financing of improved technologies in telecommunications, transportation, computers, and petroleum. Russian companies are doing reasonably well in these fields. Therefore, projects that are financed have a good chance of catching the attention of these companies.[3]

The Ministry of Economics maintains a related fund to support initial production runs for new or improved items. Manufacturing enterprises that desperately need new product lines to stay alive are sometimes beneficiaries. To avoid interagency quarrelling, the Ministry of Science and Technology does not participate in these activities, despite its expert knowledge of the innovation process in Russia. Instead, the latter ministry concentrates on individual entrepreneurs, even though they represent but a small portion of the country's technological potential, and on the State Scientific Centers discussed in Chapter 2.[4]

The foregoing funds are well known throughout the Russian research and development community, but they tell only a small part of the story. In 1998, a Russian official handed me a list of 81 other government funds set up to support industrial development. While some are limited to specific regions of the country, and almost all are directed to narrow industrial sectors, in the aggregate they cover almost all branches of industry. None of the funds have much money to distribute, but they keep alive the hope that at some future date the government will again be a reliable source of resources for industrial development.[5]

Many government agencies in the United States, Europe, and Asia also support research and development in Russia, although no one has a reliable list of such programs. Several western companies also fund research and development in Russia. One compilation identifies over 50 foreign sources of financing of technological and related commercial activities not including individual foreign companies. At least a dozen venture capital funds have been established in Russia, usually with financial contributions from abroad. Something about Russian industry, despite its weakened state, continues to hold the world in suspense.[6]

Few of the foreign venture funds are investing significant amounts in technology development. The St. Petersburg Technology Fund is a promising exception. A handful of foreign investors have pooled resources to establish a fund that takes equity positions in well-managed Russian high-tech firms. With western management philosophy and direction, the fund has invested several million dollars in small companies; and expansion of activities is a high probability.[7] While several million dollars may seem small, a good track record with limited resources is preferable to the many false starts of much larger, past investors.

Why hasn't foreign equity investment become a more significant factor in the revitalization of Russia's industrial base? Western firms had less than satisfactory experiences with joint ventures in the early 1990s—often coming to impasses with Russian partners over both management and financial issues. Most large western companies became disillusioned about the joint venture approach, although a few small western entrepreneurs investing on the order of $500,000 to $1.5 million have enjoyed significant returns despite the economic downslide throughout the 1990s.[8] In general, foreign companies—and even some Russian companies—are more attracted to short-term contracts with much less risk involved. For example, the Russian organization NPO Mashinostroenie, the Central Aerohydrodynamics Institute, and the Research Institute of Aviation Systems have been reluctant to give up equity or to provide cash as required in joint-venture arrangements.[9] Yet, growth in foreign equity investments remains an important near-term goal for Russia if sustained income streams are to be developed.

Much of the lack of interest in the West in foreign equity investment can be traced to the uncertain legal framework and the associated risks. Among the specific concerns are:

- Taxes should be based on profits not on turnover, as is now the case, and should never be retroactive, a constant worry.
- Minority shareholder rights need to be strengthened and legally binding.
- Venture funds should have the right to extend loans as well as provide equity, but now only banks can extend loans.
- Registration and approval requirements for many types of activities need to be simplified.
- A reliable banking system is essential.[10]

While foreign investors are increasing in number, they are becoming more chary in their willingness to take chances. They want good projects. But what is a good project? To most investors, a good project equates with a good business plan—a plan that emphasizes a realistic customer demand for the product and an approach that avoids entanglements with criminal elements. Unfortunately, proposals for good projects are in short supply. Support of Russian organizations as they develop candidate projects should be an activity for western organizations interested in a stronger technological infrastructure in Russia.

A European Union report issued at the end of 1999 concludes that with minor improvements in the Russian legal and taxation system and with modest economic growth, up to $4 billion dollars could be available from European venture capitalists for Russia, if good projects were developed. The report underscores the importance of investment by both public and private sectors in innovative activities and the financial systems which support those activities. Such measures can realistically boost international competitiveness of Russian industry, according to the report.[11]

Protecting Income Streams Flowing from the West

Russian specialists attempting to develop and market newly found technologies consider funding pursuant to western contracts and grants more reliable, as well as more lucrative, than payments from Russian sources. Foreign payments usually arrive on time. They are generous, given the low average salary levels in Russia. Also, they usually are denominated in dollars, which provides some protection from devaluation of the ruble.

Russian and foreign partners have successfully used a variety of mechanisms for transferring money into Russia. A principal objective is to avoid payments to customs and tax officials, to pension and social funds, and to bottomless overhead accounts of Russian organizations. Some end runs of "authorized" payment channels are within the laws of Russia while others unambiguously violate the laws. Many are on the edge of legality, with Russian law enforcement officials making arbitrary decisions every day as to whether to block financial flows that do not follow regular patterns.

A simple route to avoid diversions of funds is for the intended recipient simply to receive stacks of one hundred dollar bills handed directly to him or her in Russia by the foreign funder rather than having the money deposited in a bank account. The recipient can then direct the funds to research and development activities or other uses as he sees fit without an obligation to pay bank fees or to hassle the accountants working at his organization. At the same time, the western partner must have an astounding amount of trust in the integrity of the recipient of the bills to engage in such a practice. Also, Russian authorities may be poised to question the legality of such transactions.

Occasionally, directors of institutes arrange such payments. They cherish the flexibility of unencumbered hard currency, since they seldom receive real cash owed to them by Russian institutions. Indeed, financial transactions between Russian entities show up as entries in the bank accounts of the payer and the payee. The paper trail complicates development of concocted stories about cash histories to avoid payments to the government of one type or another.

Most foreign partners know that if they place money into the bank account of an institute rather than the account of an individual researcher, greedy hands will be reaching for a percentage for "personal supporting services," for institute overhead, or simply for paying impatient creditors who threaten to close the institute. Adding overhead, pension, health care, and income tax deductions, the researchers are lucky if they receive one-quarter of the funds earmarked for salaries after the garnishments are deducted. While western scientists are accustomed to such deductions at their home institutions, they are confident that pensions will be real, that health care will be adequate, and that overhead charges will benefit their work. Such confidence is difficult to imagine in present-day Russia.

In 1993, the International Science Foundation established in Russia by George Soros began handing funds directly to individual researchers, with the approval of the Russian government, to avoid diversion of research stipends to questionable activities such as purchases of new Mercedes automobiles for directors. In 1994, the International Science and Technology Center in Moscow adopted similar procedures. By 1999, more than two dozen western organizations were making direct payments to Russian specialists.[12] These legally sanctioned transfer routes circumvented most opportunities for either the government or an institute's management to take a cut.

Initially, institute directors hated schemes for direct payments of foreign funds to individual researchers. To them, not having personal control over salary funds meant losing control of their employees. Also, the directors feared that employees who did not have an opportunity to share in a portion of the income from foreign contracts and grants might soon revolt over the higher salaries of their favored colleagues.

In time, the directors adjusted. First, they too became participants in western projects, at least on paper. They were added to the lists of recipients of direct payments from abroad. Also, western organizations provided modest cash payments for overhead to be used at the discretion of the directors. The level of overhead funding was usually no more than 20 percent of total project costs. This was free money for the directors. While 20 percent is a very small percentage in comparison with the overhead charges of 500 percent or more to which the institutes had been accustomed during the Soviet era, guaranteed payments of even small amounts of overhead were welcomed.

Finally, many directors decided to withhold for the institute's general fund the salaries that foreign-supported researchers would have received from the institutes if they did not have western income. For example, if a researcher received the equivalent of $50 per month as an institute employee and then was awarded a foreign grant that provided $300 per month, he or she would receive a total of only $300. The institute retained $50 for overhead that in principle should benefit all researchers in some small way.

The Russian government approved the scheme for western funders to pay unencumbered salaries directly to researchers only for nonprofit organizations and international organizations that transfer funds to Russia for "technical or humanitarian assistance." Governments and private companies have no comparable payment route unless they first transfer their funds to an intermediary nonprofit organization for conveyance. To circumvent this limitation, representatives of some western companies become money mules, carrying large amounts of cash into Russia every time they make visits, and then handing the money to the designated recipients. Also, foreign governments often rely on diplomatic pouches for shipping cash for local expenses, with the embassies seldom concerned about the propriety of diplomatic dodges around the tax structure.

Another approach to circumventing Russian government claims on foreign payments is for a foreigner to hand over cash to a Russian partner for "expenses" during the latter's travels abroad. The foreigner can rest assured that the acquaintance will figure out some way to use the money without having a substantial portion skimmed off. Western scientists are small players in this game, however, transferring only hundreds or possibly thousands of dollars in individual transactions. Western companies interested in buying Russia's natural resources sometimes transfer tens of millions of dollars to Russian businessmen in transactions at overseas locations, a practice clearly outside Russian law.

For their part, Russian customs officials seem unconcerned about cash coming into the country from the West, apparently assuming the dollars spent in Russia are a plus for the economy. On only one occasion has a customs official ordered me or any member of groups travelling with me through Sheremetyevo Airport to produce the dollars indicated on an entry declaration. My wad of new $100 bills added up to $9,500 on that one occasion, the amount needed for legitimate lodging and transportation expenses for a group of visitors. The customs agent simply glanced at my bulging fist and immediately waved me through the checkpoint.

Leaving the country is a different story, however, reflecting Russian determination to cap one route for capital flight. The traveler who overestimates his financial needs in Russia and plans to go home with more than $500 in cash should beware. If he or she has more foreign currency in pocket than was originally noted on the entry declaration, the excess could be taken at the exit point. Customs officials are instructed to prevent the outflow of foreign currency, although they may not always be attentive to their jobs.

During one trip, an attractive young American friend was carrying $9,000 out of the country, cash she had forgotten to declare on her customs form during entry. When I asked her at the airport how she would get the money past the customs desk, she replied, "Just watch." After loosening the top button of her blouse, she leaned over the customs official's counter, blinked, and said in perfect Russian, "I have only $500 dollars which I don't need to declare." A grin ran off the edge of the uniformed official's face. His eyes froze in a downward stare toward his work space, temporarily hidden. After a few blinks and a long hesitation, he waved her through and wished her a pleasant flight.

Not surprisingly, the extraordinary measures associated with money transactions in Russia often distract Russian research and development managers from their primary focus on ensuring the sustainability of research and development programs at their institutes. They must pay a "time tax" of 10-20 percent of the work week for coping with financial flows. Indeed, the focus on money has forced many researchers into technical support services for people with cash-in-hand, even though these activities result in a slow erosion of research competence.

Research and development is subsidized in all countries, and research and development organizations traditionally receive tax breaks. But, in Russia, there is a large cadre of impoverished specialists unable to benefit directly from either approach. They must push the envelope of legality to make ends meet. Let us hope that their unorthodox approaches are short-term measures and that in time they will be able to concentrate on technology innovation rather than on money manipulation.

Roofs for Businesses in Russia

Several Russian acquaintances, in addition to Gennady who was introduced in Chapter 2, have tried their hands at becoming entrepreneurs, each determined to set up a business independent of the shackles of any existing Russian organization. Their logic was that ties with old-line Russian organizations would simply siphon away portions of the earnings of new businesses. Instead they would find working spaces, hire their own employees, and set up their bank accounts. Then their businesses would take off. If necessary, they would hire security guards for their premises. From time to time, they would consult Russian acquaintances to help file the proper papers with the authorities and generally stay out of legal entanglements—so was their game plan.

But it wasn't so simple. The first problem was work space. Well established organizations or simply squatters seem to have claims on all desirable working spaces in most cities of the country. Even the independent-minded "gang of four" physicists encountered in the Prologue retained an affiliation with Moscow State University so they could be assured of space with guarded entrances.

A second problem is heating, water, electricity, telephone services, and waste collection. These services are not always easy for an individual to organize for business purposes. New businesses are viewed with suspicion by municipal officials who issue the necessary authorizations. Some officials are genuinely concerned about mafia links. Others ponder how they can benefit from a new business moving into their territory.

The list goes on. Fire and health inspections may require modifications of premises, acquisition of nonflammable carpets, or eradication of pests that will not go away. Parking places for personal and customer vehicles may not exist. By the time a potential entrepreneur has a suitable place to work, he or she is so shaken by the many uncertainties of maintaining the premises that little energy remains to devote to the business. And the mafia hasn't even arrived at the doorstep yet.

It didn't take long for aspiring Russian entrepreneurs to recognize the advantage of locating fledgling businesses on premises maintained by someone else. It made sense for the new entrepreneur to find an organization that could provide a "roof" (or krysha) for the business. Some preferred institutions in similar lines of technology development in order to ease access to supplies and supporting services that were already available on the premises. However, the chosen institution could not be so similar as to be a competitor. A few decided to take advantage of sites offered by technoparks and incubators. Most have preferred to find roofs maintained by old acquaintances. Tens of thousands of small businesses of all types have been set up on the premises of enterprises, institutes, and other established organizations. Technology-oriented businesses are often located inside the premises of research institutes, where institute employees can be engaged by the firm on a part-time basis (see Chapter 2).

To some western experts on Russia, the notion of a roof has strong criminal overtones. They consider the concept an outgrowth of the communist system: one variant of corrupt patronage, confiscation, and dispensation has merely supplanted another. From their viewpoint, the roof includes the following elements:

- connections to a financial institution,
- penetration into government structures—nationally and locally—and
- availability of an armed force when necessary.[13]

However, a roof for a small innovative firm with limited cash flow seldom rests on a credo of destruction of property, beatings, and murders. More often it relies on lawyers and accountants who wend their way through the labyrinth of government bureaucracies to assist the business in moving forward. Sometimes, as has been noted, the primary purpose of a roof is simply to provide safe working space and supporting physical infrastructure.

Roofs of various types have become a permanent feature of the changing Russian economic scene where protection of assets commands the highest priority. As organized crime becomes more aggressive, a new firm without a roof can be in trouble. When threatened with annihilation, some new firms simply have no choice but to engage organizations that maintain close contacts with criminal gangs to provide roofs.

The acceptance of the roof concept is not limited to Russian entrepreneurs. When western companies establish operations in Russia, some recognize the importance of a roof. Others are determined to do business as if they were in California—and they soon return to California. A few decide to pay for favors on a case-by-case basis.

The smartest accept as the only sensible path to follow a relationship with a Russian organization that can provide a roof (e.g., Monsanto's laboratory at the Institute of Bioorganic Chemistry and Westinghouse's office at the Institute of Power Engineering). In a large city, it is often expeditious to enter into a joint partnership with the city administration (e.g., McDonalds' arrangements with the mayor of Moscow, which not only embrace hamburgers but also provide rental space for Boeing and other western companies). Russian organizations of all types are providing roofs for western firms.

Roof maintenance is clearly a cost of doing business in Russia. And the 10 percent or so of profits needed to maintain a roof simply becomes an unwritten entry in the business plan. Those who decide that such insulation from financial and other types of predators is not necessary may in time have difficulties avoiding far more costly confrontations.

Privatization and the Enterprise Managers

Money manipulations within research institutes and small firms have been modest compared to the elaborate get-rich schemes that accompanied the privatization of large state enterprises. Much advanced technology from the Soviet era still resides in these firms. While some technology may be completely out of date and other capabilities may be rusting, they nevertheless could offer springboards for economic revitalization in important fields.

As the Soviet Union splintered into 15 independent states, thousands of Soviet government officials knew they would soon be out of their government jobs. They ceded to themselves and to their friends de facto ownership of the assets of many state enterprises. The majority of the capital and perhaps 80 percent of the voting shares of the privatized companies ended up under the control of people who have milked these assets for their own ends.

At the height of privatization in 1996 more than 2,000 privatization crimes were registered. Given the notoriously weak government enforcement when powerful Russians are involved, many times that number of unregistered crimes undoubtedly took place. Government officials were themselves often involved.[14]

Key participants in privatization schemes have been enterprise directors who remained in place from Soviet times like "fixed post agents of the old regime, sentries left behind, unrelieved and forgotten by a hurriedly retreating army."[15] A considerable number are engineers. Many personally developed technologies that were critical to successful Soviet production efforts. Understandably, they believe that they should be among the beneficiaries of their contributions.

Initially, directors found themselves answerable to no one. They maintained a type of hypnotic control over workers. The workers, through their shareholdings, were supposed to become owners of the enterprises, but they often considered their paper shares worthless and turned them over to management.

Even prior to privatization, some directors took advantage of a government decree permitting the establishment of cooperatives at state enterprises. This new form of private activities, largely unnoticed among the many smokestacks throughout the country, provided cash cows for directors and their close associates, who used them as personal sales outlets for goods contributed almost free of charge by the enterprises. The transactions of the cooperatives set the stage for more extensive diversions of assets that, during the privatization process, had suddenly been put up for taking by the best-informed parties—namely, plant managers.

Reports abound as to how profits were diverted into accounts controlled by directors, how companies were allowed to enter bankruptcy after directors stripped them of their assets, and how directors arbitrarily declared illegal any shareholder meeting that criticized management. Even in cases when individual directors were painstakingly removed by the government for unseemly behavior, their successors frequently offered more of the same. Sometimes they conspired with the deposed directors.

Now barter and promissory notes are important currencies of enterprises. Legitimate owners of privatized firms and government officials responsible for state-owned firms have even more difficulty gaining control of the assets, since there are fewer financial levers to grab. Further, with increased reliance on non-cash transactions, the interest of management in investing money in activities that will result in technological advancements in the long term is at an all-time low.

Stories about the theft of enterprise assets are often connected with firms exporting natural resources—the Krasnoyarsk aluminum plant, the Norilsk nickel combine, the large oil companies. While firms engaged in aerospace, computer, nuclear, and other advanced technologies may have fewer cash assets, they too are targets of financial swindles. Indeed, by 1999 any firm with significant assets that had cash value, directly or indirectly, was on the hit list of dishonest forces in Russia.

What can be done to restore confidence of potential investors in privatized companies with strong technological capabilities? As one step, the Russian Federal Securities Commission—which has power to investigate alleged abuses—should be able to refer documented abuses to the procurator general for prompt punitive actions. The commission should approve public offerings of securities only for companies with satisfactory records in dealing with shareholders. Also, the government should embed protections for minority shareholders, as well as transparency requirements, in the corporate charters of state-owned companies *before* any more are privatized.[16]

The financial situation in most enterprises is incredibly complex and confused. Inter-enterprise debts and credits have accumulated for years. Unpaid bills for utilities and supplies are commonplace. Tax payments, however calculated, are held in abeyance as long as possible. Bank accounts are drained at the end of each month as inflation degrades the ruble's buying power. And personnel turnover clouds efforts to determine where assets have gone in the past. While many uncertainties will never be resolved, more rigorous accountability to the shareholders and to the tax authorities is a priority requirement for governmental action.

Bankers and the Flow of Money

As Russia began to move toward a market economy in the early 1990s, the banking system immediately took on new responsibilities as the conduit for flows of money into, out of, and through Russia. Twenty-five hundred banks were established. By 1999, many had folded voluntary or had gone bankrupt, and 1,500 remained. While small transactions regularly take place outside the banking system and large deals are frequently consummated abroad, the banks handle most of the nation's financial assets. Without reliable banks, a technology-based industry that draws on both foreign and domestic capital has little chance of succeeding.

Beginning in 1992, I spent two years searching for a bank in Moscow that could handle $70 million of available western funds for Russian scientists and engineers. We had two requirements. The money was to be deposited in personal bank accounts of several thousand individuals or handed to the individuals, with "reasonable" transaction fees being charged by the banks. The relevant bank records showing the money trails were to be available to western auditors. Every bank claimed it could easily handle the first requirement, although most of the banks underscored that since such small sums of money were involved, the transaction fees would be between 5 and 10 percent. Only one bank—Konversbank, which was controlled by nuclear specialists who were to be beneficiaries of the funds—agreed to the audit requirement and would accept reasonable fees. The other bankers simply wanted to take care of the transactions their own way with no one peering into their internal processes. I soon became convinced that their way was both risky and illegal.

Throughout our discussions, specialists from the Central Bank provided advice to us. These specialists knew the details of every applicable regulation and the legal limits of banking practices. At the same time, they did not know—or did not admit to knowing—the details of practices of the commercial banks.

Against this background, I was not surprised when the banking scams of the mid-1990s came to light. Nor was the deep involvement of banks in facilitating off-shore capital flight unexpected. Even the contract killings aimed at banking officials were not a surprise. As elegant bank buildings appeared, as Russian artists found bankers eagerly purchasing their most expensive paintings to decorate bank offices, and as armored car sales to the banks boomed, it became clear that a disproportionate share of Russia's wealth was supporting extravagant tastes of Russian bankers.

The banking system became a nesting area for illicit activity. Criminals were often employed by banks, sometimes unknown to bank management, while other criminals manipulated bank decisions from behind the scenes. Banks and bank customers were targets for extortion. Russian organized crime even placed moles in banks around the world with tentacles into Russia.[17]

Already in 1993, the Central Bank had transferred $50 billion of its financial reserves to a shell firm registered on the Channel Island of Jersey, reserves that should have been used to stabilize the ruble-dollar exchange rate. Instead, the firm invested, successfully, in the Russian bond market. The recipients of the profits from the successful investments, as well as the exorbitant fees that were charged for each transaction, remain a mystery. Also, Central Bank officials illegally sold federal property, used bank credit cards for personal purchases, and established a $20 million social fund for bank employees. Such practices by the regulator do not send a good signal for establishment of reliable banking institutions.[18]

The antecedents to current bank frauds go back more than a decade. In 1988, the first so-called "zero banks" were established as hideaways for funds taken from the communist treasuries by officials who were soon to lose their positions of influence. Much of the money was transferred abroad. Also in 1988, "pocket banks" were established to serve heavy industry. Such banks were in the pockets of enterprise directors.

One bank set up in Moscow simply to bilk its depositors was named Nazhebanye. If the spelling is reversed, the resulting Russian word means "screw you." During its few weeks in existence, it attracted a number of customers. It then closed, and the founders simply disappeared with the deposits. All that was needed to set up such a bank were three board members and capital of $80,000. Even if a bank were not established to take advantage of unwary customers, its management team could use it as a laundering operation for illegally obtained income.[19]

With this recent history, in all likelihood the banking system will continue to be vulnerable to counterfeit, manipulation, and fraud.[20] Still, commercial banks are critical for the functioning of a Russian economy in transition. Russian criminal elements will strongly resist any expansion of services currently authorized for western banks operating in Russia, but only a greater role for such banks can provide the necessary competitive pressure for Russian banks to clean up their act.

Turning to capital flight, 1999 estimates had up to $2 billion leaving Russia every month for offshore havens, primarily in western Europe, with Russian bankers frequently involved in these transactions. Russian specialists define capital flight as transfers of assets denominated in rubles into assets denominated in a foreign currency, either at home or abroad, in ways that are not part of normal commercial transactions.[21] Both legal and illegal behaviors are included. For example, keeping money abroad due to a lack of confidence in Russian banks may not violate any laws. Sending money abroad to avoid taxes is probably an illegal practice. And laundering money derived from the narcotics trade through various bank accounts should be a ticket to jail. Also, the propensity of Russians for hoarding cash at home in dollars rather than rubles is considered internal capital flight although, in most cases, illegal behavior is not the motivation.

Perhaps the most common type of illegal capital flight involves western buyers of Russian products who place a portion of the real payment for sales in offshore Russian bank accounts. The Russian seller then pays taxes on the much lower declared payment that is remitted to Russia. Another approach is for a Russian organization to invest illegally obtained funds abroad and let the interest accumulate there.

Capital flight is draining the country of investment capital and aggravating the balance of payments problem on a large scale. High-tech activities require such investment capital which, unfortunately, has moved offshore. Also, foreign partners are discouraged by their governments to invest in Russia when the Russian government has inadequate income due to tax evasion.

What can be done to cap capital flight? Improvements in the investment climate and financial infrastructure are fundamental requirements. Stricter laws are needed to control international transactions. Taxes on barter arrangements and requirements for immediate repatriation of revenues associated with exports will also help reduce incentives for capital flight.

One bold and sensible proposal of leading Russian economists calls for a program of amnesty for Russians with bank accounts in western Europe that contain income from illegal activities. The owners of bank accounts in some countries are having difficulty withdrawing their money as local authorities ask questions about the sources of that money. These authorities frequently turn to the Russian government for information prior to permitting further money transactions in their countries. The scheme of the Russian economists calls for the Russian government to certify the legitimacy of funds being held hostage in foreign banks, whatever the source, in exchange for a return of 50 percent of the funds to the Russian government as overdue taxes.[22]

The growth in economic crime intersects with many aspects of technology development. As to the large enterprises, illegal trade in natural resources is the dominant form of economic crime, while small entrepreneurs are constantly confronted with property theft and bribery. One chilling report in 1997 said that:

> Organized crime controls 40 percent of private businesses, 50 to 85 percent of banks, and 60 percent of state-owned companies. In Moscow, organized crime is believed to control 50 percent of commercial real estate and 80 percent of all shops, warehouses, and service industries.[23]

This situation evolved in several stages, as suggested by the following timeline:

- 1985-92: Perestroika: criminal groups sprouted deeper roots than ever before, with protection rackets encompassing embryonic joint ventures and cooperative restaurants in providing a financial base.
- 1992: Vacuum: large and sophisticated criminal groups moved in, establishing banks and solidifying their financial base.
- 1993-95: Privatization: a flea market for deep-pocketed criminal groups to take over much of the technological prowess of the country developed, with a massive wave of murders that peaked in 1995.
- 1998-?: Consolidation?: With thousands of criminal groups having become active, consolidation will be the byword of the future. And competition will lead to new conflicts among kingpins.[24]

A particularly nasty aspect of economic crime is contract killings. Common targets include officials in government, banks, or large companies who make illegal business dealings difficult. Also at risk are businessmen who either fail to pay their debts or who are reluctant to share their profits with criminal elements. Some cynics contend that contract killings are an alternative means of enforcing business contracts that are not enforceable through the judicial system.

Often, contract killings are double hits. The first killer is hired to assassinate a designated victim; a second killer is hired to kill the first assassin as soon as he kills his victim. Thus, the costs of hiring the first killer have doubled from the $5,000 price tag for assassinations in 1995.[25] This chain of events complicates the tracing of the perpetrators. And the plotters of assassinations are seldom, if ever, captured and convicted.

Bank-related crimes have included bombing of the car of the deputy finance minister, who reduced the number of banks authorized to deal with the government, and an attack on the home of the president of the Central Bank after revocation of licenses of several commercial banks. The president of a trade union bank was assassinated for refusing to launder money for Chechen rebels. Finally, a speaker at the funeral of a bank president involved in the takeover of aluminum assets was poisoned.[26]

What can be done to reverse the upward surge in crime, so banks can become more responsible and entrepreneurs can reduce their protection payments? Fortunately, in January 1997 the government and parliament adopted a new criminal code which, together with the constitution, provides a good paper framework for the development of the rule of law within the country. Many Russians still shake their heads in disbelief that the criminal code made it through the Duma. Many deputies simply were not paying attention, even those surrounded by advisers with close ties to organized crime.

What is needed now is enforcement muscle. But the law enforcement agencies are plagued with corruption, and the courts have yet to emerge as a force in combating crime. Edicts are regularly issued by the government to challenge the crime lords. They call for additional police on the streets, more and better paid judges, a federal protection program for witnesses, and removal of officials from office as soon as they are charged with corruption.[27]

These measures target the manifestations of crime, but not underlying organized crime structures. Investigations are frequently thwarted by mediocre police performance—the result of poor recruitment procedures, low morale resulting from irregular pay checks, and reliance on inadequate law enforcement technologies. Sometimes, the police, lacking vehicles, jump into taxis in pursuit of criminals leaving crime scenes.[28] Nevertheless, partially effective measure are better than no response at all.

While deeply concerned about crime and corruption in the country, neither Russian nor western reformers have considered the situation serious enough to be a show stopper for economic recovery. But with organized crime having touched every facet of the economy, often conferring a sense of legitimacy to illegal activities, they are wrong. Fear of crime and corruption has discouraged many potential entrepreneurs from undertaking legitimate activities that could lead to financial ruin. A turnaround is essential if legitimate business is to begin approaching its potential.

Multiple Challenges

Is it any wonder that the entire population is focused on money? Much of the focus is on ways to safeguard money obtained through legitimate activities. At least for now, few investors will risk long-term investments in technologies with the hope that in a few years there will be a positive return on their investments.

Raising investment capital, protecting financial and other assets, and finding and retaining paying customers for new products are talents in high demand in Russia. There are occasional successes of innovating for profit. The Russian government can help in all of these areas, as we have seen. Steady efforts of Russian leaders and western institutions to promote good government and rewards for efforts to overcome illicit activities are needed.

Transparency should become the hallmark of transactions involving money, particularly government funds. Banking laws, trading laws, and a host of other money-influencing laws need to be strengthened to provide legal pressure for such transparency. A rewards-for-reporting program could encourage whistleblowers to report illegal transactions under conditions that would not jeopardize their safety. The establishment of nongovernmental organizations, with anit-corruption as their theme, should be encouraged. As transparency evolves, corruption should subside. Then, in time, funds will gravitate toward projects that stand on their technical merit, the foundation of the innovation process.

Western governments can play a strong supportive role, both by repeatedly imploring the Russian government to clean up its act and by supporting Russian organizations with good records of integrity and responsibility. The schemes for direct payments of salaries to individual researchers work well and avoid many problems. Other innovative schemes are needed, particularly in encouraging innovation at large enterprises.

Finally, when transferring large resources to Russia, the IMF, the World Bank, and other major financial institutions must be vigilant as to how their resources flow through the Russian system and where they end up. It is not acceptable to simply say that management of these resources is a Russian responsibility. Without close oversight from abroad, few Russians in desperate economic straits can resist temptations to develop their own interpretations of what is legal and what is not. If illegal activities are permitted by western institutions, the likelihood of Russian institutions following a straighter path is low indeed.

Notes

1.   Richard Dulik, "Legal Issues of Special Concern to Technology Commercialization," *Technology Commercialization: Russian Challenges and American Lessons* (Washington, D.C.: National Academy Press, 1998), p. 16.
2.   Discussions with American and Russian officials knowledgeable about the activities of the Fund for Development of Small Firms in the Scientific and Technical Sphere that updated earlier discussions with fund officials, April 1999.
3.   Discussion in Moscow with officials of the Ministry of Science and Technology, June 1998.
4.   Ibid.
5.   "Register of Branch and Interbranch Extra-Budgetary Funds for Scientific-Research and Experimental Design Work," Ministry of Science and Technology, April 1998.
6.   J.E. Tumarkin and J.F. Kraus, *Sources of Financial Assistance for the Environmental Restoration of Former Military Lands* (Washington, D.C.: Institute for Defense Analysis, January 1998).
7.   Discussions in Moscow with science and technology experts from St. Petersburg who participate in activities of the St. Petersburg Technology Fund, November 1999.
8.   Discussions in Monterey, California, with a Seattle-based representative of a large number of small American firms that invest in companies in the Urals and Siberia, December, 1999.
9.   David Bernstein, *Commercialization of Russian Technology in Cooperation with American Companies,* Center for International Security and Cooperation, Stanford University, June 1999.
10.   "White Paper—Priorities for Private Equity in Russia," released by European Union TACIS program, Moscow, November 1999.
11.   *Ibid.*
12.   Meeting in Moscow with a representative of the Ministry of Finance, November 1998. See also "Order No. 315," Government of the Russian Federation, April 12, 1994; "Decree No. 426," President of the Russian Federation, April 27, 1992; and "Instructions No. 120," Ministry of Science and Technology, November 13, 1997.
13.   *Russian Organized Crime,* CSIS Task Force Report (Washington, D.C.: The Center for Strategic and International Studies, 1997), p. 30.
14.   *Ibid.*, p. 3.

15.   Albert Sperensky, "The Red Directors," released on the Internet by The Jamestown Foundation, HtmlResAnchor www.jamestown.org, October 1996.

16.   E. Michael Hunter, "The Russian Financial Crisis," conference in Washington, D.C., at the Carnegie Endowment for International Peace, June 8, 1998.

17.   "Moles at Banks," CNN broadcast, September 2, 1999.

18.   See, for example, Bill Powell and Yevgenia Albats, "Follow the Money," *Newsweek*, March 29, 1999, pp. 38-39. See also OMRI Service of Radio Free Europe, February 5, 1999.

19.   Timothy M. Burlingame, "Criminal Activity in the Russian Banking System," *Transnational Organized Crime*, Vol. 3, No. 3, Autumn 1997, pp. 46-72.

20.   *Ibid.*

21.   "The Problems of Capital Flight from Russia," Task Force Report, Institute of Economics, Moscow, September 1998.

22.   Discussions in Moscow with Russian economists, November 1998.

23.   Nicola J. Lowther, "Organized Crime and Extortion in Russia: Implications for Foreign Companies," *Transnational Organized Crime*, Vol. 3, No. 1, Spring 1997, pp. 23-38.

24.   See "Four Waves of Russian Crimes," *Russia Review*, March 13, 1998, p. 20.

25.   Discussion in Moscow with Russian criminologists, November 1998.

26.   Burlingame, "Criminal Activity in the Russian Banking System."

27.   *Russian Organized Crime*, p. 69.

28.   *Ibid.*, p. 70.

5

Long-Term Patent Protection and Short-Term Tax Relief

Russia needs to send 10,000 law students to the United States for training so the country can develop the rule of law.

American patent attorney, 1998

Showdowns with tax cheats and kicking in doors of deadbeat businesses are the best things I get to do in this job.

Chief of Russia's State Tax Service, 1998

I seldom spend a week in Moscow without witnessing acrimonious debates—at meetings, in private discussions, and in the press—about ownership of Russian discoveries or pirating of western inventions. Uncertainty abounds as to whether western financiers, Russian research and development organizations, or individual inventors are the rightful beneficiaries of anticipated profits from products developed in Russian laboratories. As Russian enterprises attempt to reverse engineer items developed in the West for the Russian market, they show little concern over patents that may be attached to the original items. Should Russian industry begin to revive, the conflicts over protection of patents, copyrights, and trademarks—the three aspects of intellectual property—will surely intensify.

Russian diplomats, lawyers, and research managers haggle frequently with western partners in international projects over ownership of innovations that may generate commercial products. They are relentless in their complaints that American companies providing funds for cooperative activities carried out in Russia do not let Russian partners have the opportunity to share in profits from sales or licenses based on "Russian" technologies. The Americans argue that their money supports the work and therefore they are the rightful owners of all discoveries. The Russians counter that their brain power fuels the discoveries, hence they are entitled to reap some of the benefits of their own know-how.

International sharing of intellectual property rights was one of the most contentious issues during the establishment of an international institution in Moscow to provide research grants to Russian scientists and engineers—the International Science and Technology Center. The negotiations dragged on for 18 months, with marathon arguments between western and Russian diplomats bolstered by lawyers, economists, and scientists. Who has commercial rights to the results of joint high-tech projects, rights in Russia, in Europe, in the United States, and in the rest of the world? Must the scientific results of projects that will not have commercial payoff in the foreseeable future be made available to the general public, or can researchers keep this information locked up for their own personal use? If the party entitled to patent rights for a new device won't risk its money to obtain a patent that in the West may require paying lawyers $15,000, can the other participating party then claim the rights and buy patent protection for itself, lest bystanders take over the discovery?

During this extended dialogue, it was clear that Russian legal provisions are not precise and their interpretation depends in large measure on the views of the Russian officials overseeing their implementation. Every time western diplomats thought they had achieved an accord, a new Russian lawyer would enter the fray with a different edict that, he would argue, must be observed. It was not unusual for an expert from a Russian ministry to show up at negotiations with an overriding document conveniently authorized just the preceding day.

In the end, a consensus was reached concerning intellectual property resulting from the international program that had been the center of this attention. When a western government finances a project, that government should have exclusive rights for selling the products in its own country, Russian researchers should have exclusive rights in their country, and the rights in other countries should be shared. But an escape clause was included. This clause stated that, regardless of the provisions of the agreement on division of rights that had just been so painstakingly negotiated, the participants in projects retain the option to adopt any arrangements that are mutually acceptable.[1]

Had the negotiators wasted all that time? Probably not. Even if other arrangements are considered under the escape clause, the agreed-upon formula for sharing provides a point of departure for negotiations on the new arrangements. Also, agreed-upon provisions negotiated by government representatives help Russian entities develop agreements with western companies. They can use the intergovernmental formula as an opening gambit in bargaining, whereas western companies inevitably start from the position that they should own all rights everywhere.

For almost a decade, the Russian government has experimented with modifications of long-standing laws and traditions in an attempt to improve the environment for Russian and foreign entrepreneurs interested in drawing on Russia's extensive technological resources. In recent years, the Duma has enacted special laws to help clarify situations involving patents, although uncertainties remain. The government has also taken steps to facilitate trouble-free international cooperation in research and development. They urge Russian institutions to include clear provisions concerning intellectual property in international contracts so as to avoid conflicts after the projects are under way.

All the while, Russian managers spend 24 months or longer obtaining protection of their discoveries from the Russian patent office. They are then surprised to learn that Russian patent certificates mean little overseas. Even more importantly, if no customers at home or abroad are interested in their inventions, they have simply wasted their time and money, both in the laboratory and in the offices of bureaucrats reluctant to expedite requests without special compensation. With the collapse of the economy in 1998, many managers found they indeed had wasted their time and money. They declared bankruptcy, as concerns over patents, copyrights, and trademarks soon paled in comparison with the financial realities of Russia.

A vivid example of the inadequate concern of the Russian government over intellectual property rights is its reluctance—or at least its lack of priority—to crack down on copyright theft. The U.S. and other governments repeatedly protest the expanding Russian piracy of video cassettes and complain loudly about fraudulently acquired computer software. If such pirated goods were purchased rather than stolen, western organizations would have received hundreds of millions of dollars in payments since 1992. Meanwhile, this never-to-be-collected debt continues to mount.[2]

Russian officials shrug, pointing out they are at the mercy of the omnipresent Russian mafia, which controls the entertainment and software industries. To help stem contraband trade in cassettes, the U.S. Motion Picture Association has financed a Russian Anti-Piracy Organization (RAPO) within the Russian government. In 1998, RAPO officials—typically recruited from the intelligence services and from special police units—seized 825,000 video cassettes from the pirated-products market, booming in the wake of the financial crisis that made legitimately imported products prohibitively expensive.[3] As for the sale of computer software, in June 1999 the Russian police made a statement about their determination to enforce applicable copyright law. They provided the international press with photo opportunities to document the crushing of 500,000 illegal disks by a bulldozer.[4] Despite the increase in seizures of cassettes and disks, however, fines for piracy are rarely collected.

Intellectual property rights are but one aspect of the murky legal framework surrounding business dealings in Russia. In the long run, they must be a critical factor if Russia is to have an economic future that meshes with technological achievements the world over. For the present, the Russian government is likely to continue complaining that western business partners cherry-pick the best Russian technologies while failing to provide adequate compensation for Russian inventors.

Of more immediate concern to most Russian firms and institutes than intellectual property rights, however, is the uncertain tax code and the constant threat of property confiscation should the tax police discover irregularities and pursue payment on behalf of the tax service. As demonstrated in the preceding chapter, the multiplicity of taxes and high tax rates have fueled the centuries-old Russian tradition to avoid taxes through both legal and illegal evasion schemes. To many well-connected organizations and individuals, tax collection is a concept and not a reality. But, at many research and development institutions, taxes take a heavy toll on the limited funds available for exploring the future.

Reliable patent protection and tax relief are important keys to a viable business climate. Western investors, accustomed to meaningful patents and to tax exemptions for research and development in their own countries, want to see immediate action on both fronts. From the perspective of most Russians—who live from payday to payday—tax relief is the dominant issue. Patents represent an investment in the future. As such, they are often ignored, even though the future consequences from lost claims on technologies may be great.

There are a few tax breaks for some research institutions, particularly those emphasizing basic research. Tax relief for expenditures on research should mean more funds to uncover technologies that lead to patents. These patents in turn can increase market shares and entrepreneurial earnings. The taxes from these earnings should then strengthen the government's capabilities to enforce the law, although more effective patent protection is not a current priority.

Patents, Copyrights, and Hope for Brighter Days

Why bother developing a new device or a new manufacturing process if someone else will steal your idea and undercut you in the marketplace? This has been the mantra of Russian government officials frustrated by their inability to hold western technology hunters at bay. Looking to the distant day when Russian technologies worthy of patents are commonplace, they certainly have a point.

Western businesses argue that they are playing by the rules. They add that it is not their fault that the Russian patent system is not fully developed and is poorly enforced by the embryonic Russian court system. Also, if Russian entities are eager to trade long-term rights to technologies for immediate financial income, why shouldn't foreign businesses be willing partners?

Few people, from Russia or the West, fully comprehend the workings of Russian law as it applies to intellectual property. Some regulations interpreting these laws are known only to a limited few. Provisions in the most widely disseminated documents are sometimes vague. Even when regulations are clear and a Russian inventor carefully follows procedures, with all required documents in order, redress from an infringement on the rights of the inventor is almost unknown. From time to time, court rulings in Russia recognize the misuse of property rights. But, for the aggrieved party to actually receive remuneration for economic losses due to patent infringement is indeed a rare occurrence. Once a decision is rendered, the case is filed away.[5] With no system in place to retrieve funds—and no penalty for nonpayment—it's up to the individual to collect.

Many Russian entrepreneurs simply walk away from the procedures necessary to obtain patent protection. They are convinced that any lawyers they might engage will charge large fees and deliver little in return. Occasionally, such entrepreneurs become shocked to learn that someone else had taken the trouble to patent "their" inventions.

What is so mysterious about patent protection in Russia? After all, in 1992 and 1993 the Russian government enacted intellectual property rights legislation that closely resembles similar western laws. The legislation's purpose is to promote research by ensuring that successful inventors are rewarded, to prevent duplication of research, and to clarify ownership rights.[6] The soundness of the 1992-93 legislation is reflected in the likely acceptance of Russia into the World Trade Organization. Membership requires that national legislation on intellectual property rights meets an international standard of acceptability.[7]

But, despite international acceptance of the patent law, there is a weakness in the Russian approach. The legislation does not adequately address ownership of technologies that are developed with the use of government funds—and for decades the government has financed the bulk of innovative work at Russian institutions. Correcting this weakness is central to stimulating technology development in a country where the government has a long history of financing almost all research activities. What's more, many technological innovations of commercial significance will only emerge in the marketplace if government funding is involved, at least to a limited extent. Thus, ownership of the results of government-funded projects is an issue that needs to be resolved.

The 1992-93 legislative flurry ceded all rights for results of government-funded activities to the institutions where the work is conducted. They were to decide whether individual inventors deserve a share of the proceeds. Despite protests from entrenched government officials that their ministries should be the rightful owners of discoveries they finance, under the law ownership rights could be assigned only to legal entities—research institutes, manufacturing enterprises, and innovative firms—that make discoveries. Nevertheless, the ministries kept trying to obtain pieces of financial pies that occasionally were cooked up—and divided up—within these organizations, threatening to withhold future funds unless pieces are delivered to their doorsteps.

In 1998, a Russian expert on technological development and intellectual property law, Yuri Lebedev, summarized the situation thus:

> The government has declined to control the use of scientific-technical results obtained using government funds. The consequence has been chaotic redistribution of rights to such results, ineffective use of research results, development of many undefined and contentious relationships, and violation of the legal rights of patent and copyright owners.[8]

This statement could be misinterpreted as advocacy of a return to the Soviet system of governmental shepherding of innovations from the workbench to the consumer. The government would then control all associated financial dealings. This expert, however, advocates reducing the chaos within the new market economy without turning back to the ways of the past. He is on target with his suggestions.

The framework Lebedev proposes would help ensure more equitable sharing of the rights to products resulting from government-funded projects. Underlying his solution would be legislation that assigns intellectual property rights to enterprises and institutes that develop new technologies, as was the case. In addition, however, he recommends clear legislative language specifying that individual inventors receive significant portions of any profits from patented technologies. Also, to respond to at least some concerns of government ministries, the framework calls for the government to receive the right to use patented technologies for noncommercial purposes, such as use in space exploration, through nonexclusive, no-cost licenses.

Lebedev advocated other modifications to patent practice. State-owned manufacturing enterprises had the right to appropriate research results from government-funded projects for their own use if such action is "in the interest of the industrial sector." Lebedev believes that such use should be based on licensing arrangements between the enterprises and the research laboratories. However, his proposals became mute when in 1999 new government regulations—contradicting the 1992-93 laws—vested ownership of results of government-funded activities in the ministries.[9]

An important aspect of Russian intellectual property law that directly affects individual Russian scientists and engineers is traced to a Soviet system that provided for each inventor to receive limited compensation for use of his or her discoveries based on author's certificates. In an economy that was not driven by profit, the level of compensation was usually small. Still, prestige associated with author's certificates was high, and such certificates covered approximately 80 percent of the most important Soviet technological achievements. The other 20 percent of Soviet-era discoveries were attributed exclusively to manufacturing enterprises and research institutes, particularly those discoveries with direct military applications.

Following enactment of the 1992-93 laws, owners of author's certificates were given a 20-year window within which to exchange them for patents. Some entrepreneurs have taken advantage of this no-cost exchange while others simply have not been motivated to go to the trouble of exchanging the documents. They hold on to their author's certificates, delaying action until the day when they have real value.

Even when the owner of a certificate has a claim to a technology, it is seldom clear how the claim can be exercised so the owner profits. In a rare case, a government agency may actively support an owner's protest that his or her technology is being misused. The likely response of the organization that has taken over the technology will be to pay the original inventor a token amount or simply to halt production plans, in which case no one benefits.

The roots of much technology of current interest date to the Soviet era. Controversy abounds as to ownership of the technology that is now available, including the scope of any given author's certificate. In cases where contemporary technology combines old inventions with new ones, the confusion mounts. For a specific, recently-developed technology, the ownership struggle may involve claimants from a government agency, former employees of a now-defunct institute where the work was performed, management of the new replacement institute, and members of the original scientific team who cling to their yellowing author's certificates.

Meanwhile, many technology-oriented organizations have been privatized. If privatization procedures were not followed meticulously, as is often the case, the new entities now have difficulty laying claim to the technological developments of the predecessor organizations. Then confusion as to who owns a specific technology that originated in the predecessor organization increases even more.[10]

Potential investors interested in commercializing old technology, or hybrids of old and new technologies, are rightfully wary about risking funds in uncertain investments. If they are successful in developing salable technologies and profits start flowing, they can be reasonably sure that someone else will lay claim to the technologies underlying their products.

My repeated suggestion to Moscow officials that the Ministry of Science and Technology establish a commission to address the blurs in ownership of technology has fallen on deaf ears. Such an entity, at the request of a Russian or foreign organization interested in commercializing a specific technology, would rule on the ownership aspects. The commission would identify all legitimate claimants, if any, and the extent of their claims. The technological entrepreneur with eyes on a potential market could attempt to make financial arrangements with the claimants. If unsuccessful in efforts to compensate the claimants or to develop appropriate licensing arrangements, the entrepreneur could walk away from the technology. No one would benefit or lose. If the entrepreneur decided to proceed with his or her project, there would be no surprises after he or she had spent funds.

This suggestion to establish yet another bureaucracy when there are not enough funds to pay salaries within existing offices was a non-starter. Entrenched bureaucrats claimed they were already empowered to make such judgments, although they had yet to consider a single case. They argued that they also needed supplementary pay to compensate their involvement in such complicated matters.

The suggestion, nevertheless, is sound if entrepreneurs are expected to invest in existing technologies. Granted, such a commission—probably with a small staff and an uncertain payroll—might not be very efficient. Still, it would be a start in the long process of resolving thousands of conflicting claims on technologies that might some day have real value. If the applicants pay modest fees for determinations by the commission, the mechanism for resolving uncertainties would be energized.

To further explore the impact of patent uncertainties on technology development, in the spring of 1998 Russian colleagues assisted me in determining whether uncertainty over intellectual property rights was stifling applied research activities at Russian institutes. We conducted a survey of 28 applied research institutes—from the Russian Academy of Sciences, the university sector, and the industrial sector—and then followed up with more in-depth discussions. While each institute had a differing view on intellectual property, a general consensus emerged on a number of key points.

First, the framework for intellectual property rights was important but usually not the critical factor influencing research and development in the late 1990s. Given economic difficulties, there was limited opportunity to find markets for products that would be protected by patents; and copyrights and trademarks were almost unknown to the institutes. Nevertheless, there was an occasional opportunity to lay claim to technologies that might have commercial value in the future. Clearly, according to the respondents, the situation would have been much worse had the 1992-93 laws not been in place.

Also at the institute level, protection of new discoveries was more important than resolving uncertainties in exploiting old technologies. Unlike industrial enterprises interested in selling off-the-shelf technologies developed in the 1980s and earlier, the institutes were concerned primarily about the fruits of current research activities. Uncertainty over ownership of old technologies was of less interest.

With this focus on current activities, the institutes viewed Russian patent laws as reasonably clear. As expected, they considered costs of Russian patents high, delays in issuing patents excessive, and penalties for not respecting patent rights nonexistent. Some gave much higher priority to obtaining patents abroad than to wasting time and energy in Russia—assuming they could find a foreign partner to pay the high registration and related fees.[11]

In summary, the importance of protecting intellectual property rights is widely acknowledged throughout the Russian government and the research and development community. For most enterprises and institutes, patent, trademark, and copyright protection will bring benefits only in the distant future, however, and will not relieve the pressing problem of meeting current payrolls. Foreign investors who are encouraging large Russian manufacturing enterprises to dust off older technologies seem to be the most eager to sort out intellectual property issues as soon as possible. In one area—namely intellectual property rights associated with international projects—Russian entities feel that immediate action is needed so they will no longer be at a disadvantage in working with foreign partners.

International Sharing of Intellectual Property Rights

In 1998, patent experts at the Ministry of Science and Technology confronted me with the following assertion:

> During the past two years, not a single patent application has resulted from the 450 research projects financed by the U.S. Department of Energy in Russia. The Americans insist on taking possession of all patent rights that might flow from the projects. Therefore, Russian researchers have no incentive to search for market applications of their work. If they cannot share in the profits from their research, why should they try to make Americans richer?[12]

Total U.S. ownership of intellectual property rights resulting from activities supported in whole or in part with U.S. funds is the position most commonly taken by U.S. government agencies as well as by

American companies. There has been an important exception, however.

A ground-breaking model for the division of rights for western-financed projects at Russian institutes was adopted in 1994 by the International Science and Technology Center (ISTC), established in Moscow by the United States, the European Union, Japan, and Russia. Box 5.1 sets forth the division of rights in the ISTC model for a project financed by the U.S. government. In this case, the U.S. government

---

Box 5.1
Sharing Intellectual Property Rights from International Projects

• All intellectual property rights flowing from a project belong to the Russian institute where the research is carried out.

• The rights to background technologies—technologies that were in the possession of the Russian research institute prior to initiation of the project—remain unchanged by the project.

• The U.S. government (or its designee) has the right to an exclusive no-cost license for commercializing the results of the project in the United States.

• If the U.S. government (or its designee) does not take steps to use the results in the United States after the Russian institute indicates an interest in this market, the Russian institute can exploit the results in the United States.

• The Russian institute has exclusive rights in Russia.

• The U.S. government (or its designee) has the right to purchase from the Russian institute an exclusive license on "fair and reasonable" terms for using the results in Europe, Japan, and other countries.

• Russian inventors are entitled to a share of any royalties received by the Russian institute.

• If the Russian institute makes no effort to promote commercialization of the results within two years after completion of the project, the U.S. government (or its designee) has "march in" rights to use the results as desired.

Source: Statute of the International Science and Technology Center, adopted in Moscow, 1994.

passes on its rights to an appropriate U.S. institution that has demonstrated special interest in the project. This approach diverges from the more common formula whereby the western provider of funds receives all rights. The ISTC model calls for a genuine sharing of rights between the funder and the Russian institute that carries out a project. (This formula is the result of the 18-month negotiation cited at the beginning of this chapter.)

For the first few years after these ground rules were adopted, few research results were patented in Russia or abroad. Beginning in 1997, however, the ISTC undertook a concerted effort to both fund projects with commercial potential and pay more attention to the patent aspects of project results. By 1999, commercialization of technology had become a major concern of the ISTC, and the need to protect technological developments took on a high priority. It seems likely that, in the not too distant future, financial returns will be flowing both to Russian institutes and U.S. collaborators from some projects.[13]

The position of almost all western companies doing business in Russia is quite firm. They are not prepared to share intellectual property rights with anyone, even rights for marketing made-in-Russia products in Russia. In many cases, western firms reward individual Russian researchers responsible for important discoveries—most often with bonuses and trips abroad rather than with a percentage of profits from sales of products.

To date, western companies have been operating in a buyers market, with Russian institutes and researchers so desperate for funds they will not object to any arrangements concerning patents. At the same time, the position of the companies has not gone unnoticed by the Russian government. Some Russian officials resent what they consider to be exploitation of "their" talent, and politicians continuously threaten to block western access to Russian technologies rather than to continue tolerating technology bazaars that benefit western firms. Neither the concerned politicians nor the resentful officials have been able to muster enough support in Moscow to be able to change western habits. However, one-sided patent arrangements certainly do not encourage assistance from these officials when companies encounter administrative problems that hamper operations in Russia.[14]

That said, western firms intending to establish a permanent presence in Russia should reconsider their extreme positions on intellectual property. In the long run, a western company's recognition of the entitlement of Russian entities to share in the fruits of Russian know-how may help pave the way to new discoveries with financial returns for the company. But, whatever the commercial agreements that are reached on intellectual property rights, both foreign firms and Russian partners should insist on written contracts that include provisions to fill in blanks not addressed in Russian legislation and regulations.

The intransigence of western companies with regard to intellectual property rights sometimes motivates Russian organizations to seek access to intellectual property through whatever channels they can uncover. In response, western high-tech firms with substantial investments in Russia are well advised to have a continuing presence in the country to resolve problems that inevitably arise over infringement on property rights. Also, western companies should hesitate in taking proprietary products to Russia for demonstration or other purposes lest they be compromised. Finally, western companies cannot rely only on legislation and contracts to adequately protect their technologies, and they should develop networks of officials both in Moscow and at the municipal level whom they can call upon when controversies arise.[15]

Sharing of intellectual property rights is an investment in the future of Russia. While western governments cannot be expected to interfere in commercial arrangements of western companies, they should set an example by acknowledging that international projects are only truly international when there is an equitable division of profits from innovation. An adoption of the ISTC model by western governments in their bilateral programs would go a long way toward supporting the struggling research and development sector. Also, the approach would improve the political climate for continued western engagement with important Russian institutions.

The Tax Man Cometh

For years, every Russian manager has been waiting for legislation that will take some of the tax burden off his or her back and simplify accounting procedures. There are more than 200 different types of federal, regional, and local taxes in Russia. Most firms involved in innovation must cope with at least several dozen. These firms, hopeful of earning income from their innovations well into the future, are obliged to pay their taxes now.[16]

Several tax breaks are bestowed on some scientific institutions, in recognition of the fact that in the long run scientific research benefits society as a whole. They are exempt from paying value added tax (VAT) on goods and services, federal profit tax on income from research contracts, and regional property tax. Smaller, but still significant, local taxes that can be avoided by an institute engaged in scientific research include land, forestry, animal, and water taxes if natural resources are the object of scientific study.[17]

Several categories of scientific institutions have special tax exemption status: the State Scientific Centers and the institutes of the Academy of Sciences, the Academy of Medical Sciences, and the Academy of Agricultural Sciences. In addition, tax exemptions may be granted to other institutions demonstrating that at least 70 percent of their total income is derived from research and development activities. This usually means that most of an institute's income must come from government research funds. At the beginning of 1999, certification of scientific institutions meeting the 70 percent criteria was well underway, indicating a governmental intention to verify the legitimacy of claimed exemptions. At the same time, a few research institutes that are heavily engaged in commercial activities have spun off daughter companies where they concentrate their commercial income so the entire institute will not be subject to all of the taxes levied on commercial organizations.[18]

Some research institutes believe the 70 percent rule to be unfair. Their core research budgets from government are very small, and they must raise funds from a variety of sources. They argue that if such income, whatever its sources (e.g., property rental to commercial organizations), is reinvested in research programs it should be considered within the 70 percent rule. Otherwise, they will simply be discouraged from raising private funds.[19] Then, in 1997, Russian officials opposed to any types of exemptions from taxes took aim at the universities and attempted to levy taxes on research grants and graduate student stipends, but they were overruled by the Duma.[20]

In 1999, the Russian government and the Duma took steps to lighten the tax burden on all sectors of the economy. These measures were important for research and development institutions and researchers with little cash flow. The maximum personal income tax rate was reduced from 45 percent to 35 percent. The required contributions to the pension and other social funds by employers was reduced from 39 to 33 percent of the employee payroll.[21] The national VAT is being reduced from 20 to 15 percent, although a small comprehensive sales tax has been introduced to compensate for loss of some income from this primary revenue generator. Taxes on company profits were reduced from 35 to 30 percent. Finally, emerging businesses (fewer than 200 employees) producing consumer goods or engaged in public works projects have a two-year start-up holiday from federal taxes. To help ensure that tax revenues remain steady, additional regulations were designed to reduce tax evasion and improve tax collection.[22]

New spotlights have focused on more limited tax exemptions that would benefit technology-oriented firms. Local officials, for example, have persuaded the Duma of the need for 30 tax havens established as either (a) special economic zones to attract foreign investment through tax holidays and import/export privileges or (b) administrative territories encompassing nuclear and other defense towns that permit local jurisdictions to reduce the share of tax collections sent to Moscow, as we shall see in Chapter 8. With each such exemption, financial officials in Moscow deplore the loss of tax revenues while they watch favored businesses prosper. In the nuclear cities, scientists also derive direct benefits. Most tax havens have became money laundering enclaves, however, with only a few cities achieving their intended objective of stimulating local industrial and technological development.[23]

Another type of tax exemption came into public focus in the summer of 1999 when banners appeared in several Russian cities and in the press. "Ban Tolling: Stop Robbing Russia," the banners proclaimed. Unknown parties, and perhaps the tax service itself, protested the practice of trading companies acting as tollers—bringing into Russia the inexpensive mineral alumina to be processed into aluminum at Siberian smelters and then exported to customers in the West. The alumina is imported at $120 per ton, a fee of $250 per ton is paid to the smelters, and the aluminum is sold on the London metals exchange at $1,400 per ton. The tax code exempts well-heeled tollers from import duties, export tariffs, and VAT.[24]

At the same time, under a presidential decree internal tolling is also exempted from VAT. Alumina mined in Russia is processed along with imported alumina in the Siberia smelters. Altogether, 90 percent of Russian aluminum is linked to tolling. Without tolling, Russian officials have estimated there would be a drop of 30 percent in Russian processing of alumina and a loss of tens of thousands of jobs.

It is not surprising that shady companies have gained substantial control over activities at Russian smelters. Politicians attempting to change the generosity of the law may be subjected to blackmail and death threats. In principle, nevertheless, the concept of tax breaks to encourage industrial activities in Russia that add value to natural resources is a sound policy in moving away from a Russia that simply exports raw materials. Better legislation is needed to regulate tolling, but more transparent accounting practices of the enterprises would also reduce temptations to bilk shareholders of their rightful earnings. Then in a surprise move in early 2000, several Russian aluminum producers abandoned tolling, allegedly in response to public criticisms of the practice.[25]

Tax credits for investments to encourage innovation are also a lively topic within government circles. In 1999, after lengthy debate, the Duma rejected a proposal to exempt from federal taxes industrial profits that are reinvested in research and development or in modernization of facilities. Debate on the length of the amortization period for expenditures on new industrial equipment was also intense. These discussions will undoubtedly be revived in the months and years ahead.[26] At the regional and local levels, investments in improving manufacturing facilities—particularly high-tech facilities—are often deductible from regional and local taxes, usually at 50 percent of the total investment.[27]

Russian companies, including many technology-oriented companies, probably owe more than $50 billion in back taxes. According to tax authorities, only 25 percent of taxable personal income is declared. One report noted that, of 24,000 firms in Moscow subjected to audits in 1997-1998, 16,000 were fined for tax evasion.[28] Lower estimates were presented in late 1999 by the minister responsible for tax collection, who claimed that only one of six firms cheat on their taxes and that the arrears were only $8.7 billion. The first estimate seems more reliable, given the well-known history of tax evasion. The minister also stated that one-half of income earners—including many of the wealthiest Russians—cheat on their personal income tax. This number is also probably low.[29]

Against this background, in 1998 the tax service promised the:

- arrests of 10 major tax offenders within a few months;
- 700,000 audits by the end of 1999;
- increased tax collections from companies that are able to pay;
- crackdowns on the gray economy, especially informal traders who have not paid taxes; and
  - aggressive collections of VAT.

Whether these objectives were met was never reported.[30]

Tightening up on tax collection spells bad news for Russian researchers. Many large Russian enterprises, with legal advisers and easy access to Russian financial officials, will continue to find ways to limit their tax burdens—through offshore accounts, through money diversion schemes, through barter arrangements, or through bribery. Although considered small fish and therefore not singled out as targets in public statements, both research institutes and individual inventors will be under siege. They are not well equipped to fight back. Scientists and engineers have more difficulty than big business in concealing budgets. Their budgets are generally known at several levels of government since they receive most of their funds through the Russian banking system, where secrets are protected only for friends of the banks.

For the foreseeable future, the executive and legislative branches will continue to be engulfed in efforts to revise the tax code. As we saw in 1999, each proposed exemption to the tax code has its advocates. The government's general goal of eliminating exemptions will remain but a distant thought; and, from the point of view of innovation, tax exemptions are sometimes warranted.

Taxation and Technical Assistance from Abroad

Tens of thousands of Russian scientists and engineers depend on foreign grants and contracts related to international projects as their primary source of income. The largest category of contributors to these projects is western governments, with most government funds dispensed through western, private-sector, intermediary organizations. The second largest category of foreign financial supporters is private industry. Both intermediary organizations and private industry depend heavily on representatives based in Russia to identify project opportunities, to monitor project implementation, and to troubleshoot administrative problems. Thus, when the tax chief targets foreigners living in Russia for special attention, many international programs designed to upgrade innovation capabilities in Russia could be in jeopardy.

Foreign residents in Russia with responsibilities related to financial transactions have repeatedly been accused by the Russian government of avoiding personal income tax obligations, primarily through receiving their salaries in off-shore transactions. In the words of the tax chief:

> I think that our visitors from abroad will start paying taxes after a couple of them are arrested at the border and told that they are going to have to spend a few years in Siberia because they did not want to pay their debts to the Russian Federation.[31]

In addition to possible hits on individual employees who may not pay enough income tax, western firms worry they will be unfairly targeted by the tax service for failures to pay VAT, profit tax, or some other form of duty. Indeed, American companies usually cite taxes—both the number of taxes and the level of taxation—as the principal challenge in doing business in Russia. The tax system is far from transparent, which greatly complicates efforts to comply with the rules.

The case of Johnson & Johnson is often cited as dramatic justification for western anxieties. In 1998, the tax service confiscated 89 automobiles belonging to the firm and started criminal proceedings against two former managers. The tax service claimed that the company owed $19 million in back taxes. The company, which has always been proud of its squeaky-clean image, cried foul. While the details of the case are still not public, different interpretations of the vague tax laws are undoubtedly at the center of the dispute. It seems likely that Johnson & Johnson will try to settle since it has no other recourse except to abandon its presence in Russia.[32]

In 1998, a law was enacted that provides tax exemptions for Russian organizations that receive "technical assistance" from foreign governments, international organizations, and nonprofit foundations. According to this general legislation, Russian entities are exempt from paying VAT, import duties, and several other types of taxes on funds, services, and in-kind contributions designated for humanitarian aid and technical assistance.[33] Given the vagueness of the law, it was up to the Ministry of Economics to determine which programs qualified for the tax exemption while the Customs Service determined which incoming shipments were exempt from import duties.

Then, in May 1999, a watershed law was enacted. This law provides exemptions from profit tax, VAT, the road tax, personal income tax, and contributions to pension and social funds for humanitarian assistance and technical assistance provided free of charge by governments, international organizations, and nonprofit organizations. This law also provides retroactive amnesties for unpaid taxes. It is a major breakthrough in freeing many western programs from the overhanging threat of tax collection on technical assistance activities, with all types of scientific and technological cooperation eligible for classification as technical assistance. Of course commercial transactions do not fit under this law.[34]

There are many twists and turns in the search for legal routes to avoid payment of Russian taxes. Regardless of the provisions of laws and regulations, exemptions are only exemptions if the officials at the working level are convinced that the exemptions are legitimate. These officials often change jobs. This argues for a western provider of assistance or promoter of cooperation in order to accumulate as many officially stamped documents certifying the legitimacy of activities and the right for tax exemptions as possible to buttress claims at the working level.

Other Hurdles in Carrying Out International Programs

Customs charges are another tax that complicates cooperative technology activities and thus may discourage foreign investment involving imports of high-tech equipment. Since 35 percent of the Russian budget depends on collections of duties on imports and exports, the customs service has considerable political clout.[35] In general, import duties can reach 30 percent of estimated value (although in special cases a rate of 250 percent has been applied). In any given case, the tariff depends on the type of goods, the legal status of the importer (a Russian company, an office of a western firm, a joint venture), whether the items are intended for use by the importer or by someone else, and the final destination for the goods, such as a research facility in a free economic zone.[36]

Clearing items through customs has always been a tedious chore in Moscow and other ports of entry into Russia. Customs officials are well equipped to address general issues and to search out regulations concerning various types of charges. But, when it comes to handling items imported under programs that are supposed to have special exemptions—particularly technical assistance programs recently certified by the Ministry of Economics—the officials may be uninformed about the specific programs. That is when documentation, persuasion, and negotiation take over. Off-line payments often expedite the process.

Seemingly legitimate fees are routinely encountered at international airports and other customs clearance points. These include a customs clearance fee and a fee for storing items if they are not picked up immediately upon arrival. But every foreign program manager in Russia will probably concur that customs clearance procedures have a long way to go if international programs are to run smoothly while following the rules.

As discussed in Chapter 1, a significant dimension of conducting business in Russia is reliance on barter. For some foreign companies, barter may provide the only means to receive payment for engineering products and services. In the tax arena, barter sometimes benefits both the provider of goods and services and the recipient. Swapping goods is simply an inventory transaction not reported on a balance sheet. Barter activities cannot be detected without detailed audits, and barter strips off liability for VAT and other taxes. While finished goods go into inventory, they never show up as sales. Tax authorities then may end up looking for cash that, officially, isn't there.[37]

For foreign companies, barter transactions are often more trouble than they are worth. Even if a firm receives products at agreed intervals without difficulty, problems with selling these products may be severe. Many companies prefer to use brokers to mediate countertrade. This practice also has risks and downsides. But, in the absence of Russian cash, it may be the only available course to take advantage of either market opportunities or unique Russian capabilities to develop products.

An important legislative action was the granting of authority to government entities at all levels—federal, regional, local—to enter into cooperative agreements with foreign organizations for economic purposes. Such agreements are to be registered in Moscow, but shortcuts around Moscow authorities have often been the rule, with complicated tax avoidance implications.[38]

A final tax-related issue relates to foreign equity investments in Russia. In 1987, Russia passed its first decree regarding the joint venture. Intended to pave the way for such investments, this decree has been modified many times. The idea was that if the division of rights between Russian and western investors were clarified and tax implications simplified, western companies would go to Russia.

A few joint ventures were established. However, financial squabbles among the participants and between the investors and the government prior to establishing the joint venture and then after it was in place were commonplace. Some joint ventures were simply paper creations that the Russian participants viewed as a safe channel for an influx of western dollars—funds that often failed to materialize.

Within a few years, most western firms had learned that the extensive efforts needed to put a joint venture in place before meaningful activity could begin were not worth the effort. Therefore, straightforward contractual arrangements became far preferable for these firms. Such arrangements include licensing agreements, turn-key construction projects for which foreign companies provide engineering services, Russian manufacturing of agreed-upon quantities of product, production-sharing arrangements, and a host of other contractual approaches. Although the joint venture approach never caught on in a major way, it was an important step toward a still-evolving legal regime for foreign commercial activities in Russia.[39]

A Legal Environment to Facilitate Innovation

Fair and enforceable laws and regulations that provide the framework for a safe business environment are essential if new generations of Russian technology entrepreneurs are to adopt western business standards and practices. Only then will these entrepreneurs be able to find their way in a western-style market economy. Until that time, they will need help and protection, not harassment, from the Russian government if they are to survive in a tumultuous milieu of corruption and financial deprivation.

Uncertainty over patent rights will remain a major question confronting technological progress in Russia. Few doubt that, under favorable economic conditions, some Russian technologies will be of widespread interest at home and abroad. At a less practical but still important level, Russian patent certificates that are of no interest to foreign experts looking for technologies with greater payoff can have substantial meaning for Russian inventors. They are viewed as measures of personal success and as claims, however small, on the future of the world's progress.

Meanwhile, for a decade western voices have been cheering for the tax police to do their job. All are convinced that without tax collection Russia will never recover. An easy strategy for the tax authorities will continue to be to make pronouncements denouncing all tax deadbeats but then confronting those who put up the least resistance. This latter category includes many technology entrepreneurs.

Proposed changes in the tax code that could ease business dealings will be debated for years. Some will be enacted piecemeal. For example, in 1997 the requirement to pay tax on anticipated income from a contract as soon as the contract is signed rather than when the money is received was changed. Then, in 1999, tax on sales-below-cost was eliminated. Also, the law now states that in disputes between tax authorities and the taxpayer the latter is presumed innocent until proven guilty—although recent Russian visitors to the offices of the tax service laugh when they learn about this turnabout on paper.

Whatever the laws and regulations, successful marriages of diverse interests between Russian and foreign investors will help solve many problems, including equitable arrangements to share intellectual property rights and joint efforts to minimize taxes. One American expert who has been involved in over 700 proposed and completed business marriages observes:

> An extremely important predictor of success has been the quality of the Russian business partner. The ideal partner is one who has a sound understanding of western business standards and practices, can effectively navigate the labyrinthine Russian bureaucracy to obtain required approvals and registrations, is trustworthy and reliable, and is willing to learn and embrace foreign financial reporting and other business practices.[40]

In short, Russia remains a country where the rule of relationships is supreme and the rule of law is still being born. Successful marriages will help convince influential politicians and seemingly intransigent bureaucrats that governmental actions to facilitate joint efforts can, in fact, pay off. Only with their leadership will the rule of law become one of the keys to technological development of Russia.[41]

Notes

1. Negotiations in Moscow from November 1992 to March 1994 on the Statute of the International Science and Technology Center.

2. Vladimir Smoylenko and Ian Spence, "The Current State of Tax Reform in Russia," *Russia Business Watch*, Spring 1999, pp. 38-9.

3. Nick Holdsworth, "Video Pirates To Walk the Plank," *The Moscow Times*, August 14, 1999, p. 24.

4. Vladimir Merkushev, "Microsoft Sales Slump 38% in Russia, CIS," *The Russia Journal*, September 27-October 3, 1999, p. 9.

5. Vladimir Meshcheryakov, "Development of Legal Regulations for

Technology Commercialization in Russia," *Technology Commercialization: Russian Challenges, American Lessons*, National Academy Press, 1998, pp. 60-66. This report describes the legal basis of the protective documents issued by the patent agency while pointing out the necessity for stopping violations of exclusive rights in receiving infringement disputes, as well as mechanisms for enforcing the decisions of the courts.

6.   Andrei A. Baev, "Protection of Intellectual Property Rights in Russia," *Cooperative Business Ventures between U.S. Companies and Russian Defense Enterprises,* Center for International Security and Arms Control, Stanford University, 1996, pp. 267-285.

7.   Meshcheryakov, "Development of Legal Regulations for Technology Commercialization in Russia."

8.   Yuri Lebedev, "Problems of Taxation and Technology Commercialization in Russia," *Technology Commercialization: Russian Challenges, American Lessons* (Washington, D.C.: National Academy Press, 1998), pp. 50-54.

9.   *Ibid.* "On the Use of Results of Scientific-Technical Activity," Decree of the Government of the Russian Federation, No. 982, September 2, 1999. Also, "Conception of State Policy on Introducing into the Economy, the Results of Scientific-Technical Work Carried Out with Funds of the Federal Budget," Interagency Commission, Protocol No. 6, April 7, 2000.

10.   Baev, "Protection of Intellectual Property Rights in Russia."

11.   Glenn E. Schweitzer, Field notes from survey of 28 applied research institutes in Russia conducted in July and August 1997.

12.   Discussions in Moscow at the Ministry of Science and Technology, July 1997.

13.   Discussions in Moscow with staff members of the International Science and Technology Center, April 1998.

14.   Discussion in Moscow with patent expert and foreign relations officials at the Ministry of Science and Technology, July 1997.

15.   Baev, "Protection of Intellectual Property Rights in Russia."

16.   While the U.S. Department of Commerce has considerable information on the various tax requirements at the national level, there is no authoritative source of all tax requirements either at the national or local level. Both Russian and western entities are well advised to consult frequently with the authorities as to their legal obligations, as well as relying on the growing cottage industry of tax lawyers in Russia.

17.   Lebedev, "Problems of Taxation and Technology Commercialization in Russia."

18.   Discussions in Moscow with a number of Russian research managers and tax specialists, November 1998.

19.   Schweitzer, Field Notes.

20.   "Russian Grants to Remain Duty Free," *Science*, April 16, 1997, p. 1197.

21.   Glenn Geffner, "Income Tax Rates Due for General Overhaul," *The Moscow Times*, July 27, 1999, p. 14.

22.   "Commercial Overview of Russia," *BISNIS*, Department of Commerce, September 1999, pp. 16-18.

23.   Igor Emenenko, "Sheltering Havens," *Business Review*, September 1999. At the end of 1999, the Duma was attempting to drastically reduce the number of tax havens in connection with the need to increase tax revenues.

24.   Brian Humphreys, "Campaign Targets Aluminum Firms' Tax Breaks," *The Moscow Times*, September 28, 1999, p. 14.

25.   Vladimir Merkushev, "Internal Tolling Likely To Be Extended One Year," *The Russia Journal*, November 22-28, 1999, p. 15. Oleg Kirsanov and Sergey Padalko, "Good Changes in Russian Aluminum Sector?" *The Moscow Courier*, No. 1, June 2000, p. 4.

26.   Smoylenko and Spence, "The Current State of Tax Reform in Russia."

27.   Alexander Chmelev, "Recent Developments in Russian Tax Legislation," *Russia Business Watch*, Fall 1998, pp. 26-7.

28.   "Tax Evaders Targeted," *The Moscow Tribune*, November 4, 1998, p. 8.

29.   "Tax Minister: A Sixth of Firms Cheat," *The Moscow Times*, August 14, 1999, p. 12.

30.   Karl Emerick Hanuska, "Make My Day," *Russia Review*, September 11, 1998, Vol. 5, No. 16, pp. 25-28.

31.   *Ibid.*

32.   Margaret Coker, "Grab the Band-Aids, Get Ready to Fight," *Russia Review*, September 11, 1998, Vol. 5, No. 16, pp. 29-30.

33.   "Federal Law on Introducing Changes and Amendments in Specified Laws of the Russian Federation Concerning Taxes and Obligations in Connection with Nonreimbursable Assistance to the Russian Federation," No. 2439-II GD, May 14, 1998.

34.   Nicole N. Nelson, "MPC&A Tax Status Report," U.S. Department of Energy, June 3, 1999, updated and corrected by spokesman for Ministry of Foreign Affairs, Monterey Institute of International Studies, Monterey, California, December 1999. For background on procedures that had been in effect until this time see "Agreement on Exclusions from Payment of Taxes in Connection with the Realization of Programs of Assistance Agreed on a Nonrepayment Basis between the Russian Federation and the Government of the United States of America," originally signed by Minister of Finance V.G. Panskov and U.S. Ambassador Thomas R. Pickering, April 17, 1996, and subsequently extended on several occasions; and "Letter on Excluding Grants from Personal Income Tax that Are Provided by International and Foreign Institutions and International and Foreign Noncommercial and Humanitarian Organizations for Support of Russian Science," Russian Ministry of Finance and State Tax Service (and signed by Z.A. Yakobashvili, Ministry of Science and Technology), May 21-22, 1997.

35.   Discussion in Washington, D.C., with Deputy Director of Customs Service of Russia, June 1999.

36.   "Russian Customs: How Much—and How—To Pay," *BISNIS* Bulletin, Department of Commerce, July 1997, p. 6.

37.   "Barter in Russia: How To Protect Your Investment," *BISNIS* Bulletin, Department of Commerce, May 1998, p. 3.

38.   "Federal Law on Coordination of International and Foreign Economic

Relations of Subjects of the Russian Federation," adopted by Duma on December 2, 1998, and signed by President Yeltsin on January 4, 1999, No. 4-f3.

39. Jeffrey A. Burt, "Joint Ventures in Russia: The Ten-Year Lesson," unpublished manuscript distributed by Arnold and Porter, Washington, D.C., September 1998.

40. Richard N. Dean, "The Russian Legal System: Ten Years Later," unpublished manuscript distributed by the firm Coudert Brothers, Washington, D.C., April 1998.

41. Ibid.

Redirection and Erosion of Russian Brainpower

The main wealth is our people who take very good care of the genetic code.

Chairman of the Federation Council of Russia, 1998

Ivan the Terrible sent 17 young men to study abroad to make Russia "rich and strong," but none ever returned.

Russian historian, 1994

At the end of 1998, two American journalists reported widespread recruiting by Iranian officials of Russian scientists who had been involved in the Soviet biological weapons program. The investigative reporters discovered Iranian business cards at a number of former bioweapons research institutes in the Moscow region. The institute leaders acknowledged the visits but disclaimed any personal interest in contributing to development of biological weapons capabilities in Russia, Iran, or anywhere else. Two interviewees reported, however, that they knew a "half-dozen" colleagues who had traveled to Iran, adding that other Russian scientists had entered into contract arrangements with well endowed Iranian institutions. The details of the Iranian overtures were vague and uncertain, although salary offers of $5,000 per month seemed unambiguous. One Russian microbiologist reported he had been bluntly asked to return to his previous profession of developing biological weapons, but not for Russia.[1]

A few months later, during a visit to Tehran, I raised with several well informed Iranian acquaintances U.S. government concerns over Iran's international shopping for expertise to help develop weapons of mass destruction. They replied that Washington suffered from paranoia on this issue and saw hidden facilities behind every rock in the Iranian desert. At the same time, Iran had the right to defend itself. Like the United States, the government was obliged to investigate modern weaponry. My contacts argued that Iran is surrounded by hostile forces and is within easy range of the Israeli nuclear arsenal. It only made sense for the country to be ready for any type of attack. They attached considerable importance to good relations with Russia although they steered clear of discussing cooperation in biotechnology or other sensitive fields.

The U.S. government is convinced that Iran is developing biological weapons. Another interpretation of developments is that the Iranian government is trying to create a biodefense program. Most likely, Iran wants a capability related to biological weapons to be used as the international situation dictates. Its leaders probably do not embrace the fine distinction made by the international community between an "offensive" capability, banned by international conventions, and a "defensive" capability, considered necessary and permissible. The details of the Iranian program undoubtedly are known to only a handful of direct participants. In any event, the account of the journalists of activities in Russia is unsettling.

At the very time the reporters were making the rounds of the Russian institutes with their questions about connections with Iran, I was visiting the same institutes and meeting with the same Russian scientists. My task was different, however. I was searching for opportunities for U.S.-Russian cooperation in redirecting the skills of the biological scientists and technicians to address public health problems.

Many viruses and microbes that have been considered for use in weapons occur naturally in the wild. They pose a threat to the public in some regions of the world. For example, anthrax contaminates large agricultural areas of Russia where it has infected cattle and sheep, and is a short step from reaching human populations. Anthrax is also occasionally encountered in the United States by American veterinarians, and it infests other regions of the world as well. Anthrax not only poses possibilities of tainted meat; some think bioterrorists might attempt to disperse anthrax through postal systems or subway tunnels in the United States or elsewhere.

Russian authorities are rightly concerned that this agent be brought under control, particularly in their agricultural areas. Anthrax, when transferred to humans, can spread quickly and lead to sudden and painful death. Successful control requires research on the prevention, detection, and treatment of anthrax infections. Russian colleagues are particularly interested in novel approaches to development of anthrax vaccines that could counter infections by different anthrax strains, a development that could benefit both countries.

United States offers of collaboration in this kind of work should be an appealing alternative to employment in the Middle East for Russian scientists who want to be in the mainstream of world science. First, for centuries Russians have been wary of Moslems. Second, in recent years they have been ambivalent toward cooperation with their southern neighbors—even those in Central Asian countries that had been part of the Soviet Union. The relatively unsophisticated state of biology in most of these countries further dampens the enthusiasm of Russian scientists to travel south. That said, nations with weapons ambitions may bid high, and offers from the United States must be quite attractive, particularly in guaranteeing reliable incomes over a number of years.

At one time, thousands of Soviet scientists and engineers were engaged in biological weapons activities. The residual of that workforce is simply too large—with skill levels ranging from world class to mediocre—not to expect some orientation of bioweapons brainpower toward countries with nascent bioweapons programs. These countries may well have money to put into the hands of researchers with little documentation required.

Development of biological weapons is only one of the skills the Soviet Union left behind that is of interest to rogue states. Some regimes with hostile intentions are expanding their capabilities related to chemical weapons, nuclear devices, and missiles. Thus far, few Russian weaponeers have sold their secrets, although tens of thousands have left their laboratories to seek fortunes as traders and handymen in the cities of Russia.

Western countries are rightfully concerned about weapons expertise flowing from Russia to trouble spots of the world. Still, the mass exodus of technical talent from science and engineering to business pursuits within Russia is even more significant for the future of Russia. Highly experienced specialists from civilian institutions have joined displaced weaponeers from the downsized nuclear weapons complex to seek their fortunes in professions far removed from research laboratories.

Some Russian specialists have moved to Europe, Israel, and the United States. They have mixed experiences. A handful of internationally known researchers and their protegés enjoy scientific success. Skilled computer programmers, in particular, easily find jobs that use their talents, but many emigres consider themselves fortunate to have any type of challenging employment.

The overwhelming majority (i.e., more than 95 percent) of researchers searching for new professions remain in Russia, though often disillusioned by what they find there. Whatever professions they choose, there simply are not enough financial rewards at fulfilling assignments to go around.

The number of young students entering Russian science and engineering faculties is on the rise after several years of decline. However, the percentage of graduates who pursue careers in their fields of study for more than a year or two is appallingly low, probably less than 20 percent. With many of the most capable young researchers changing professions, Russia's technical manpower base is aging quickly.

Russia simply cannot aspire to regaining a place among the world's technological leaders without cutting-edge brainpower to spark the effort. In the years ahead, brainpower must encompass not only technical know-how but also entrepreneurial savvy. The key to ensuring that the manpower pipeline is adequately stocked with a combination of technical and entrepreneurial expertise is to provide a university experience that convinces students that technology endeavors will pay off for them personally while at the same time benefiting their country.

New Income Streams for 60,000 Weaponeers

At the end of 1998 and during 1999, new revelations reached the West about the vulnerability of Russian aerospace institutes to aggressive recruiting tactics of countries seeking to tap Russian military know-how. For example, a Moscow institute previously involved in anti-ballistic missile programs had fallen on such hard times that the work force had plummeted from more than 10,000 employees to a mere 2,500, with even managers going unpaid for three years. The only way the institute managed to remain open was through rental of four floors of space to Chinese shuttle traders, who used the facility as a staging area for penetrating the Moscow consumer markets with leather jackets and furs. A number of physicists at this and other institutes in Moscow—people prepared to repair VCRs, tape recorders, or electronic systems of automobiles to survive—were approached by representatives of Middle Eastern countries soliciting their services to pursue more serious physics experiments for yet-to-be-revealed purposes. The physicists claimed they rebuffed the offers.[2]

This situation is not surprising. As discussed in Chapter 3, Iraq, India, and other countries have been eagerly seeking technology transfer arrangements with Russian aerospace institutes that have long histories of development of rocket engines.[3] It is a little surprising, however, that the extreme economic conditions faced by the physicists did not inspire some level of interest in international overtures to pay for their skills.

Russian nuclear institutes have constantly been in the headlines for flirtations with visitors from other parts of the world as well. Strange sounding names like Arzamas-16, Mayak, and Krasnoyarsk-26 have become common grist for journalists looking for incidents of leakage of nuclear materials and nuclear know-how from behind guarded fences.[4] There are few documented cases of violations of Russian regulations concerning protection of state secrets that reside in the heads of nuclear specialists. But Russian security services may relax stringent interpretations of regulations so as to permit transfers of sensitive information if officials in Moscow consider that the price is right.

Overall, there are tens of thousands of Russian scientists and engineers with skills relevant to the development of nuclear or other dangerous weapons systems who have been and remain potential targets for expanded recruitment efforts from abroad. In the early 1990s, U.S. experts were reluctant to acknowledge that such a high number of weaponeers accurately reflected the proliferation threat. The experts argued that only a handful of Russian specialists had the wherewithal to lead a weapons program, whether it be nuclear, chemical, or biological.

Commonly accepted estimates in Washington during that time as to the number of scientists that should be of proliferation concern equalled 200 nuclear scientists, 100 chemical and biological scientists, and 200 rocket scientists.[5] But these estimates were grossly off the mark. While only a few Russian specialists may have the capability to lead a weapons program, most countries of concern already have their leaders. They are looking for more narrowly oriented specialists to fill in important technical details. In even greater demand for most countries with fledgling weapons programs are engineers and technicians with experience in the weaponization process, a process that in particular requires skills in electronics and mechanical engineering.[6]

The importance of engineering experience in solving problems associated with effective delivery of biological agents to designated targets, for example, is illustrated at a former bioweapons laboratory near Moscow now engaged in research that will benefit public health. Whatever the biological agent of choice by military commanders or terrorists, there is a problem with precisely introducing the agent on the target. The engineering group in the laboratory has constructed mechanical devices for spraying minuscule particles of dust that can serve as carriers of bacteria as the dust floats in the air. Experimenting with these devices, that permit the infection of rats and mice with bacteria-laden fine sprays, allows the engineers to better understand the reaction of the rodents to dangerous bacteria. They have designed highly effective spray nozzles, as well as small metal boxes for holding the rodents in the midst of the sprays.

A key bottleneck in the weaponization process is the capability to produce such a spray for dispersal in urban areas. The spray is supposed to carry infectious bacteria in very small breathable globules.

This is precisely the problem the engineers have solved. Fortunately, these specialists intend to globulize bacteria for use in the laboratory and not in cities.

At one time, technical facilities in Russia housed nearly one million scientists, engineers, and technicians who dedicated their careers to nuclear, biological, and chemical weapons and to missiles and other delivery systems. Among those former Soviet weapons specialists, some 60,000 have skills that are potentially of interest to rogue states attempting to assemble and use weapons of mass destruction. About 30,000 learned their trades in the aerospace industry, 20,000 in the nuclear complex, and 10,000 in the chemical and biological sectors. Of the 60,000, perhaps one-third are still engaged in weapons work, one-third have retired or become commercial traders and other types of businessmen, and one-third are still in their laboratories trying to find civilian applications for their talents—relying in large measure on grants from abroad. All of them have honed their skills for many years throughout an extensive network of research, development, and production facilities established during the Soviet era.[7]

As I noted in 1996:

> Almost all countries of proliferation concern have a number of well-trained scientists with skills relevant to weapons programs. Many studied in elite institutions of the United States and Europe. Therefore, most of the one million Russians with skills important, but not unique, to weaponry would not be of interest to countries with hidden agendas involving weapons. The additional insights that they could provide would not warrant the difficulties in recruiting them. But 60,000 core specialists had many years of direct hands-on experience in the laboratories and on the test ranges where components and materials for thousands of real weapons were developed and fired. Such experience is lacking in most countries.[8]

Few scientists and engineers still affiliated with sensitive laboratories will respond to overtures from unknown foreign sources without official permission of the Russian government authorizing participation in such international contacts. They will continue to be driven by a loyalty to Russia and to their institutes, aware of the dangers to the world should they or their colleagues transmit secrets to foreigners who could misuse them. But if economic deprivation or enticement by criminals encourages only a few to behave otherwise, the consequences could be severe.

Corralling the large numbers of scientists, engineers, and technicians with important weapons-relevant skills who have already left their institutes offers a special challenge. For example, there are reports that Chinese aerospace enterprises and research institutions have recruited retired weaponeers living in the Urals. This is not surprising, given the massive budget shortfalls in that region and the need for grandparents still capable of earning money to contribute to the financial well being of their extended families.[9]

Turning back the clock, in 1993 I discovered in Russia a leaflet intended for circulation in many regions of the world. It was a recruitment advertisement of the Sun Shine Industrial Company. This Hong Kong firm had a long history of arranging arms shipments to China and apparently had developed access to former Soviet weaponeers. In part, the advertisement said:

> We have detailed files of hundreds of former Soviet Union experts in the fields of rocket, missile, and nuclear weapons. These weapon experts are willing to work in a country which needs their skills and can offer reasonable pay.[10]

Were recruitment efforts successful? Six years later we did not know. Perhaps the Chinese firms recruiting in the Urals received leads from Hong Kong. We may never know. Or we may wake up some day to incidents of mass casualties that are traced back to Soviet know-how. What we do know for sure is that Russia's economic slump is only heightening the proliferation pressures on former and current weaponeers.

Growing Pressure on Weaponeers

Despite press predictions in 1992 of a mass exodus of weapons specialists from Russia, none occurred. Salaries for senior scientists had declined to less than $50 per month, and all of the foregoing proliferation concerns were at the center of international concern. Transfers of information seemed most likely, not through emigration, but during short-term, officially sanctioned trips by Russian specialists abroad. Reports of Russian missile technology being transferred to Algeria, electronics specialists being hired in Syria, nuclear contracts being negotiated with Iran, and even scientific exchanges taking place with Libya had heightened western apprehensions.[11]

There was a significant difference between the Russian environment at that time and in 1999. In earlier years, almost all government officials from both Russia and the West, as well as the weaponeers themselves, were convinced that the economic crisis would last but a few years. Then budgets of federal ministries would be restored, Russian industry would be searching for new technologies, and research and development institutes would again be in a growth mode. In short, officials and weaponeers alike thought they could see some light at the end of a dark tunnel.

The emphasis of nonproliferation programs financed from abroad was on short-term measures to stem the outflow of brainpower from military-oriented enterprises and institutes. If only support could be provided for a few years, permanent and productive jobs would be found for former weaponeers in a prospering economy. This was the conventional wisdom.

Thus, work by former weaponeers on civilian projects supported by the United States and other western governments was based on one- and two-year projects. Russian specialists would draw steady salaries for a short time, while also contributing either to international science or more directly to Russian economic development. *Keep them busy* so they will not have time to look to rogue states for support; this was the doctrine. Cynics described these efforts as a form of bribery of scientists that could not be maintained in the long term.

In the end, the cynics proved correct in predicting that many projects would not be renewed when initial grants and contracts came to an end. While international programs have been remarkably successful in engaging tens of thousands of former weaponeers in civilian activities, most individual projects have been too oriented toward basic research to be of priority economic interest. The Russian government simply does not have financial resources to support science for the sake of science, while the private sector wants reasonable assurance of near-term returns from their investments.

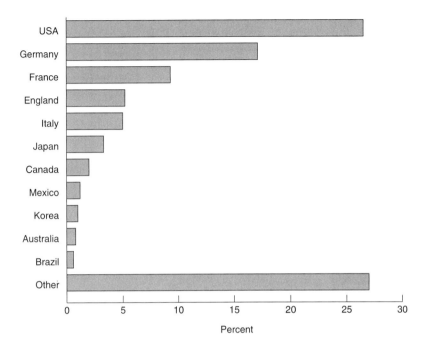

FIGURE 6.1 Foreign countries where Russian researchers work on temporary assignments, 1996. Note: Total of 4084 researchers. SOURCE: E.F. Nekipelova, *Emigration and Professional Activities of Russian Scientists Abroad.* Center for Science Research and Statistics: Moscow. 1998, p. 37.

By 1999, both Russian and foreign governments realized that economic turmoil was well ingrained in the landscape. Hesitations of Russian institutions over the source of funds to support projects—whether it be a state of questionable reliability or a western country—were receding. Indeed, despair was turning into desperation. Figure 6.1 reflects the increase already apparent by 1996 in the number of Russian scientists and engineers working abroad on contracts extending more than three months. Unfortunately the number who traveled to countries engaged in activities of concern to the West is masked under the general heading of "other countries." Several hundred probably fell into that category.

Meanwhile, the Russian government's commitment to pick up,

within a reasonable period of time, costs of programs started with foreign support has not materialized. From the geopolitical viewpoint, Russia should be concerned if the countries to its south obtain nuclear, biological, or chemical weapons or missiles that can hit targets in Russia or the territory of its friends. In practice, such thinking does not drive Russian efforts to limit the outflow of technical skills and technical information.

Russia does have regulations to curtail sales of hardware that are prohibited by international agreements. Also, Russian security services prevent leakages of state secrets unless pressured by government officials to reclassify information to accommodate new financial opportunities. However, the Russian government has left to the West the task of providing cash for supplementing meager salaries of scientists and engineers who might otherwise establish contacts in countries with malevolent intentions.

In Russia, the enterprises and institutes give ever-increasing weight to the financial dimension of proposed international projects. Even when the United States or other western countries threaten to cut off assistance funds in retaliation for Russian transfers of high-tech know-how to blacklisted countries, Russian organizations are not intimidated. They carefully weigh the cash flow aspects of dealing with all foreign partners in deciding on their responses.

Given these conditions, what is the near-term future for former Soviet weaponeers? Will there be an exodus of a few specialists who accept weapons-related work abroad? Will contracts with governments with hostile international intentions penetrate Russian institutions more deeply? Or will under-employed weaponeers simply be content to pass idle time as best they can at their country dachas? All of these scenarios seem likely.

Even if western efforts continue, Russian weaponeers will remain a proliferation concern during the next decade and probably longer. We must accept the reality that some will sell their dual-use technology skills for application at home and abroad, with concerns over misuse of these technologies taking a back seat to immediate economic needs. We urgently need strategies to reduce the demand for high-tech know-how from Russia and from other countries—including our close allies—by parties with grievances against their neighbors and the United States.

To this end, effective engagement of scientists and engineers in rogue countries by western specialists through cooperative projects in these outcast nations could be an important complement to efforts to contain dangerous technologies at their sources in Russia and other industrialized countries. Such engagement, initially through private channels, should be possible if we pay the bill, and might well record successes in encouraging previously isolated scientists and engineers to work on civilian activities that enhance the standard of living of their people. Engagement in rogue states, even on a limited scale, would improve western understanding of developments in these countries of concern. Clearly it is preferable to create the opportunities for a realistic assessment of evolving capabilities than to sit on the sidelines and predict the worst possible scenarios.

An Aging Manpower Base for Space Exploration

Proliferation of Soviet and Russian military know-how will continue to be an international security threat that attracts western attention, but replenishing Russia's scientific and technological expertise is critical to the future of the country in many spheres. An example of the need to upgrade existing capabilities arose in September 1997, when *The Christian Science Monitor* asked for my stand on whether the U.S. government should entrust the life of yet another American astronaut, David Wolf, to a flight on the rickety space station, Mir. Mir's computer systems had already crashed on three occasions, a small flash fire had erupted in the cabin, and mechanical failures had become commonplace. Still, Mir was providing useful experience for both Russian and American astronauts as an important stepping stone to launching the International Space Station (ISS).

The technical issues were clouded with conflicting information. My view on the immediate problems aboard Mir would have been little more than uninformed speculation. Opinions on the safety of the Russian vehicle were better left to three expert panels assembled by

NASA to recommend whether Wolf should participate in this shaky Russian adventure. And he did, successfully.

However, no one in Washington had addressed the related issue of the long-term importance of Russia replenishing its cutting edge technological skills as a prerequisite to remaining a reliable partner in manned space flight. The leading nations of the world have banded together in a 13-year program to launch the ISS. Russia, with a decade of unique experience in operating Mir, is scheduled to provide key components for the station. To meet this commitment over many years, an infusion of new technical blood into the Russian space program must begin immediately. There are too many space research and production facilities in Russia with tired faces and aging skills to think otherwise.

My specific suggestion to NASA was to invest $100 million over a period of five years, or longer, in support of the education and early research efforts of a new cadre of young Russian scientists and engineers. This investment, if focused on specific critical skills, would help ensure a secure technical footing for Russian participation in providing components, services, and manpower for the ISS. Five hundred up-and-coming specialists, committed to aerospace technology and current on worldwide developments in the field, could make a significant difference in key institutes and enterprises among the Moscow region and several other industrial areas.[12]

Such an expenditure would be less than 0.3 percent of the U.S. investment in the ISS. Russian participation has been repeatedly justified to the U.S. Congress as saving the United States $3 billion. If Russia does not perform as intended, those costs—and probably much more—will eventually flow back to the United States. Without new talent to maintain competency in high technology, the likelihood of failures of Russian equipment or operational procedures that will affect the investments of more than a dozen countries is unacceptably high.[13]

Three years have passed and NASA has not responded to these concerns. A few, but not enough, bright Russian students are still attracted by the lure of space exploration. But by 2005 or sooner, Russia may not be able to hold up its end of this technological bargain. The hardware will be only as good as the designers and construction personnel and the operations only as good as the launch and flight crews.

Widespread Decline of the Research and Development Workforce

The problem of tired blood is not unique to the aerospace industry. Prominent Russian leaders say they cannot prevent the loss in many scientific disciplines of an entire generation of talent lured from science by higher-paying jobs elsewhere. In 1997, the Minister for Science and Technology was vigorously pressing for a commitment of sustained government support for the 10,000 leading Russian scientists to preserve and expand world-class achievements in their disciplines, called "schools of science." He subsequently reduced his goal to 1,000 scientists, assuming that they could each share a portion of their support with other members of their research teams. But even that modest goal seems out of reach for a government committed to cutting expenditures on every front.[14]

During the early 1990s the exodus of young scientists and engineers from research and development institutions was dramatic. Those who stayed in the institutes experienced nothing but boredom, with little useful activity and little or no pay in most Russian laboratories. After the economic collapse of 1998, many who had switched to the private sector were suddenly out of jobs and saw the security of the old-line institutes in a new light. In fact, some who lost private sector jobs, playing on old friendships with institute directors, were able to rejoin their former institutes. By now, elation over minimal pay is fast disappearing; and increasing numbers see emigration as their only hope.

Russian statistics, while often uncertain, nevertheless help describe technical manpower developments. About one million scientists, engineers, technicians, and support personnel were engaged in research and development activities in 1998. About 500,000 were classified as researchers, with two-thirds engaged in engineering research. One decade earlier the workforce was double this size. My estimate is that only one-fifth, or 100,000 of the researchers, were active researchers in

1999, spending at least 50 percent of their time carrying out specific projects. The remainder were on the rolls of research and development institutes to retain social contacts and partake in health and retirement benefit plans, however modest. They only rarely engaged in serious scientific endeavors in lighted offices or laboratories (see Figure 6.2). [15]

The mix of employees of the institutes is also changing. According to 1996 statistics, 38 percent of the personnel leaving the facilities were researchers while 50 percent were support personnel other than technicians. An estimated 26 percent of new hires were researchers and 66 percent were support personnel. In short, the research and development facilities are becoming more heavily populated with administrative staff. [16]

External Brain Drain

External brain drain from Russia encompasses two traditional categories: emigration for permanent residence abroad, and long-term (more than three months) employment abroad that sometimes leads to emigration. After the exodus of large numbers of Jewish specialists at the beginning of the 1990s, fewer than 1 percent of the remaining researchers have emigrated (as indicated in Figure 6.2). In mid-1999, there was a brief upswing of computer programmers leaving the country under a special visa quota for computer specialists to accept employment in the United States. The U.S. Embassy in Moscow and the three U.S. consulates were issuing about 60 visas per week to Russians headed for long-term employment in the United States, primarily at computer software firms. The embassy estimated that about 50 percent of these long-term workers will remain in the United States permanently. [17] On a broader basis, Figure 6.3 characterizes the overseas employment of about 4,000 Russian scientists and engineers in 1996. Again, about one-half of these specialists probably stay abroad for permanent residence.

But external brain drain should also include employment of research and development specialists by foreign firms that claim intel-

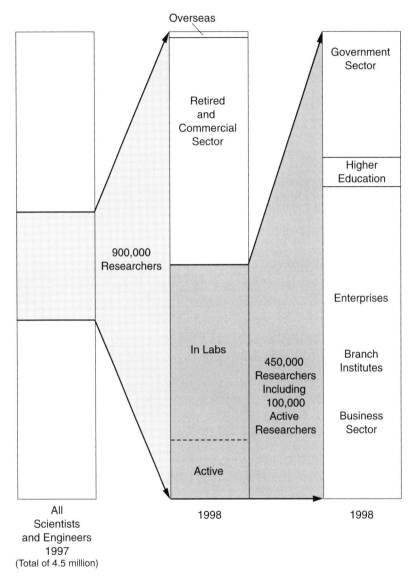

FIGURE 6.2 900,000 researchers. SOURCE: Russian Ministry of Science and Technology, April 1999. Supplemented by author's observations at many research organizations.

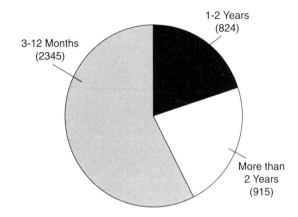

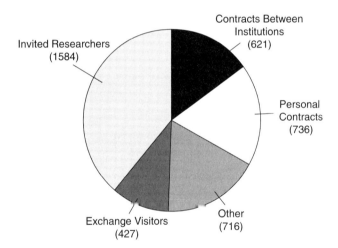

FIGURE 6.3   4084 Russian researchers working abroad in 1996.
SOURCE. E.F. Nekipelova, *Emigration and Professional Activities of Russian Scientists Abroad.* Center for Science Research and Statistics: Moscow. 1998, p. 34.

lectual property rights and do not publish the resulting findings. In addition, publication of Russian research and development results only in foreign journals not widely available in Russia is a form of information emigration.[18] These two types of activities, even though some science policy analysts are reluctant to call them brain drain, reflect the loss of intellectual prowess when researchers cast their lot with foreign institutions.

Also of concern to some officials in Moscow has been loss of technology through Russian specialists working on defense-oriented contracts sponsored by the U.S. Department of Defense and Department of Energy. One seemingly accurate estimate is that, in the mid-1990s, 8,000 Russian researchers were working on these contracts. The annual cost to Russia was several hundred million dollars, since the Russian institutes shared expenses of almost all projects. Many projects were of little interest in Russia other than as income sources for the participants, so this activity too should be considered a form of brain drain.[19]

The majority of researchers who went abroad and found relevant career opportunities in the early 1990s were well known Russian leaders of science and talented young researchers with ties to these leaders. The loss of leading researchers, even if limited in number, can devastate specific fields, as has been the case in theoretical physics and mathematics. But this development is not evident in engineering.[20]

Recent science and engineering emigrants have been primarily undergraduates, graduate students, and young researchers under the age of 35. Some have succeeded without the benefit of support from eminent Russian mentors.[21] The recent example of 462 researchers emigrating from the Physical Technical Institute near Moscow, one of the country's premier research universities, shows the youth of recent departees: 51 percent were under 30 and 22 percent were between 30 and 35. In all age groups most of the emigrants went to the United States, although a significant portion of the youngest and oldest emigrants went to Israel.[22]

Before concluding that Russia's scientific loss equates to the West's scientific gain, it is important to realize that many researchers seeking immigrant status abroad have little interest in continuing to work in science. They simply want a new way of life. They now know that jobs are not easy to find, and many rely primarily on their language skills and their willingness to work in other fields to find appropriate employment niches.

An interesting development has been the movement abroad of Russian research groups that at the same time retain a foothold in Russia. The Institute of Microbiology of the Russian Academy of Sciences has established a laboratory of 10-15 researchers from Moscow at Argonne National Laboratory near Chicago, for example. Their work is supported by a large grant from the Pentagon's Defense Advanced Research Projects Agency. They use sophisticated equipment in designing impregnated microchips that detect biological agents of possible use to terrorists. At the same time, the Russian researchers retain tight links with their home base, probably uncertain as to how many more years the financial support for research in the United States will continue. A second arrangement is the outpost in Paris of the Landau Institute of Physics, where a dozen Russian researchers press the limits of mathematical physics. The French government provides support to "twin" laboratories in Russia with counterparts in France.[23]

Do foreign grants encourage Russian recipients to remain in science or engineering in Russia in the long term or do they simply whet appetites to seek a better life abroad? Such grants certainly are welcomed by recipients, and some researchers are building their careers on grants. As an extreme case, in November 1998, a young Moscow biologist informed me she was working simultaneously on six grants from U.S. and European organizations. Still, availability of grants is probably not a pivotal factor in the determinations of most researchers as to whether they should continue to pursue scientific careers in Russia.[24]

Other factors influence individual decisions whether to remain in science and engineering, whether to seek emigration to other countries offering work in these fields, or whether simply to abandon any hope of using years of specialized training. The long-term outlook is important to many who had been accustomed to commanding respect in their communities. Now at the top of the list of respected professionals in Russia are businessmen, bankers, and politicians and at the bottom of the list are soldiers, scientists, and engineers.[25] Working conditions have become difficult and often impossible as equipment breaks down and supplies run out. Finally, housing difficulties almost always prevent young researchers from accepting positions at facilities distant from their residences.

Under these conditions, a "prosperous" researcher in the academic city near Novosibirsk has been described by a Russian sociologist as follows:

> He is a doctor of science, rather young, with fairly good housing conditions. He receives a comparatively large salary at his institute and teaches at a higher educational institution. He has close connections with domestic as well as foreign scientific funds and business partners. He successfully combines the energy of youth and a high level of scientific training, and he is in demand on the market.[26]

A poverty-stricken scientist is described as follows:

> He is either relatively young or a man of many years, usually without an advanced scientific degree. He has poor housing conditions. His basic source of income remains the institute salary, which is paltry, and he is forced to spend most of his time working in his garden plot.[27]

Education, drive, and connections—particularly international connections—still pay off. Such connections are often important in encouraging Russian researchers to remain in the laboratory. But these connections must be sustained or their impact will quickly vanish.

Role of Russian Technical Universities

Given the internal and external brain drain, universities are on center stage in efforts to replenish the pipeline with young specialists who have both technical talent and entrepreneurial zeal and skill. The universities are now aware of the need not only to train students but also to expand efforts to place them in jobs, since the state is no longer a matchmaker. At the same time, the universities are seeking new income streams through contracts and grants with domestic and international funders and through adoption of tuition systems for students.

The 50 or so leading technical universities of the Soviet Union and now Russia have long provided the core cadre for industry, relying on work-study programs, guest lecturers from industry, and industrial research projects to stimulate student interest. A few universities were tightly linked to Soviet military programs, and they developed dual-use technologies they currently are attempting to market to all comers. Their industrial links belie assertions by some western scholars who view Russian universities as isolated from both research and industry.

Also, when the economic shocks of the early 1990s shredded the federal budget for higher education, almost all Russian universities took several important steps to help cushion the impacts. They changed their policies of providing tuition-free education for all students. They instituted two-track systems whereby a portion of new enrollees, perhaps one-half and purportedly chosen on the basis of merit, receive tuition scholarships. The remainder are required to pay substantial tuition, usually several thousand dollars per year. Thus, rich Russians are generally assured places for their children, since competition for the second tier is not intense. Other Russians have difficulty finding resources to enroll children who fall below the tuition-free cutoff. Many universities have expanded recruitment programs for foreign students, who are now expected to pay full tuition for education previously provided free of charge to students from countries where Soviet influence was important. Overall, competition for enrollment at the country's leading technical universities is on the rise after a sharp dip in the early 1990s. Part of the increase is explained by the fact that student status provides a lawful way to avoid the military draft—a more important factor than previously, due to the war in Chechnya and the overall poor conditions that currently exist in the Russian military services.[28]

To strengthen their budgets, universities have turned to their alumni for help—almost always through informal contacts. Organized fund raising targeting wealthy graduates remains an unknown art, but some alumni respond to more informal requests. They arrange for their universities to obtain contracts with government agencies or industry. Once in a while they even arrange cash donations for scholarship funds.

Despite these efforts to maintain viable education and research programs, in 1999 the overall situation was very poor—deterioration of facilities, low and uncertain pay for faculty, and a slow decline in the quality of instruction as the faculty ages and loses enthusiasm for working for very small salaries. There were some bright spots. Researchers from technology-oriented research institutes, in search of income supplements, spent more time as adjunct faculty. Also, the universities have paid more attention to the responsiveness of their curricula to employment opportunities within the economy.

While enrollment is up, less than 50 percent of science and engineering graduates enter the technical workplace. At some universities fewer than 25 percent pursue technical careers and, for those that do, one-half or more drop out within a year or two. The perceived payoff from private business dealings is simply too much of a draw, even for physicists and engineers.[29] Meanwhile, the number of enrollees in graduate engineering courses is on the rise, probably representing a significant return to the classroom by older engineers with time on their hands (see Table 6.1).

One realistic Russian researcher believes that a "successful" university should be shoring up its teaching staff and not recruiting more

TABLE 6.1 Growth in Graduate Students in Engineering

	Seeking Kandidat (Ph.D.) Degree			
	1994	1995	1996	1997
Enrollment	12,560	15,183	18,980	22,537
Entrants	4,840	6,400	7,918	8,729
Graduates	2,642	2,423	2,548	3,185

	Seeking Doctor of Science Degree			
	1994	1995	1996	1997
Enrollment	531	634	742	887
Entrants	221	257	316	354
Graduates	97	124	163	197

SOURCE: Research and development in the Russian higher education sector. Center for Science Research and Statistics, Moscow. 1998, pp. 32-33, 40-41.

researchers. This researcher notes the increasing need to customize student programs and the decreasing amount of research funds. Not more than 50 percent of the university's income should come from federal funds, and the university should be content to rely on its own equipment to the fullest extent possible. She adds that foreign grants and contracts can be helpful but are not essential.[30] Several examples of recent developments in a few technical universities generally support these conclusions but, at the same time, show how individual universities must take advantage of their special capabilities and historical strengths.

The Gubkin Oil and Gas Academy in Moscow has long been proud of its role in providing the bulk of the specialists that built the Soviet gas and oil industry. The academy established affiliates in the country's oil and gas producing regions that have now become independent universities. Many faculty members in Moscow and in the affiliates moonlight as consultants to the gas and oil companies. At the beginning of 1999, two-thirds of the students in Moscow were being sponsored by future employers—a remarkable record. At the same time, the research program of the academy has not kept pace with worldwide developments in the industry, and researchers are slowly falling behind in their knowledge of many advanced developments. The Russian energy companies, recognizing the rapid technological progress abroad, are turning to western consultants to gradually replace faculty members as advisers, a development that does not bode well for the academy.

The Moscow Institute of Technology (Bauman), often called the MIT of Russia, has recently made considerable effort to market technologies developed over many years. But, because these technologies were often the result of military contracts, adaptation to civilian markets has not been easy. To further this effort, the institute has established seven industrial research centers intended to link the faculty and associated researchers with industrial organizations. Many prominent Russian captains of industry are graduates of the institute and have interests in the centers, but success of these new efforts is still to be demonstrated.

The Moscow State Institute of Electronic Technology provides an umbrella framework not only for students but also for a major state scientific institute and an innovation center that supports small electronics firms. Across the street are the two leading electronics firms in the city of Zelenograd, and the integration of research, education, and production in this city has repeatedly been touted by Russian officials as a model to emulate. To visitors from Silicon Valley, the Russian research efforts seem primitive, but the excellent educational experiences of Russian students cannot be denied. And the small firms are finding domestic niche markets (e.g., electronic switches, connectors, sensors, integrators) that are not totally dominated by imports from the United States, Europe, and Asia.

A visit to Russia's oldest technical university, the St. Petersburg State Mining Institute, is an uplifting experience. Beginning with the courtyard where Catherine the Great selected her night-time companions from among cadets assembled at attention, this institute has been a cornerstone of the nation's technological efforts for several centuries. While providing specialists for the oil, gas, metallurgy, and coal industries, the institute has pioneered ways to supplement its income streams. Hallways of new classrooms are bedecked with plaques commemorating generous donors. Honorary degrees are accorded for both technical achievements and for support of the institute. Research contracts with foreign partners reflect the international interest in gaining access to the lucrative natural resources industries of Russia.

These technical universities, like Russian research institutes, are scrambling for money from foreign as well as domestic sources. All the while, the U.S. government is watching to detect any efforts to transfer technologies to the Middle East through Russian faculty members traveling abroad or through visiting foreign students. In early 1999, the U.S. government decided that faculty members of the Mendeleyev Institute for Chemical Technology and the Moscow Aviation Institute crossed the line of acceptable technology transfer in their dealings with Iran, and therefore declared the institutions ineligible for receiving U.S. government funds. This is a rather unusual position, since hundreds of Iranian students were in residence at American universities in 1998, including students studying aerospace and other high-tech subjects. A number of Iranian students were identified by the FBI as extreme Shiite Muslims considered to be terrorist threats.[31]

For their part, Russians continue to cherish education even though less than 1 percent believe it will be a decisive factor in enhancing the country's stature in the near term.[32] Only 2 percent pin their hopes on science, believing science will contribute to economic development.[33] Nevertheless, the majority of the population has an intrinsic belief that education has been and will continue to be a pathway to success.

In 1998, the son of good Russian friends was accepted at the Bauman Institute on the tuition-free track. Neither the father nor mother had received paychecks for six months, and they couldn't even pay their utility and telephone bills. They remained confident that they would not lose these services. If they did, they would move to the countryside while their son became a successful Russian engineer with skills of the highest order. Two years later, little has changed. My friends remain in their apartment with sporadic income and unpaid debts, and their son is doing well at the Bauman Institute.

Bill Gates gave an unexpected boost to the spirits of all university students engrossed in science and engineering courses. Widely heralded throughout Russia as the world's richest person, his presence in Moscow in 1998 signaled that technical careers can be rewarding. He stirred the hopes of the Russian population by boldly pronouncing that within a decade all Russians would have Internet connections in their homes.

The universities will be an important key to unlocking Russia's capability to become an industrial force. *Russians will continue to invest in their children no matter the financial hardships.* Many students will carry on the traditions of science and engineering that date to the time of Peter the Great, but most are increasingly oriented to emulating Bill Gates and other contemporary technology entrepreneurs.[34]

Meanwhile, a few forward-looking Russian science and education leaders are doing their best to support the current generation of young researchers. For example, each year the Moscow Institute of Power Engineering of the Ministry of Atomic Energy recruits 25 new university graduates, guarantees them steady paychecks and interesting work for three years, and helps them find long-term financial support so they will remain at the institute. This commitment to the future of Russia is striking.[35]

Future of the Russian Manpower Base

The international community—particularly the United States—is steering large numbers of former Soviet weaponeers in nonthreatening directions through financial support for international projects. Even if projects are of only marginal technical interest to the United States, the costs of employing highly talented manpower will continue to be incredibly low—probably on the order of $5,000 per workyear. The commitment by the United States and other western countries to supporting such bargains is of considerable national security importance. At the same time, these programs can be of greater importance for Russia if the Russian government adopts policies that improve the marketplace prospects for deriving profit from innovation. For their part, western partners should emphasize support of applied research projects with commercialization potential.

The commercialization challenge should not be underestimated. Perhaps 15 percent of current projects among the best Russian researchers have a chance of raising interests in international business circles. Another 15 percent might have marketing potential in Russia.[36] But, at present, most projects have little commercial value.

The other options for productive work are limited. A few Russian specialists may be able to conduct contract research for western governments, such as developing devices for detecting nuclear smuggling at international airports or flight testing new components for spacecraft. Also, particularly talented Russian research teams should be able to compete successfully for international funds to advance the frontiers of science. But such possibilities will engage only a few specialists of proliferation concern.

As time passes, former weaponeers will become rustier. Their interests in weapons will decline. Thus, they will become less of a national security problem. But for the next few years the problems of unemployed weaponeers cannot be dismissed lightly. They simply want to have jobs, and they are less and less particular as to where they work.

With delayed paychecks for faculty members, out-of-date laboratories for students and faculty, and unpleasant dormitories for life away from home, higher education institutions are not very inviting for young, ambitious Russians. But, in contrast to many other institutions in the country, the universities are making a slow recovery. Some are expanding work-study programs, providing new opportunities for student experiments in laboratories of the Academy of Sciences, and helping students line up employment months and even years in advance of graduation. Overall, the universities will not be the brakes that hold back economic progress in the short term. But in the long term their success in inspiring youth to pursue technical careers will be extremely important.

Western programs to support outstanding faculty and young students can help maintain local competence but in some cases may simply open new emigration pathways. Longer term contracts and grants (e.g., five years) with less rather than more international travel for Russian recipients should increasingly characterize these programs. Western institutions can be most effective by stressing cooperative programs that relate student interests to the near-term needs of the country and to technology-oriented businesses with a future.

Most important, both students and specialists need work, not welfare.

Notes

1.   Judith Miller and William J. Broad, "Bioweapons in Mind, Iranians Lure Needy Ex-Soviet Scientists," *The New York Times*, December 8, 1998, p. A1.

2.   David Hoffman, "Idle Arms Experts in Russia Pose Threat," *The Washington Post*, December 28, 1998, P. A1.

3.   Schweitzer, *Moscow DMZ*, p. 130.

4.   See, for example, Glenn E. Schweitzer with Carole C. Dorsch, *Superterrorism: Assassins, Mobsters, and Weapons of Mass Destruction* (New York: Plenum Press, 1998), chapter 2.

5.   This topic was frequently debated within and outside government in Washington, D.C., in 1991 and 1992. While there was no formal consensus on the number of weaponeers of proliferation concern, the discussions were dominated

by a narrow vision as to ways in which technical specialists might be used by rogue states.

6.   Hoffman, "Idle Arms Experts in Russia Pose Threat." This article gives a good perspective of the range of skills within one speciality that have been of interest.

7.   My estimates were developed in consultation with Russian specialists who were familiar with personnel in the nuclear, aerospace, chemical, and biological communities of Russia. We reviewed both national statistics on the size of the manpower base and then considered each of the key institutes where most of the specialists were located.

8.   Schweitzer, *Moscow DMZ*, p. 103.

9.   Discussions in Moscow with Russian weapons specialists from the Urals, November 1998.

10.   Schweitzer, *Moscow DMZ*, p. 35. This quotation was subsequently used in U.S. Congressional hearings by senate staff members who stated they had confirmed the activities of the company with intelligence community experts.

11.   S.I. Simanovskiy and M.P. Strepetova, "Role of International Cooperation in Turning Around the Brain Drain from Russia," *The World of Science and Technology and Education* (Moscow: International Engineering Academy, 1994), p. 11.

12.   Glenn E. Schweitzer, "Aging Mir Isn't So Worrisome as Russia's Long-Term Technological Decay," *The Christian Science Monitor*, September 26, 1997, p. 18.

13.   *Ibid.*

14.   Meetings in Moscow with Russian Minister for Science and Technology, March 1996 and October 1998.

15.   *Russian Science and Technology at a Glance, 1997*, Center for Science Research and Statistics, Moscow, 1998.

16.   Irina Malakha and Igor Ushkalov, "Drainage of Intellectual Potential," *NG-Nauka*, April 1, 1998.

17.   Discussions in Moscow at the U.S. Embassy, June 1999.

18.   Irina Dezhina, "Adjustments of Russian Science and Brain Drain," unpublished paper, Science, Technology, and Society Program, Massachusetts Institute of Technology, 1997.

19.   Malakha and Ushkalov, "Drainage of Intellectual Potential."

20.   *Ibid.*

21.   Dezhina, "Adjustments of Russian Science and Brain Drain."

22.   *Ibid.*

23.   Discussions in Moscow with Russian scientists involved in these programs, November 1998.

24.   L.M. Gokhberg and O.R. Shuvalova, *Public Opinion about Science,* Center for Research and Statistics on Science, Moscow, 1997.

25.   *Ibid.*, p. 28.

26.   Anatoli Ablazhey, "What is Siberian Science Living On? Wages of Scientists at Academic City Today Lower than Average for Novosibirsk," *Vecherniy Novosibirsk*, August 1996, p.4.

27.   *Ibid.*

28.   Discussions at six Russian universities during the fall of 1998.

29.   *Ibid.*

30.   Dezhina, "Adjustments of Russian Science and Brain Drain."

31.   Schweitzer and Dorsch, *Superterrorism,* p. 137.

32.   Gokhberg and Shuvalova, *Public Opinion about Science,* p. 46.

33.   *Ibid.*, pp. 31, 46.

34.   Discussions in Moscow with a number of Russian acquaintances during the 1998 Bill Gates visit.

35.   Discussions in Moscow at the Institute of Power Engineering, June 1999.

36.   Comments by Boris Milner of the Institute of Economics in Moscow during a meeting at the National Research Council in Washington, D.C., November 1999.

7

Sixty-Five Science
Cities with
Three Million People

The science cities are experiencing tough times and may become ghost towns unless granted special status and government assistance.

The Russia Journal, 1999

Making science cities economically self sufficient is dangerous. Priceless technologies and equipment will be destroyed if facilities are converted to produce commercial goods.

Mayor of the science city, Dubna, 1999

In 1964 I first visited Akademgorodok, the famous Soviet science city located 2,500 miles east of Moscow and 25 miles south of the industrial center of Novosibirsk. The building of the city began in 1958 and, by the time of my visit, 15 research institutes had opened their doors and lit their laboratories. Another half dozen were in various stages of planning and construction. Tens of thousands of scientists and their family members were already living in this forested hideaway where researchers were to be unshackled from political and economic constraints as they uncovered the secrets of nature. Many young Russian researchers who had moved east eagerly anticipated new personal challenges and greater advancement opportunities away from dominating mentors in Moscow and Leningrad. Their mentors had insisted on taking personal credit for each research achievement, no matter how small, regardless of which scientist was responsible.

But the collective aspirations of the Russian visionaries who were relying on generous budgets with no strings attached were not entirely realized at this scientific outpost. In the words of an American scholar:

> The utopian design of the scientists and Communist Party leaders to build a city of science fell prey to the same handicaps endemic to Soviet science in general. Ideological constructs, political desiderata, and economic uncertainties dogged the efforts of Akademgorodok's founders to create a unique scientific community in the west Siberian forest. The community of scientists never fully escaped the constraints imposed by a centralized command economy and a party apparatus that grew increasingly conservative and ideologically vigilant in the Brezhnev years. As in other societies, the power of the purse always shapes the face of research; and the USSR was no different as the state pressured scientists to abandon basic science in the name of accountability to Siberian economic development.[1]

Thus, despite noble sentiments about the benefits from unfettered basic research leading to discoveries that could not possibly be predicted, the pressure for near-term economic payoff from research was clear from the outset.

Already in 1964, the Akademgorodok mathematicians boasted about their contributions to computer programming. The geologists claimed they were leading the national search for mineral deposits. The physicists were proud of the instrumentation they had designed and built. The research economists tied their analyses directly to requirements of the central planning system. Even though theoretical studies dominated the scientific publications of Akademgorodok, the researchers knew that transformation of discoveries into practical applications was the name of the game. As a result, they tried their best to be politically correct in their remarks to officials from Moscow that Siberian science would have a short-term payoff.

While the best known, Akademgorodok was not the first science city. To many Soviet officials it was of relatively minor importance in comparison with science cities established to support the military-industrial complex. It captured the imagination of other government leaders largely because it was located in the midst of the untapped natural resources of Siberia. Their expectation was that scientists would soon transform dormant towns into production centers to strengthen the nation's military might and to fill the treasury with export earnings.

By the early 1950s, science cities were springing up in the Urals and the Moscow environs to harness the most modern and often the most destructive technologies that could be devised. These company towns, established primarily by production-oriented ministries and occasionally by the Academy of Sciences, became homes for the nation's best-trained applied researchers. Without hesitation the Kremlin provided the necessary facilities and materials for the research and development endeavors of these specialists. Additional incentives for moving to some of the more remote cities included personal benefits, such as privileged access to high-quality consumer goods and services, to the best educational and recreational opportunities for children, and to the most coveted medals from a Soviet leadership that closely followed the launch of every spacecraft, the test of every nuclear device, and the development of every new vaccine.

Now, the 65 science cities (see Appendix C) are having great difficulties adjusting to the new social and economic conditions in Russia. The termination of defense contracts and the severing of subsidized supply lines of consumer goods have forced a dramatic change in the privileged lifestyles in these protected havens. The cities still cling to the parent ministries or other Moscow organizations that established them in the first place, hopeful that more rubles will flow in their direction. Many continue their national defense responsibilities, although sharply reduced, providing both financial relief at home and heightened proliferation anxieties in the West. Education remains a high priority even though the youth have become less and less interested in following in the footsteps of fathers who made their reputations in research laboratories. Finally, the cities are gripped by many problems inherent in their efforts to commercialize home-grown technologies. Particularly unhelpful are geographic remoteness from potential customers and security limitations on access by foreigners to many of the cities.

Innovating for Profit in Siberia

For two evenings during my 1964 Akademgorodok visit, several American colleagues and I were guests in the living room and at the dining table of the founder of the city, mathematician Mikhail Lavrentyev. He lived in a small log cottage in the midst of the remnants of a birch forest that had given way to new residential areas. He had personally garnered support for the Akademgorodok project from Nikita Khrushchev, who was enamored with the concept that science would provide political pillars for a Marxist state stretching from Europe to the Pacific Ocean.

During our dinners, Lavrentyev was surrounded by a phalanx of admiring Russian scientists who had moved with him from Moscow. He regaled the gatherings with stories of how workers had carved the city out of the forest despite shortages of equipment and material, a harsh climate, and no transportation or communication networks. Most important, he claimed, was a new freedom in Siberia for scientists to follow their instincts, despite countervailing views in Moscow that advocated highly-directed research.

He noted that many scientific leaders in Moscow thought a science center in Siberia made little sense, that he had taken resources away from the "real" centers of research in Moscow and Leningrad, and that in the long run his experiment was doomed to failure. He then beamed. He reported that the leaders of Soviet science had visited Akademgorodok. During their adventures on the frontiers of both nature and science, they became convinced that the investment would pay off handsomely.

During our tour of the city, Lavrentyev demonstrated the capabilities of a high-pressure water gun designed at his Institute of Hydrodynamics. He repeatedly directed a compact water jet at targets of stacked bricks located about 60 feet away, shattering pile after pile. Although he was silent on practical use of such a device, this activity by one of the nation's leading scientists could not possibly have been simply "boys with toys." Was he confirming design principles for a Soviet weapon to be used selectively against targets that could not be easily demolished with explosives? We would never know.

Twenty-two years later, in 1986 during my next visit, the town and the institutes looked much the same. The water gun was reported to be in a storage shed, apparently overtaken by more sophisticated devices for destroying bricks. There were more park areas, more apartments, and more shops. But the general layout was undisturbed.

However, in the intervening years, the scientists of the city had pioneered impressive marriages between education and research. At our meetings, each presentation by a Russian specialist emphasized the importance of building up the educational capabilities of Siberia. Student achievements were on display. The university in Akademgorodok attracted the best students in Siberia. These new arrivals had opportunities to use the excellent research facilities of the many institutes in the city, despite the Soviet tradition of separating higher education institutions from scientific research activities. Also, the university had become the focal point for science olympiads that, each year, featured spirited mathematics and physics competitions among the region's best young brains.

At that time, the Soviet Union lagged 5-10 years behind other industrialized countries in information technology. Impatient with Soviet progress in a vitally important field, the staffs of several institutes had diverted money from their accounts to buy Japanese and American desktop computers for local high schools. Students in Moscow were just beginning to take courses in the theory of computer programming using notebooks instead of keyboards and screens. Meanwhile, the Akademgorodok students were glued to workstations under the tutelage of the best mathematicians in the city, reflecting the conviction of the scientists that students were the key to Siberia's future.

When I next visited the city in 1994, the institutes had lost their military contracts and were struggling to find civilian customers. By the time of yet another visit in 1998, most institutes had gone sharply downhill as their budgets declined dramatically and inflation galloped upwards. The advent of democracy and free market economics had not been kind to scientific research in Siberia. In the wake of economic decline, communism had re-emerged as a political dogma in the Novosibirsk region. Even the senior representative of the Academy of Sciences in Akademgorodok had cast his lot with the new undefined

brand of communism, usually characterized for the national media simply as a form of government that would restore the good life of the
1980s. Also, most research institutes were struggling with limited success to find sponsors for their projects.

Two institutes were able to prosper in the new environment. The
Boreskov Institute of Catalysis had established a money-making market niche, at home and abroad, in the automation and improvement of
catalytic processes for oil refining and for pollution control. By the
mid-1990s, the institute had developed contacts with more than 100
foreign firms, and more than ten companies (e.g., Dupont and
Monsanto) provided financial support through those contracts. This
favorable situation dates from the 1980s when the institute began selling licenses for catalytic processes for air pollution reduction equipment to firms in Switzerland and the United States. Also, about 20
Russian firms have purchased related technology from the institute,
and the scientists have attracted an array of small research grants from
both the Russian and foreign governments.[2]

The institute experimented with organizational adjustments for a
market economy. In the early 1990s, the institute directorship established a number of small firms on its premises to facilitate the commercialization of its products. Despite the early successes of several ventures, most failed. As commercial entities, they did not qualify for
research grants from Russian and western funding organizations and
therefore had no scientific underpinnings for their activities. Also, being outside the main research stream of the institute, they were not
aware of the details of basic research under way in nearby laboratories
and soon fell behind their western competitors in exploiting the latest
technical developments.

Now, small firms play a very limited role. Almost all development
as well as research activity is carried out within the institute itself. The
institute is in the fortunate position of being able to consolidate overhead funds from its western contracts to sustain long-term (five years)
basic research that enriches its short-term (two years) applied programs.

Each year the institute recruits high-quality university graduates to
bolster its staff of about 400 scientists—young researchers eager to

work with modern equipment for steady paychecks and for opportunities to stay abreast of new scientific and engineering developments. Thus, the biggest personnel problem has not been a lack of new blood, but an excess of tired blood. The older scientists simply do not want to retire, even though they may have fallen woefully behind in their fields, because of the miserable pension situation. Many seniors are retained as consultants, as inspectors, and as other supernumeraries in view of their decades of loyal service to the institute.[3]

Another anchor institute since the founding of the city has been the Budker Institute of Nuclear Physics. Always sensitive to western research priorities in shaping its programs, the institute's leaders remember when it was "a capitalistic institute in a socialist environment," sending its scientists to Europe and western Europe where they could help arrange different types of financial support for the institute. They note that it is now more of "a socialist institute in a capitalist environment," with an obligation to provide support for all its employees regardless of their success in winning international contracts.[4]

With 600 scientists in residence in 1999, the institute depends heavily on emigrants who have departed from its ranks to provide an overseas support network. This network has brokered many contracts and grants from western institutions. The network belies the notion that brain drain is always a bad development for Russia. Finally, like the Institute of Catalysis, the Institute of Nuclear Physics recruits young scientists every year (60 in 1998), with the average age of the staff in 1999 being 42. When staff reductions are required due to a lapse in contracts, however, older scientists are usually given job preference.[5]

In recent years, the institute has obtained about one-half of its income from scientific equipment that it manufactures and sells to research and commercial organizations around the world. For example, China has been a customer for its nuclear accelerators at a cost of $700,000 each. These accelerators operate as high-precision heat generators, ideally suited to sealing wires within insulated cables in jet fighters but with other applications as well.

The institute is also pursuing a line of products for environmental and health applications that have attracted foreign interest. These include irradiation equipment to eradicate bacteria in logs earmarked for processing abroad, portable irradiation devices to guard against salmonella poisoning in fast food restaurants, and new types of accelerators to destroy dioxin in municipal incinerators. Customers for these and related applications of the institute's accelerators have been found in Germany, Italy, Poland, Hungary, and India. In a development that depends more on the engineering than on the nuclear physics skills of the staff, an insulin injector for testing blood sugar levels has also attracted attention in Europe.[6]

Still, the institute has difficulty making the transition to operating with a reduced core budget from Moscow. It considers basic research as its primary mission, research that should be paid for by a government that has few funds and higher priorities. On the commercial front, the institute has not been successful in efforts to become a provider of components for scientific instruments that western firms could assemble into finished products, a tactic used by some institutes. Indeed, too many institutes are competing for such markets.[7]

Science Cities Encircling Moscow

The histories of the 29 science cities founded in the 1940s and 1950s around Moscow are intimately linked to the military buildup of the Soviet Union. With populations ranging from 20,000-100,000 and situated 20-100 miles from the Kremlin, the cities were to be self-contained enclaves. The degree of isolation from the general population varied from city to city depending on the sensitivity of the experimental work that was under way.

Amenities were important. Each city obtained funds to construct housing for the researchers and their families, thus greatly easing problems of recruiting good scientists and engineers. At the same time, housing seldom was adequate and, despite the never-ending construction effort, to this day there is a shortage of housing nearly everywhere. Special consumer goods and services, including theater tickets, were less of a problem, usually provided from Moscow.

After the collapse of the Soviet Union in 1991 and the cutbacks in federal budgets for research and development throughout the country, life on the fringes of Moscow changed dramatically. As paychecks became smaller and less certain, dacha gardens suddenly took on new significance. Many young scientists saw a brighter future in the commercial rather than the science sector and migrated to Moscow to work in banks or become traders.

The Ministry of Defense lost most of its interest in the science cities, and technologies that the institutes had secretly developed were shown to the world. Some countries would surely be interested in paying for the right to use at least a few of the technologies for civilian purposes, or so thought the institute directors. But, in most areas of commercial applications, comparable or superior civilian technologies were readily available in the global marketplace.

One valuable asset could not be denied, however. There was considerable land available within each of the cities even after accommodating the apartment buildings. If all else failed, land could be rented to foreign firms interested in manufacturing products for the Russian market, an approach quickly adopted in many of the cities.

In contrast to Akademgorodok, cities near Moscow have a number of advantages over more remote settlements. The first attraction is access to both the Moscow market, with 10 million inhabitants in 1999 and each with an insatiable appetite for goods and services of all types, and to the markets surrounding Moscow, with an additional 6.5 million residents. One-half of Russia's industry is located in this geographical area, and almost every foreign investor in Russia has an office in or near Moscow. The region has lower prices, rents, and production costs than in Moscow proper. The transportation infrastructure (air, rivers, rail, and highways) and the communication networks (phone, e-mail, courier services) are excellent by Russian standards. Also of interest for importers and exporters is the large number of customs stations and warehouses in the region and the well-developed networks of banks, some with reputable international connections and others with connections of another ilk.[8]

One dilemma confronting these cities is that advantages for technological entrepreneurs can also be exploited by organized crime. The more attractive a city becomes for business interests, the more attention the city commands from mafia leaders who often take up residence in the cities near Moscow. But having a ganglord as a neighbor is not always bad. Many rich Russians who amassed their fortunes outside the law now seek a degree of respectability. They usually deplore street crime in their neighborhoods and, if necessary, employ their private security forces to help bring tranquility to previously tumultuous urban areas.

Of special importance for small businesses, the regional government has enacted several laws to provide tax and other incentives for investors in technology-oriented activities. For scientific organizations, the regional profits tax—which is added to the federal profits tax—is reduced by 50 percent. And, the regional government provides a two-year tax holiday for investments of $5 million or more in production of selected products. For example, genetically-engineered human insulin has been singled out as a desirable industry, one that could benefit from tax breaks during the start-up periods.

Despite the importance of tax exemptions and other incentives that local officials might offer businesses, investment decisions in the region are also driven by the potential customer base and the availability of financing. A regional approach can be helpful. Directing government procurements at the regional and municipal levels to the most qualified local firms through a competitive bidding process can be particularly important in this regard.[9]

Snapshots of several science cities near Moscow encapsulate most of the problems faced by the research and development community throughout Russia. They highlight opportunities that officials and entrepreneurs have recognized for developing reliable income streams. The tensions between selling dual-use technologies for profit and protecting such technologies to limit proliferation of dangerous items and expertise are also apparent. But only in one city cited here is there recognition of the critical role in technology development that the youth of Russia must play with more enthusiasm than at present.

Dzerzhinsky

The Luberetskoe Production Association adjacent to a well-preserved monastery in Dzerzhinsky, a one-hour drive to the south of

Moscow, developed solid propellants for Soviet rockets. Drawing on their expertise in how to launch missiles, the scientists are convinced that rocket technology can be adapted to propel large quantities of water through high pressure hoses mounted on aircraft or situated on the ground to fight forest fires.

Despite the institute's dramatic film showing how an unrelenting stream of water could systematically extinguish an advancing fire line, foreign specialists lost interest when the feasibility and cost of deploying such a technological innovation were calculated. Firefighters want their planes to land as close to the fires as possible to reduce costs and delays in refilling water tanks. However, the large Soviet-era planes that were equipped with water cannons require long runways. Also, while a water gun adds considerable precision to the laying down of a liquid blanket, dumping water from bags suspended from aircraft has the advantage of simplicity and reliability in covering a blazing forest.

Fighting forest fires is only one area of interest to the institute. Looking to the future of the Russian gas industry, the chemists developed a new type of electric generator driven by natural gas, explosive devices that help delineate seismic profiles in the exploration for gas deposits, and reliable and powerful fire extinguishers to combat gas fires. The rocket scientists also became biochemists and polymer chemists, turning out new pesticides, cleansing agents, construction material, and even camping and boating gear.[10]

Such technical ingenuity has not assured a high-tech future for the town of Dzerzhinsky. The institute's technical base is too specialized, and the military customers have disappeared. Each innovation out of the institute's previously defined box runs headlong into an imported product. Finally, the workforce has shrunk and aged considerably, and the charismatic academician who founded the institute and commanded great respect from the Soviet scientific community has passed into the history books.

Zhukovsky

Just a few miles to the east of Moscow is the Central Aerohydrodynamics Institute, often referred to as the birthplace of Soviet aviation technology. For decades, the institute carried out highly classified research in some of the most advanced wind tunnels and related experimental facilities in the world. But already by 1994, less than 0.2 percent of the institute's budget came from military sources, in contrast with more than 50 percent several years earlier. Some facilities have become obsolete, but others are highly functional and would seem to offer important research and development opportunities.

Dozens of customers come from abroad. Foreign aircraft manufacturers pay modest fees to use the wind tunnels and related facilities. However, the institute promotes with little success the use of new types of seaplanes, installation of highly automated greenhouses, and construction of sophisticated stands to test truck performance in rough terrain. These capabilities, while possibly attractive to other countries, all have international competitors.

The list of other services the institute offers to world aviation is impressive: airframe tests, flight simulator experiments, creation of flight control systems, and fabrication and installation of data acquisition systems, for example. But, again, American and European organizations are stiff competitors. Many institute facilities simply have not been used for a number of years.

A profitable activity for the institute during the mid-1990s was production of parquet flooring. The institute's high-temperature ovens provided an excellent capability for this successful business. Products appealed to both commercial firms and wealthy Russians building large homes, but the market eventually declined in the face of foreign imports.[11]

Despite the downsizing of the technical workforce, the town of Zhukovsky will remain an important center for the Russian military and civilian aeronautics community. In addition to the aerohydrodynamics institute, the Gromov Flight Research Institute is located in Zhukovsky with its extensive facilities for flight testing in extreme conditions, for developing computer-based simulation systems, and for training test pilot for airplanes and helicopters. Also, being close to Moscow, the city is a popular venue for international exhibitions of Russian achievements in aeronautics.[12]

Kaliningrad

The Institute of Machine Building on the northern edge of Moscow had for many years played a central role in the design and testing of components for Russian missile systems. As the institute began to search for new outlets for its technological capabilities during the 1990s, the imagination of the researchers ran in many directions.

During the Gulf War, engineers in Kaliningrad developed a unique approach to extinguishing fires in oil wells that had been ignited by retreating Iraqi forces. They built a flying saucer—two feet in diameter—that could be launched from a helicopter. The whirling projectile would hit and crimp the vertical pipe in the oil shaft just below the surface of the ground. The crimping would cut off the oxygen supply, and the fire would quickly die out. They sharpened their aim during a series of helicopter practice flights. However, by the time they were ready to take the technology to Kuwait, fire fighters from the United States and Western Europe had already earned $500 million by using older, but proven, techniques to extinguish all 500 fires.

Another proposal from the Kaliningrad scientists calls for nations of the world to unite in preparing for the impact of a meteorite on the Earth's surface. The Russian way to prevent such an event is to deploy around the Earth a network of rocket launchers that can shoot down the meteorite as it approaches. Institute scientists are ready to build 200 low-cost launchers deployable from many countries so destruction of the meteorite would be assured regardless of the direction of impending impact.

During several visits to the institute, I hesitated to mention other global problems, knowing the researchers surely would develop a solution given the slightest encouragement. They have long been convinced, for example, that manufacturing synthetic diamonds using their shock tubes built in the 1920s is easily within their grasp, if only given a small amount of money to begin. In 1994, focusing on a totally different track, they tried in vain to convince visitors that their high-temperature combustion chambers were precisely what was needed to rid the world of toxic wastes.[13]

Finally, they were able to obtain the financial support to demon-

strate the effectiveness of high-temperature destruction of toxic materials. They proved themselves right. The research team received
awards at an international ecological forum in Las Vegas in 1997 and
at a UN-sponsored conference in Moscow in 1999, where the technology was considered an excellent candidate for use in the UN Persis-
tent Organic Pollutants Program. Presumably, the next step will be to
enter into a licensing agreement with a western firm to market the
technology.[14]

Chernogolovka

Two hours to the north of Moscow, the science city of
Chernogolovka is home to 10 research institutes and 25,000 residents.
Beginning in the 1950s, research on rocket fuels was the city's main
theme. In time, more diverse activities became ingrained in the programs of a wide variety of institutes. In the mid-1980s, there was a
surge of interest in research on lasers that could be used in systems to
destroy incoming missiles. Observing that the concept of national missile defense is now being revived in the United States, some of the
town's physicists believe they may again have contracts with the Ministry of Defense. This seems a long shot, however, given the ministry's
priority of simply sustaining current activities on military bases.

My two visits to Chernogolovka focused on the work of the combustion engineers who had tested the ignition characteristics of rocket
fuels. This was highly delicate work, since a mistake could have easily
triggered an explosion. The engineers justifiably believe they have become the leading experts in Russia, and indeed in the world, on the
causes of explosions, including explosions in industrial plants. Their
problem has been that no one is interested in paying them to redirect
their talents to preventing industrial explosions despite the frequency
of such accidents. And, in truth, most of the engineers are nearing
retirement age, many locked into their technical discipline with little
interest in retraining.

Fortunately, a few of the most promising young engineers have
succeeded in obtaining invitations to conduct research in the United
States and Western Europe. Many specialists have found profitable

ventures buying and selling apartments and real estate in Moscow and in Chernogolovka.

Before the conclusion of my visit, the former rocketeers presented me with a wooden carving fashioned into the shape of a brain. For me it symbolizes both the brain drain that has depleted the town's young talent and the brains still in Chernogolovka that need financial resuscitation. At the same time, I can't help but see in it the form of a mushroom cloud from a nuclear explosion, perhaps symbolizing missile technology proliferation concerns surrounding the city.[15]

Pushchino

"We can't rely on the agricultural authorities to solve our food problem. Just give us the land, and we will increase productivity overnight." This was the repeated plea of microbiologists at Pushchino to U.S. Agency for International Development representatives in Moscow in the mid-1990s. The scientists received substantial funds, and they planted new varieties of potatoes on their experimental plots of land.

But their effort to increase agricultural production was a failure. It takes more than science and enthusiasm to increase agricultural production. It takes political clout to obtain large tracts of unencumberd land with good growing potential. It takes capabilities to produce crops efficiently on a large scale and to move them from the fields to the stores in an edible form. Historically, more than 50 percent of Russian agricultural produce has been unfit for consumption by the time it reaches the stores—some crops remaining in the fields, others rotting at distribution points waiting for trucks that do not arrive, and still others molding in storage areas because food processing cquipment is not functioning properly.

The science city of Pushchino is unique in that it never was defense-oriented. A few contracts with the Ministry of Defense were dispersed among several of the institutes. The city was designed to be a center of scientific excellence for microbiologists and related researchers concentrated in about a half-dozen institutes of the Academy of Sciences.

Pushchino is close to Moscow but not so close as to be plagued with housing problems and other diversions from research, thought the founders. But now housing is at a premium, with families of some senior scientists confined to one- or two-room apartments, more accurately described as modified dormitory rooms. Being distant from Moscow is no longer an advantage. Most funding organizations—Russian and foreign—are located in Moscow, and frequent trips to their offices are essential if there is to be research.

Pushchino's prowess in basic biomedical research cannot be denied. Despite difficult times, a few excellent biologists are the scientific core of several institutes that comprise the backbone of the city. A few lucrative grants from western organizations play key roles in maintaining a modest level of activity. Indeed, in 1999 the only laboratories with significant activity were those that were recipients of western grants.

The city's residents are quite proud of the university that has been established there during the past few years. This graduate-level university is tied tightly to the research institutes. The institutes provide the laboratories for the students who in turn provide high-level technical support for the institutes' biologists. The university draws many students from the region who simply cannot afford to study in Moscow.[16]

Overall, the living conditions in Pushchino are poor and are emblematic of the plight faced by most researchers throughout the country. Aside from the handful of biomedical superstars, the most successful researchers are those that are addressing environmental problems of concern to western organizations. They have succeeded in obtaining limited financial support to explore both the biology of ecosystems and related degradation of agricultural soil throughout the region.

Fryazino

The electronics city of Fryazino is located 25 miles to the northeast of Moscow. A branch of the Moscow-based Institute for Radioelectronics and Radioengineering has long been a mainstay of the city. But it is only one of 48 institutes and enterprises located throughout the area encompassing Fryazino.

For decades, the electronics laboratories and factories kept the Soviet Union near the forefront of developments in radar systems, microwave networks, fiber optic and coaxial connections, and laser technology. In recent years, a particularly popular area with commercial payoff has been the development of medical diagnostic equipment. This has required supplementing electronics know-how with specialized knowledge from health professionals. Also, the enterprises have branched out into the metal construction, canned fish, and confectionery industries, hardly areas that feature high technology but areas of consumer interest that are stable income generators.

In 1994, the U.S. Department of Defense, supported by several other U.S. departments, attempted to convert a military electronics plant into an enterprise that produces hearing aids. Even though partial deafness is common in Russia, the firm has had great difficulty developing a customer base. While the need is there, the cash to cover production costs eludes most of the people who might benefit from this modern electronic device.

On the brighter side, several small firms in the city have succeeded in penetrating the international market. For example, with high-tech skills available at low costs, a group of scientists from the Institute of Radioelectronics and Radioengineering developed a high precision device for measuring currents generated during physics experiments that rivals the best equipment available in Europe. To avoid trouble in Russia with financial transactions, the firm established an affiliate in Frankfurt, Germany, using the Fryazino base as the source of technological innovations that could be incorporated into the equipment. Several dozen engineers from Fryazino enjoy satisfactory lifestyles through profitable participation in this successful international endeavor.[17]

This sampling of research activities throughout the Moscow region has but a few bright spots. With no place to go, many scientists and engineers will continue efforts to obtain financial support from whatever funding sources they can uncover. A handful are succeeding, although their successes have been little more than short-term respites from the intellectual boredom that hangs over most science cities and gradually erodes the vitality and capability of the technical workforce.

Ten Nuclear Cities

Of the three million inhabitants of the science cities, 760,000 live in 10 closed nuclear cities. In the fall of 1991, the western press reported the existence of these secret cities—10 cities where the core facilities of the Soviet nuclear weapons program were located. The nuclear cities were to be opened to the Russian population and eventually to the world. The scientists and engineers were reported to be diversifying their capabilities from simply supporting military efforts to also making new contributions to economic development in Russia. (The 10 cities, originally known only by post office box designations, are identified in Appendix C.) In general terms, the cities have the following characteristics:

• Their populations are slowly increasing. They have become attractive for pensioners retiring locally or moving from other areas of Russia to live with relatives in the cities. They need not worry about crime or narcotics, and housing conditions for extended families are good by Russian standards

• Defense expenditures, which have been the backbone of the cities for decades, have declined significantly. While some defense contracts remain and no cities will be abandoned, downsizing of the military commitment will continue to erode the capabilities of the municipal governments—through loss of the tax base—to support the populations.

• The cities are remote from large industrial centers. This remoteness has engendered a high degree of internal comradery, but it does not encourage outreach to commercial opportunities outside the fence.

• The cities are sites of both weapons-grade nuclear materials, thought to be within relatively secure storage areas, and radioactive contamination that in some cases covers large territories outside as well as inside the fence. Local authorities will not pay the bill to address these problems, which they rightly contend are rooted in Moscow policies.

• Each city has unique technical capabilities but, in many areas of interest to the West, they compete against each other—high-energy physics, nuclear fuel cycle safety, and software development. Other research areas where there are overlapping capabilities are medical technologies, laser technologies, microelectronics, and automated control systems.[18]

Overall, the 10 cities are storehouses of technology with major security dimensions, particularly the vulnerability to proliferation beyond the borders of Russia. These cities are also homes to dual-use technological achievements. While the Russian government usually overestimates the potential of technology for development of high-tech industry in Russia, there should be opportunities for developing and selling some technology-based products.

In 1994, I made my first visits to three of these cities—Sarov, Ozersk, and Snezhinsk. While their high fences are intimidating, inside the fences they resemble other Soviet-era cities. For me, the big surprise was that all pedestrians seemed headed for important meetings or essential shopping visits, with little suggestion of the idle time so often encountered in other Russian cities. Perhaps this purposeful demeanor is simply a characteristic of people raised in a military-type environment or, more likely, it reflects a general attitude among high achievers.

As to security, by the time of my visit several dozen westerners had already been to each of the cities for brief periods of a few days. The Russian security services had become accustomed to organizing programs for foreigners that would show off the institute's technical strengths without compromising military secrets. In short, escorts were always ready to take me anywhere I wanted to go outside the secured areas.

My visits were part of the efforts of western governments to develop for nuclear specialists civilian-oriented job opportunities that would help prevent social turmoil among the populations as salary levels plummeted. At the same time, these governments were reluctant to consider cooperative ventures that could set the stage for more broadly based redirection of the cities' high-tech resources toward the commercial marketplace. They simply did not know how to accomplish such a goal. In any event, it seemed more appropriate for Russia rather than the foreign governments to take on this responsibility.

Following my visits to Sarov, Snezhinsk, and Ozersk, I thought it was important to focus greater international attention on the dangers of economic decline within the nuclear cities. In 1995, Russian colleagues and I designed an international study of the social, economic, and security trends in the 10 cities to develop data that would support our case. The specific objectives of the study effort were two-fold: to improve understanding of the demographic, educational, commercial, and crime trends in the cities in recent years and to highlight policy and program approaches that worked well in improving the standard of living, while identifying those that worked poorly in each of the cities. Such "lessons learned" in one city should have relevance for other cities as well.

Finally, after delays in obtaining financial support in the United States and hassles over administrative approvals in Russia, by 1998 the study effort was under way—but on a pilot basis. Studying the workings of an entire city was too complicated to immediately begin well-designed investigations in 10 different locations. So, the pilot effort examined three cities, one of the 10 closed nuclear cities (Snezhinsk) and two "control" nuclear cities that were not surrounded by high fences (Obninsk and Zarechny).

The fact that Snezhinsk suffered from more physical and intellectual isolation made its economic problems worse. Such cities, with highly specialized technological capabilities located at great distances from potential customers, will have difficulty maintaining political stability without substantial governmental subsidies for the indefinite future. Yet, as demonstrated in the control cities, entrepreneurial zeal can open new commercial doors. International contacts can be particularly helpful in this regard.

Russian teams carried out the analyses; American participants served as "quality control" to promote analytical objectivity. We were quite successful in ensuring that the effort did not turn into an advertising campaign of technical capabilities within the cities. (Chapter 8 presents highlights from the study and addresses in more depth the specific challenges the nuclear cities are confronting.)

Cities that Supported Biological Defense Activities

Another subset of science cities consists of biology towns, housing institutes that supported the Soviet program to develop biological weapons. Only two (Koltsovo and Obolensk) of the dozen or more small towns and villages where laboratories, institutes, and production facilities were located are on the formal list of science cities. But all of these settlements face the problems that characterize the formerly militarized science cities.

The patron for these activities has been the Moscow-based organization Biopreparat. In the spring of 1995, Major General Yuri Tikhonovich Kalinin, the director general of Biopreparat, invited me to his headquarters. It was located in a district of Moscow that for decades had been off limits to foreigners. He wanted to discuss a proposed U.S.-Russian seminar on redirection of former Soviet biological weapons researchers to civilian tasks. Biopreparat still exerted considerable control over its institutes, although a devolution of Moscow's authority had greatly complicated the organizational structure that had been in place.

Kalinin has presided for two decades over the sprawling Biopreparat complex established during the 1970s. At its peak, Biopreparat employed more than 60,000 people working at 100 facilities. As many as 5,000 of the technical personnel had significant understanding of the workings of biological weapons, and therefore could be attractive targets for the intelligence efforts of other states trying to develop the so-called poor man's weapon of mass destruction. The network of facilities included several dozen research institutes and several industrial plants capable of producing large quantities of deadly ingredients for biological bombs and shells. The Soviet arsenal of destruction that rested on Biopreparat capabilities could deliver hundreds of tons of plague and anthrax bacteria, smallpox viruses, and other infectious agents if given the command.[19]

Until the early 1990s, the activities of Biopreparat located in secluded towns and in closed enclaves in large cities had been cloaked in secrecy. Then Biopreparat lost most of its support from the Ministry of Defense and, like other Russian defense-oriented organizations, struggled to find a new niche in the civilian marketplace. Our proposed seminar fit with Kalinin's objective of searching for new markets for Biopreparat products and new sources for financial support of research activities.

A Biopreparat car delivered me from my hotel to Kalinin's headquarters, a yellow mansion that many decades earlier had been the home of the vodka merchant Pyotr Smirnov. The Smirnov factory next door was continuing its tradition of serving the population of Moscow while extracting handsome profits despite economic problems everywhere around it. Over the years, of course, Smirnov's legacy has probably done more than any historical invader to undermine the health of the Russian populace.[20]

Kalinin received me in a spartan conference room, bedecked with samples of pharmaceutical products that Biopreparat was trying to sell on the Russian commercial market. Sale of generic pharmaceuticals, made in Russia, would help stem the tide of imported products while providing new income streams for Biopreparat. Biopreparat was working closely with struggling Russian pharmaceutical plants as the field of public health became the target for new entrepreneurial initiatives.

The discussion of the seminar's details was brief and to the point. Kalinin instructed his staff to ensure a successful meeting, and I agreed to bring leading American specialists to Moscow and to arrange for the financial aspects of the event. Throughout the encounter, Kalinin showed no signs of the financial pain engulfing his complex, a complex that spread from villages 1,000 kilometers to the northeast of Moscow, to downtown St. Petersburg, to small urban centers around Moscow, and to outposts in Siberia. His confidence indicated he was still in charge of activities at dozens of facilities despite decentralization forces in play.[21]

A few facilities in the biological cities have found market niches in the pharmaceutical and public health research fields. Several institutes are focusing on veterinary concerns. However, other biotechnology complexes are rapidly fading into simple job shops in urban centers, with all signs pointing to continued economic decline.

Certainly the science cities that possess remnants of the Soviet biological weapons program deserve attention. Some western experts worry they can again be closed to outsiders and revert to dangerous activities. Others see a steady stream of foreign visitors to the cities, including Middle East visitors, as opening new highways for an outflow of technologies. The best hope of ensuring that bacteria and viruses cultured in the biology cities are not diverted to nefarious purposes is through a program of international cooperation and transparency. Such transparency will only become reality if western countries help, through financial means, to harness biological assets of the cities for peaceful purposes. This is a formidable task, but it is one that must be undertaken.

Future of the Science Cities

There are no rigid criteria for designation of a science city. One pragmatic approach is to accept the "official" list of 65 science cities recognized by the Russian Association for the Development of Science Cities. The list reflects both technical considerations and the political persuasiveness of local leaders.[22]

Two criteria suggested for designating science cities that would benefit from special-purpose legislation are the percentage of the workforce engaged in science and education activities and the percentage of the city budget devoted to supporting science and education. However, these criteria are far from precise. It is likely that the government will continue to compile lists as in the past and that legislation singling out cities will be heavily influenced by the parliamentarians who are involved.

While many of the science cities are located in the Moscow region, hideaways with potent military-related capabilities are in the Urals (10) and Siberia (13). In those areas the classification of "closed city" may be more significant for the populations than the designation, "science city," since worker benefits are higher in closed cities than in science cities. The 10 nuclear cities are classified as closed cities as well as science cities, with the municipalities having the right to retain some federal and regional taxes collected from the population rather than sharing them with Moscow. While there is no publicly available list of all Russia's closed cities, at least 20 cities, towns, and villages under the patronage of the Ministry of Defense would be on such a list.[23] Most of the science cities are now considered open, although in many instances Russian security services ensure that they are not too open, particularly to foreigners.

An encouraging development is the growing attention within Russia to the regional context for activities within the science cities. Regional governors are increasingly active in seeking tax breaks and in helping convert facilities from military- to civilian-oriented activities that can benefit the region as a whole. High on the priority list of some regions is development of communications networks that improve links between the science cities and remote areas of the regions. Also, there are increasing calls for concerted federal, regional, and municipal policies to support economic and technological progress in the science cities.

The highest priorities of the science cities themselves are increased subsidies from the federal government and special status—akin to the status accorded to closed cities—that will reduce the flow of their tax revenues to Moscow. In the spring of 1999, the parliament passed legislation that would accord all science cities certain financial and tax privileges, legislation that was later vetoed by President Yeltsin. The government has had difficulty acknowledging that the science cities were indeed any more important than other cities—at least in terms of the need for financial breaks.[24]

For at least the next decade, almost all of the science cities will do their best to remain technology-oriented municipalities. They will be reluctant to abandon any facilities. They will continue to search for special dispensations so their banks of brains and equipment will have a better chance of being used in the rebuilding of Russian science and of the economy. A few will provide strong educational opportunities for youth to pursue careers in science and engineering despite growing skepticism as to the job market.

Several reasons for western support of the revival of these cities are compelling: humanitarian concerns over populations under stress, security concerns over proliferation of dangerous technologies, and scientific concerns over loss of results from Soviet research investments of billions of dollars. Russian interest, of course, is directed toward wastage of facilities and talent and toward potential turmoil amidst a population that feels overlooked in favor of the residents of the large cities. This view should also drive the West's list of priorities for programs in Russia.

Notes

1.   For this quotation and a more extended discussion of the early days in Akademgorodok see Paul R. Josephson, *New Atlantis Revisited, Akademgorodok, the Siberian City of Science*, (Princeton, NJ: Princeton University Press, 1997), pp. iv-xv.

2.   The discussion of the Institute of Catalysis is based on three visits and is updated by discussions at the U.S. Embassy in Moscow in April 1999. See also "Boreskov Institute of Catalysis," brochure released by the institute, 1998.

3.   *Ibid.*

4.   The discussion of the Institute of Nuclear Physics is based on three visits to the institute and is updated by discussions at the U.S. Embassy in Moscow in April 1999. This quotation was provided by the Embassy. See also "Budker Institute of Nuclear Physics," brochure released by the institute, 1998.

5.   *Ibid.*

6.   *Ibid.*

7.   *Ibid.*

8.   Olga Ananina, *BISNIS Report*, U.S. and Foreign Commercial Service, Moscow, June 1999.

9.   *Ibid.*

10.   Schweitzer, *Moscow DMZ,* pp. 150-1.

11.   *Ibid.*, pp. 156-7.

12.   "Gromov Flight Research Center," brochure released by the center, 1998.

13.   Schweitzer, *Moscow DMZ,* pp. 54-6.

14.   Personal communication from the information office of the International Science and Technology Center, Moscow, December 1999.

15.   Schweitzer, *Moscow DMZ,* pp. 50-1.

16.   Discussions during two visits to Pushchino in the spring of 1999.

17.   Visit to Fryazino in 1996, updated by Ananina, *BISNIS Report*.

18.   Lev Ryabev, "Meeting the Challenges of Russia's Nuclear Complex," Conference at Carnegie Endowment for International Peace, Washington, D.C., January 1999.

19.   Ken Alibek with Stephen Handleman, *Biohazard*, (New York: Random House, 1999), p. 10.

20.   *Ibid.*

21.   *Ibid.*

22.   A.V. Dolgolaptev, "Conditions and Perspectives of Development of Science Cities of Russia," *Material from the Fifth International Conference of*

Science Cities of Russia-97, Obninsk, State Central Institute for Raising Professional Qualifications, Minatom 1997.

23.   Georgi Lappo and Pavel Polyan, "The Closed Cities of Russia," *The Population and Society,* Institute of Economic Forecasting, Moscow, No. 16, January 1997.

24.   "Yeltsin Vetoes Special Status for Russia's Scientific Cities," *The Russia Journal,* April 5-11, 1999, p. 16.

8

Three Nuclear Cities with an Abundance of Technologies

One of every ten residents of Obninsk, including children and pensioners, has a private business.

Journal of the City, Obninsk, 1998

The advent of the market economy doomed Zarechny. The city's economy crashed. The city managed to find a way out and became an example of the effectiveness of the principle of local autonomy.

Business in Russia, 1996

Why do highly talented students enroll in difficult physics faculties at Russian universities and, five years later, turn their backs on careers in science? Why have so many high-tech companies established by leading Russian scientists and engineers gone bankrupt while a few scientific entrepreneurs have found lucrative markets in western Europe? How can scientists with incomes of less than $100 per month afford to own automobiles? Why has street crime declined in a small nuclear city with open borders in the Urals at the same time that criminals run rampant in other cities of the region? Why do residents living next to a nuclear power plant have longer life expectancies than the average Russian? In 1998, three American colleagues and I worked together with three teams of Russian specialists to find the answers to these and other questions. Our two-year investigation of the social and economic conditions in three nuclear cities—Obninsk, Zarechny, and Snezhinsk—provided insights into these and other puzzles surrounding the future of the technology born in the Russian, formerly Soviet, nuclear complex.

Each city has a nuclear pedigree. Highly talented scientists and engineers have spent many years in each city's largest institute as researchers in nuclear programs, including programs supporting weapons development. Laboratories are packed with sophisticated equipment to probe the structure of the atom. Storehouses contain highly enriched uranium and plutonium that can be used to create nuclear weapons whether or not the materials were intended for that purpose. In each of the cities, the Russian Ministry of Atomic Energy (Minatom) is a major force in determining research priorities. And, in Moscow, Minatom is the principal voice in gaining budgetary and legislative support for the cities.

Nuclear scientists and engineers spend much of their time attempting to adapt technologies to civilian markets, and the cities have become homes for a wide variety of technology endeavors unrelated to the nuclear industry. However, the Soviet legacy of considering all nuclear developments as having security implications complicates the efforts of the specialists to enter into the mainstream of the country's economic life. City and institute leaders have difficulty convincing Russian security forces that the cities house more than merely military assets. Security mindsets will not change easily.

Access by Russian visitors and foreigners to enterprises and institutes in the cities varies greatly and is sometimes unpredictable. Large areas of Snezhinsk, for example, have never been seen by outsiders. Even entry into the residential parts of Snezhinsk requires special permission to pass through the main gate. At the other extreme, almost all districts in Obninsk are open to casual visitors, with only a few laboratories completely off limits. Zarechny, while officially open to visitors, has limited entry points where unwelcome visitors are quickly spotted.

Until the collapse of the Soviet Union, the futures of the three cities were assured. Then the Russian government, strapped for financial resources and under international pressure to take steps to expedite arms control agreements, began downsizing the nuclear weapons complex. Many residents of the cities confronted the realities of economic survival for the first time. During the 1990s, hopes within the three cities have risen with each pronouncement from Moscow of yet another program to support conversion to civilian activities. Aspirations have then promptly fallen when the Ministry of Finance withdraws its funding commitment for the proposed program.

The cities range in size from 33,000 to 110,000 residents. They are located in contrasting geographic and environmental settings. Most importantly, their leaders have traversed different roads in making the transition to a new type of economic order in Russia. They all search in their own ways at home and abroad for funding sources to help maintain a semblance of financial viability.

Our two-year study assumed that a review of lessons learned in one city about the role of science and technology in regional development, about innovation centers, and about working with foreign partners should benefit not only those planning the future of that city but officials in other municipalities as well. However, we found that local Russian leaders often perceive their cities and problems as "unique," and they may not be interested in approaches of other officials regardless of their success. But federal policies concerning pensions, taxes, and a host of other issues cut across all cities. International programs that provide grants and purchase equipment or that support foreign travel are open to institutions throughout the country. In addition, costly mistakes in one city that lead, for example, to bankruptcies and brain drain should pique the interest of officials of all cities with similar problems.

An Experimental Science City under Market Conditions: Obninsk

In the Soviet era, few pleasures exceeded a two-week, all-expenses-paid holiday at a sanatorium. On three occasions during the era of the new Russia, I spent the night at the sanatorium in Obninsk—no longer well-polished, no longer teeming with attendants, and no longer free. Bring your own ping pong paddles, tennis rackets, and chess set, as recreation equipment has disappeared. Still, the whirlpools, electrical stimulation cubicles, and massage parlors are usually busy, primarily servicing short-term vacationers who live nearby but need an escape from their daily routines. The food and accommodations are adequate, and life may not be as desperate as suggested by western investigative reporters who warn of a precipitous collapse of Russia's nuclear empire.

The history of Obninsk dates from 1946, when the Communist Party established Laboratory V 60 miles south of Moscow. "V" is the third letter of the Cyrillic alphabet, and Laboratory V was the third research center in the Soviet nuclear weapons complex. (Laboratory A had just been established in Sukhumi on the Black Sea to investigate the properties of plutonium. The southern Urals was the site of Laboratory B, where biophysics and radiation chemistry were emphasized.)

Laboratory V slowly spawned a substantial city. By 1956, the scientists south of Moscow were ready to make the transition from a settlement that was simply an outpost of a government ministry to a genuine municipality. On July 24 of that year, a governmental decree conferred city status on Obninsk.[1] Forty-one years later, President Yeltsin issued another decree, this one declaring Obninsk to be Russia's first experimental science city. Even though the concept of science cities dates back several decades (as shown in Chapter 7), the Russian government realizes that new approaches are critical if these cities are to survive and eventually thrive in a market economy. Obninsk has become a symbol of this new approach.[2]

Obninsk was originally established as a center for designing nuclear reactors. These reactors were to propel Soviet submarines, to power space satellites, to generate plutonium for weapons, and to provide electricity for the country's grids. The world's first reactor to provide electricity for commercial use remains a city landmark.

Breeder reactors, long an Obninsk specialty, generate plutonium that can be recycled as fuel for continued operation of the reactors. The world's first breeder began operating in the 1960s in Aktau (now in Kazakhstan) on the shore of the Caspian Sea. Until it closed in 1997, it had the dual tasks of providing electricity for the city and power for a desalination plant. The second Soviet breeder was commissioned in the 1980s and still operates in Zarechny, one of the three cities included in our study.

Of course, the Chernobyl accident set back reactor development in Russia, as it did throughout the world. Nevertheless, the scientific leadership in Obninsk is confident that nuclear reactors will again be in favor, at least in Russia, France, and Japan, and that the city will continue to live up to its reputation as the leading international research center for breeders. New designs worked out at Obninsk envisage reactors that use as their fuel plutonium and uranium removed from nuclear warheads. But the scientists have not yet convinced authorities who control purse strings in Russia and abroad that investing billions of dollars in new nuclear reactors in Russia makes political, financial, and environmental sense.

The city has more than just nuclear reactors. It also boasts the world's largest artificial cloud chamber. Entering this chamber of the Russian Hydrometeorology Service, the unsuspecting visitor feels as if transported to Star Trek's Enterprise. At the medical radiology center, views of cancer patients being subjected to intensive radiation engender immediate respect for the practical applications of nuclear science. In the agricultural radiology laboratories, the tedious task of cataloging soil conditions from every acre within wind distance of Chernobyl, and of measuring the radiation levels in the milk and vegetables taken from that land, has been under way for more than a decade. Finally, at the Obninsk branch of the Moscow-based Karpov Institute of Physical Chemistry, sales to western customers of medical radioisotopes produced in Obninsk have kept the entire institute solvent.

The importance of these activities seems clear. But, only the Karpov Institute has found reliable cash cows for its work. The Russian ministries of both Health and Agriculture—as well as the Hydrometeorology Service—are the logical sponsors of many activities in Obninsk, but they have few resources to support innovative work. Meanwhile, foreign grants keep some laboratories in business.

Since 1991, the bustle of this city of 110,000 inhabitants has attracted many new young residents. Most arrivals, together with local young scientists who have grown impatient with low paychecks and have abandoned research, now see their futures in the business sector. Overall, the active scientific workforce of Obninsk, for decades the backbone of the city, has declined by 23 percent. While most older scientists stick to their professions, most younger ones look for other types of jobs.[3]

Residents have faced shortages of goods and services at work, in

Box 8.1
Principal State Research Organizations in Obninsk

- State Research Center for Physics and Power Engineering
- State Research Center at the Scientific-Production Enterprise "Tekhnologiya"
- Medical Radiological Scientific Center
- Affiliate of the State Research Center for Physical Chemistry, named after Karpov
- Scientific-Production Association "Typhoon"
- All Russian Research Institute for Hydrometeorological Information
- All Russian Research Institute for Agricultural Radiology and Agroecology
- All Russian Research Institute for Agricultural Meteorology
- Geophysics Service of the Russian Academy of Sciences

Source: M.V. Shubin, Presentation at the City's Scientific Conference Commemorating the Fortieth Anniversary of Obninsk, Obninsk, 1997, pp. 1-2.

the home, and in the schools. Yet, with 4,000 registered enterprises, a number of state research institutes (see Box 8.1), and 300 small businesses in the scientific and technical sphere, city leaders believe that this technology-oriented city can rebound. They point to several of Obninsk's favorable features.

The city has established an infrastructure to support small innovative businesses. Two cornerstones are a Center of Natural Sciences and Technology and a Business-Incubation Center. (Box 8.2 identifies small firms linked to these centers, firms that had promise of succeeding at the end of 1998.) A venture capital fund has also been sponsored by the city and region.

The city's overall "business plan" is cast within the context of regional development. Such an approach is often adopted in the United States when cities are trying to adjust to the closing of military bases.[4] Priority areas for contributing to the region's development include telecommunication networks, computer technologies, energy resource development and energy conservation, laser technologies for use in medi-

---

Box 8.2
Selected Small Enterprises in Obninsk

Totally owned by individual entrepreneurs
- EXSPRESS-EKO: filtration elements from modified polyethylene
- ERIDAN-1: devices for ultraviolet measurement of trace air pollutants
- POLYOT: complete interior for new generation of automobiles using composite materials
- EKSPOPRIBOR: portable plasma apparatus for cutting and welding of metal
- INTEKH: modernization of rear view mirrors for automobiles
- ROSSISKAYA NARODNAYA TELEKOMPANIYA: optical wave network for tranmission of information
- RESURS-PRIBOR: acoustic and technical equipment for modernization of industrial and power plants
- MOBITEK: modular production line for drugs
- TEPLOPROYEK: battery for electrical heating
- GEOLOID: computers for telecommunications
- BIOSAD: high quality wood products
- OBNINSKY TSENTR POROSHKOVOGO NAPYLENIYA: equipment for producing metal and metal ceramic powder coatings

Mixed Ownership: entrepreneurs and institutions
- KONVERSTSENTR: improved methods for cleaning gallium
- ADVI-ALMAS: diesel motors
- GIDROMET: devices for monitoring levels of natural and waste waters for water supply systems of small towns
- TEKHNOLOGIA: tubular electrical heating devices
- EKON: gas analyzers for monitoring boiler wastes
- EMMI: medical kits using laser infrared and ultrasound

Source: Obninsk City Administration, November 1998.

---

cine, polymer and other high-strength materials for light and heavy industry, and filtration technologies. This outreach is a promising departure from narrower marketing approaches of the past.

The Russian government has agreed to transfer federal facilities to municipal ownership, or at least local control, on a case-by-case basis.

Also, the city must approve any actions by the federal government to change the status of state enterprises located in the city—including closure of enterprises. This primacy of local authorities may be unique in Russia.

Higher education opportunities have increased, with 3,100 students enrolled at nine university-level institutions—a growth of 35 percent from 1990. The city has identified management training as a top priority. The city leaders recognize that the Soviet approach to training managers, practiced for decades in Obninsk, is no longer appropriate, and they have turned to western countries for assistance in their effort. Whether this concern over education will translate into graduation of technology-oriented entrepreneurs has yet to be determined.[5]

The veil of optimism of city leaders is paper thin, however. Funding to launch most planned activities is missing, with the city contending that the federal government has reneged on its commitment to support the science city experiment. The centers for innovation are barely surviving. The venture capital fund has yet to operate.

Turning to taxes, the city's situation has gone from bad to worse. Tax payments in kind rather than in cash have become the norm. The city may receive large quantities of building material from construction firms, but the mayor can't meet his payroll using bricks and unfinished doors. As to tax breaks promised for innovative firms, federal designation of Obninsk as a tax-free zone for investors in high-tech activities may not survive, and claiming any type of tax exemption for research activities is difficult for entrepreneurs.[6]

Meanwhile, the influx of mafia groups into the residential areas of Obninsk, which is within commuting distance of Moscow, is both a blessing and a curse. They purchase goods and services locally, with some contribution to the city's tax base. But many unsavory people gravitate toward mafia strongholds, contributing to the growth of the city's crime rate by more than 50 percent since 1994. Some local residents compare their city to the wild west of the late-19th-century United States, noting that those with guns run roughshod over a vulnerable population that has no ability to fight back and few assets to share.

Obninsk also has a special problem stemming from its nuclear heritage. The Institute of Physics and Power Engineering has storerooms packed with tons of highly enriched uranium and separated plutonium which could be used directly in producing nuclear weapons. Such material is routinely used in the institute's reactor tests and related experiments. In the Soviet era, this material was protected by reliable guard forces. However, in the absence of regular paychecks, current guard forces are less reliable.

Additional means—such as physical protection barriers and accounting systems—are needed to ensure that even small amounts of nuclear material are not stolen or diverted by any insiders who may be feeling the economic squeeze or by any outsiders who may be able to penetrate the security fences. In 1994, a small amount of highly enriched uranium showed up on the black market in Germany. This material is generally believed to have come from Obninsk. While it may be difficult to find customers in advance for a few hundred grams of uranium, local thieves may assume that once they have such material in hand, a customer will appear. Alternatively, with foreigners of all stripes omnipresent in Russia and with criminal elements well entrenched within Obninsk, interested foreign buyers might orchestrate a theft scenario.

One American journalist recounted the challenge of protecting nuclear material at the institute:

> The headache is little round tablets or disks containing weapons-grade plutonium and uranium. In the Fast Critical Facility building, there are 100,000 disks or about ten tons of bomb-grade material, theoretically enough to make hundreds of bombs. A dozen disks could easily fit into a pocket. But the old Soviet accounting system for them is a nightmare. About 6,000 disks have duplicate numbers. The Soviet-era records were kept in paper notebooks, some decades old, that record the weight and "price," an absurd measurement for bomb-grade material. In short, there is no full record of the current physical condition of the massive pile of uranium and plutonium disks.[7]

During my visit to the institute in 1995, a Russian TV crew was preparing a commendatory report on bar coding the disks in the Fast Critical Facility. Each time a disk was taken into or out of a laboratory of the facility, a physicist scanned the bar code with a supermarket-type device and entered into a computer the disk's old location and new destination. The computer system then had an up-to-date record of the locations of the disks. At the time, 10,000 disks had been bar coded, with the remainder to be labeled within 18 months. By the end of 1998, however, more than half of the disks were still not labeled. What happened? "Other priorities," pleaded the scientists.

The Obninsk experience in protecting dangerous materials and in using technological wherewithal for commercial purposes is typical of developments at institutes and enterprises throughout Russia. Russian institutes come up with new ways to employ modern technologies and projects begin with great fanfare. Most commonly, the projects run out of money, as Russian or western financiers conclude incorrectly that they have jump started a process that will continue on its own.

In some cases the Russian scientists have become relegated to the status of technicians. Bored and with no opportunities to develop yet other new technologies, they look for more challenging tasks. The project then becomes the responsibility of less talented specialists. This explains, at least in part, why so many disks remain in dusty barrels.

Another major institute in Obninsk is struggling to find new customers. The Research and Production Enterprise "Tekhnologia" has a proud history of producing unusual types of glass, ceramics, and polymeric composites. These innovations have been used in Russian aircraft, the space shuttle Buran, and rocket engines. But Russian customers no longer exist. Efforts to find foreign customers in competition with western manufacturers have proven too difficult for most products.[8]

Overall, Obninsk has transformed itself from a closed nuclear city where secret experiments were the order of the day to an open city obsessed with attracting foreign participants to conferences and consultations. These gatherings provide local specialists with opportunities to find like-minded colleagues with access to western funds in which they might share. Indeed, many researchers have become addicted to western grants.[9] While there are compelling reasons for foreign grants, little attention is given to how research activities will continue once a grant ends.

Overall, Obninsk is an economically depressed community with an industrial base working well below capacity. In contrast to the poverty in the surrounding rural areas, however, life in the city is good. The population increases by about 1 percent each year, largely due to the abundance of goods and services, which outweighs the crime, pollution, and job uncertainty. As to the priorities of the general public, improved medical services and better public transportation are at the top of the list.[10]

Finally, the scientific workforce is somehow managing to stay largely intact, with more than 70 percent of the researchers fully intending to remain in the city. The most prosperous institute is the Institute of Physics and Power Engineering, with dozens of western contracts that have led to annual incomes of $50,000 or more for a few senior institute managers. Economic conditions for other employees at the institute are much more difficult, with annual incomes of $1,000-2,000 being the norm. Nevertheless, almost all scientists have telephones at home, 90 percent own dachas, and 76 percent have automobiles. And they are not the only city residents who have some material wealth: registered within the city are 30,000 automobiles.[11]

How can this paradox of low pay (at least official pay) and a reasonable lifestyle be explained? There are two important reasons. First, Obninsk is near Moscow, where Russian and foreign representatives of funding organizations are located. Related to this geographic advantage are strong technological capabilities in Obninsk that are of interest in the West, and a large number of the city's specialists participate directly and indirectly in western-funded projects with payment arrangements frequently not officially recorded. Secondly, there are many opportunities for moonlighting in the small business sector. While few such jobs involve innovative activities, they do pay the bills, enabling researchers to keep their day jobs.

Astride the Transiberian Railway: Zarechny

The Beloyarsk nuclear power station dominates the town of Zarechny, 30 miles east of Yekaterinburg. This is a company town. Ten percent of the population of 33,000 are employed at the nuclear plant, and the plant provides the financial backbone of the local economy. The plant's income, while much reduced due to long-overdue customer payments, has been essential in cushioning for the city the economic shocks of the last several years.

In terms of electrical output—600 megawatts—this breeder reactor is not particularly noteworthy. But in terms of technology, the station has been a pacesetter for the world for almost 20 years. In contrast, the United States spent billions of dollars on breeder research and construction but failed to solve the problem of safely circulating quite dangerous sulfur through the cooling pipes of a power station. Thus, environmental concerns over the safety of such a reactor stopped the U.S. program 30 years ago.

Soviet engineers, perhaps less concerned about safety and costs during their experiments, figured out how to handle sulfur. The Beloyarsk power station became their showcase for demonstrating world leadership in that area. Small problems have included minor sulfur leaks and even flash fires. Overall, however, the plant's performance has been excellent. One of the biggest problems has been the periodic attempts of Russian environmental activists to sneak onto the reactor's territory as a sign of general protest over the uses of nuclear power. To date, no intruders have been able to get close enough to the nuclear components of the plant to cause damage.[12]

The Russian minister of atomic energy during 1999 was, earlier in his career, in charge of research activities in Zarechny. He may view as his legacy a still larger breeder at the Beloyarsk station, a project begun in the early 1990s. After the site was cleared for a new reactor and support buildings were erected, the project came to a halt due to a shortage of cash. The concept, however, is still very much alive—at least in Zarechny—since a new reactor complex would mean more jobs and a cut for the city of the revenues of those utility companies that distribute the electricity.

But where will the minister find $3 billion? His formula is simple: the regional and city governments should provide $1 billion in loans, $1 billion should come from loans from commercial banks, and $1 billion should be contributed by the Russian government, since the reactor will provide a national service by burning nuclear material taken out of weapons slated for destruction.[13]

In principle, the project makes sense. Also, the minister's commitment to funding only from Russian sources is admirable, although at least partial financing from abroad would seem more likely. I have no doubt that Russian designers and engineers could solve the technical problems and build a good station.

But, even in the unlikely event that $3 billion were available, several problems rooted in corruption would be difficult to overcome. First, ensuring that the available funds were used as intended would require an international accounting firm of the highest reputation to control all expenditures. Secondly, component suppliers and construction crews would undoubtedly attempt to cut corners on goods and services, and intensive monitoring by a corrupt-proof organization— again probably an international firm—would be essential. Finally, once the power plant was in place, monitoring to ensure that the managers and the operators do not cut corners, again to benefit themselves, would be essential.

Tucked behind the original nuclear plant is the Zarechny branch of the Moscow Institute of Power Engineering. For years, these laboratories operated in secrecy, despite Russian claims that they were always open.[14] They were located adjacent to the reactor where they could test the resistance to radiation of materials being developed for the Soviet weapons and space programs. Today the beams of radiation provide new opportunities for the laboratories to produce radioactive isotopes for international markets.

At the time of my first visit in 1993, this branch of the Moscow institute was becoming that institute's cash cow. The scientists had developed inexpensive processes for manufacturing the inert gases xenon and krypton that were in demand by physics laboratories and industrial companies in the West. The first shipments of krypton went to the Center for Nuclear Research (CERN) in Switzerland, and contracts for other shipments were promptly negotiated with customers in England, Germany, France, and the United States. The key to competing in this international market is the purity of the gases. Russian researchers rightfully boast of their super-pure products.

In 1997, the researchers attempted, with limited success, to expand their export line to include carbontetrafluoride and sulfurhexafluoride. The primary application was to be dry etching of silicon used in integrated circuits, but the international competition was too intense. A potentially more rewarding activity is providing hospitals in Moscow with xenon as an alternative anesthesia. According to the scientists, xenon has a powerful narcotic-like property with no known side effects.[15] In 1999, clinical applications were expanding, although still on an experimental basis, with particular attention to possible side effects, if any.

A daughter firm of the Moscow institute, also located in Zarechny, provides the commercial framework for producing the gases and handling financial transactions.[16] Buoyed by the success of its gas products, this firm also began producing laser analyzers of gases with the first foreign customer being the California company, Aerojet. One line of lasers can identify carbon layers in certain steel alloys, and another can be used for diagnosing cancer malignancies in humans. However, these applications have yet to attract customers.

The daughter firm and the nuclear power station are the technological cornerstones of an ambitious plan to transform the entire city into a Technopolis—a proposed technological rebirth of a city near its death bed in the early 1990s, when subsidies from Moscow began to dry up. The original idea was to develop products of interest to nearby industrial and agricultural enterprises, as well as for the international market. A core company was established to both support specific projects and provide a physical infrastructure within Zarechny that would enhance the effectiveness of small firms—with an emphasis on providing telecommunications linkages.

The core company, the Technopolis-Zarechny Development Fund, was established by Minatom, the regional administration, and the city administration. The company manages an industrial incubator and an agricultural incubator for small enterepreneurs.[17] However, the initial flurry of interest in establishing small firms was not successful. More than 500 registered firms never operated in the black. Markets for a wide variety of products simply did not develop, due to both the poor state of the economy and the lack of marketing skills among the new entrepreneurs.

In further pursuit of its ambitions, the city was the first in Russia to obtain authority to prepare a region-wide industrial program that would be recognized at the federal level as the area's authoritative program. The program does not call for transfers of government funds from Moscow, as is the conventional practice. Rather, the hope is to stimulate investments in high technologies and production processes with short recoupment periods that can then lead to capital growth. Given this ambitious undertaking, is the city really prepared to forego subsidies from Moscow if it might obtain them?[18]

In March of 1999, the regional governor gave his blessing to yet another scheme of the city's scientists to develop a profitable enterprise. The target is the international market for rare-earth metals such as lanthanum, yttrium, and scandium—malleable and durable metals now found in bumpers, trimmings, and other components of automobiles, among other uses. During the 1980s, the Soviet Union was the second leading exporter of these metals, but the four manufacturing plants—as well as the raw materials—were located outside the Russian part of the USSR. Thus, Russia now has almost no exports in this field. However, thousands of tons of monazite—enough raw material for several decades of rare-earth production—have been uncovered at a dormant storage facility several hundred kilometers from Zarechny. This material, mined in Brazil, was en route to Germany during World War II when it was seized by the allies and deposited in Russia.

The idea is to construct a manufacturing facility for the metals near Zarechny, with the profits to be divided among the regional administration, the town, and a new scientific-production enterprise. In the offing are jobs for local residents, technical challenges for scientists and engineers—and the probability of many a financial nightmare for managers responsible for dividing profits three ways while coping with Russia's banking system. Still, Zarechny entrepreneurs are confident they can not only succeed but pay off investment costs within several years.[19]

As to life in the city, Zarechny may not be a closed city with high fences, but it is certainly a guarded community. There are only three roads into the city, due to the configuration of the nearby lake. A police car is parked at each entrance day and night. Thus, the possibility of unknown persons entering the town undetected is rather remote.

In 1995 the mayor organized a festival in the town's stadium that attracted 15,000 people from the city and the surrounding area. A handful of young thugs became unruly and disrupted the celebration. An immediate telephone call to the police in Yekaterinburg brought a heavily armed response team. The troublemakers were promptly arrested, tried in a very public manner, and given harsh sentences. This quick retribution carried a message, and there has been little crime in the city since.

The resulting confidence in personal safety means less personal stress for Zarechny residents than for those in many other cities. This factor may contribute to the unusually high life-expectancy rate of 64 years for Zarechny's males, in contrast to the national average of 57. Other reasons include a reliable food supply, both home-grown and imported from nearby towns, and a well-functioning hospital. Despite economic hard times, the population seems quite satisfied with life next to the nuclear station.[20]

With these attributes and its regional orientation, Zarechny has a good chance to become a high-tech commercial center in the Urals, a center that penetrates both domestic and international markets not only with its inert gases but also with other products. One young high-tech entrepreneur, for example, has developed a handheld device that concentrates infrared waves on portions of the body that require heat massage. He moved to Zarechny because the city provided a safe working space at reasonable rates. He does not attempt to sell the device directly to consumers, given the difficulty of establishing a marketing network, but rather provides components and associated technology to a factory in Tomsk which, in turn, assembles and markets the devices.[21]

While one success does not outweigh dozens of failures, city leaders seem confident that they can help up to 100 private firms in the city become customer friendly and customer successful. If even only one-half that number are successful, the experience will offer "lessons learned" of wide interest.

In short, Zarechny is a bright spot on the bleak financial horizon of Russia. It has a number of advantages. It is small, and the communal services for its residents have been functioning well for some time. The nuclear power station is an essential facility for the region. At some future time, electricity users will be more diligent in paying their bills—probably following threats of losing their connections. Being astride the Transiberian railway and near a major airport are helpful. Finally, and most importantly, a number of Zarechny specialists now have experience in competing in the domestic and international marketplaces. They know the realities of competition, and they should be able to make reasonable judgments as to the marketability challenges for new products.

A major concern, however, is the orientation of the city's youth, a dilemma facing the entire country. The current economic conditions dictate a move away from technology to the sales of goods and services in order to survive. Added to that is the sense of isolation young people feel from the action in Yekaterinburg and other large cities. It's no surprise, then, that they spend their leisure time watching television broadcasts from other parts of the country and abroad, and only 4 percent of schoolchildren use computers on a regular basis. Our study shows that one-third of the young people want to remain in Zarechny, another one-third believe they would prefer life in larger Russian cities with greater opportunities for education and social life, and the remaining one-third want to live in foreign lands. For this latter group, Canada is the preferred destination, undoubtedly due to the highly popular student exchange programs supported by the Canadian government.[22]

Ironically, a key to the sustainability of technology-oriented programs will be a new wave of technology entrepreneurs. Without young specialists who perceive rewards from technology innovation as rewards rivaling those in trading and banking, the likelihood of sustaining technological leadership over the long term is not high. International competition will be intense and, in Zarechny, young talent will be essential to gaining and holding market niches.

Diversification of Research in the Southern Urals: Snezhinsk

For 35 years, the Institute of Technical Physics was masked by the innocuous post office address, Chelyabinsk 70. Only in the 1990s did the Soviet government finally acknowledge the existence of a municipality of nearly 50,000 inhabitants located in the southern Urals. The city adopted the name Snezhink (snowflake). Established in the 1950s as the second nuclear weapons design institute (the first was in Sarov, several hundred miles east of Moscow), the institute recruited many of the Soviet Union's best and brightest physicists and engineers. Behind the imposing fence, which encircles an area of more than 120 square miles, the nuclear scientists designed and directed the testing of weapon upon weapon in the race to stay abreast of the United States.[23]

Several of the original Soviet bomb designers have written memoires about the city's 1955 founding and the rivalry between the Snezhinsk and Sarov laboratories.[24] In recent years, rumors have circulated in Moscow that the defense establishment would cast one of the two institutes adrift in view of duplicate expenditures and the dwindling need for more nuclear weapons. Consequently, the rivalry intensifies as each rallies all its allies to protect its place in the nation's military budget.

The Snezhinsk team outpaced colleagues in Sarov in one technical program that has received little attention in recent years. This program demonstrated how nuclear explosions can be used for peaceful purposes. During the course of two decades, the Soviet Union set off more than 100 underground nuclear tests for peaceful purposes, with Snezhinsk scientists responsible for designing 70 percent of them. The tests were geophysical experiments involving the search for natural resources, the creation of storage cavities for oil and gas products in underground salt domes, the stimulation of flow in oil and gas wells, the fracturing of rock ores that can be mined, and the excavation of disposal areas for hazardous wastes.[25]

The aspirations of the Snezhinsk scientists to realize economic gain from the gas, oil, and excavation industries as the result of such nuclear explosions were shelved in the mid-1990s. At that time, Russia and the United States—along with China, the United Kingdom, and eventually France—agreed to a moratorium on nuclear tests, whatever the purpose. Disguising a weapons test as a test for peaceful purposes has always been a concern. The diplomats insisted there would be no loophole to permit tests for any purpose.

On a broader basis, the Institute of Technical Physics is going through a painful process of downsizing, with displaced scientists scrambling for new ways to use their talents. Of course, some weaponeers—perhaps one-half of the the institute's 18,000 scientists, engineers, and workers—will continue to practice their military trade at the design laboratories, two experimental plants, and experimental field site.[26] However, even the most critical and best paid personnel have become discouraged by their erratic and shrunken paychecks. Some have joined in street demonstrations protesting frequent delays in pay.

Since 1992, the institute has been a major target for programs in the West to provide alternative employment opportunities for disgruntled weaponeers lest they look to unsavory sources for income. The largest projects have been supported through the International Science and Technology Center (ISTC) in Moscow. One popular line of research is redirection of strong mathematical capabilities, originally devoted to weapons design, to modeling of many processes involving physics and chemistry that have little relevance to weapons. Modeling projects supported by the ISTC have included transformations of brittle materials under heat and mechanical stresses, dispersion of pollutants in the atmosphere, and fallout of radioactivity from two major nuclear accidents 30 and 40 years ago near Karachai Lake, less than 75 kilometers from Snezhinsk.[27]

More than 2,000 specialists from Snezhinsk have received salary support during participation in western-funded activities. In March 1999, programs financed by the West provided 10-15 percent of the institute's budget. But not all international programs have been considered by Russian specialists to be of equal importance.

Programs sponsored by the U.S. Department of Energy, in particular, have been tinged with Russian suspicions of intelligence missions. Too often the teams sent to sensitive areas have included excessive numbers of U.S. participants with no obvious legitimate tasks to perform. In group settings, Russian specialists refer to such personnel-padded activities as "nuclear tourism," whereas privately they blame U.S. intelligence agencies for complicating exchanges of real scientists.

When undertaking conversion programs, the scientific leaders of

Snezhinsk are surprisingly unconcerned about the handicaps of being located a great distance from potential customers for products they might develop and of having a workforce with little experience in marketing commercial technologies. They undoubtedly assume that public funds, and even foundation funds, will flow their way. Thus, most of their ideas to diversify from their military profile are not oriented toward the private sector marketplace. They emphasize either high-quality science to advance the frontiers of knowledge or applied projects that help government agencies responsible for environmental protection, nuclear safety, or health services do a better job.

Throughout 1999, Snezhinsk scientists marketed to international organizations, government agencies, and foundations both in Moscow and abroad several projects that, while interesting, continue to reflect a hesitancy to compete in the private sector marketplace. The projects include:

• *A test site for investigating sources of underground tremors.* Snezhink would become a test site for trying out inspection techniques to investigate suspicious tremors. International inspectors could check the effectiveness of sampling air, water, and soil for uncovering recent releases of fissionable materials associated with nuclear tests by rogue states.

• *An environmental survey of radiological conditions in the city.* Such a survey would likely confirm that radiation levels in Snezhinsk are minimal, thereby reassuring potential investors that there is no nuclear hazard in doing business in the city. The survey would also demonstrate for other cities a practical approach to monitoring urban areas where nuclear activities have thrived for years.

• *A center to study nuclear policy issues.* Among topics of interest are the strategic implications of large reductions in the nuclear arsenals of the United States, Russia, and other countries; techniques to monitor compliance with international agreements to terminate production of weapons-grade plutonium; preparation of international standards for physical protection and accountancy of plutonium and highly enriched uranium; and analyses of successes and failures in attempting to convert military-industrial activities to commercial activities in the nuclear cities of Russia.

• *A training center for personnel from institutes throughout the Urals interested in upgrading capabilities in physical protection and accountancy of weapons-grade nuclear material.* Such an activity would be analogous to training programs being carried out in Moscow and Obninsk.

• *A program to analyze export control issues.* The institute is committed to assisting Minatom in assessing the technical aspects of proposed international transfers of nuclear technology.[28]

Even if such projects are supported, they will have little direct impact on near-term economic revival of the city. The numbers of full-time participants are too small to help very much in the search for jobs. Nevertheless, such efforts have significant national security implications. They could enhance Snezhinsk's standing as a center of international importance with the potential to become a magnet for other activities as well.

As to taking a technology to the commercial marketplace, the Snezhinsk scientists are still looking for their first high-tech success. Four of their strong candidates are prosthetic devices, diamond powder for industrial applications, perforated tubing for use in the gas industry, and electrochemical sources of energy. But cost and market considerations are, as always, the keys to commercial viability.[29]

Part of the problem has been the institute's organizational approach. In the early 1990s, a number of stand-alone enterprises were established to spin off promising technologies developed within the institute. But these firms soon ran short of startup funds, encountered controversy over the extent to which the institute should share in any profits for technologies it had developed, and gradually disappeared. Most were led by entrepreneurs who moonlighted from their institute jobs and, upon the initiative's collapse, returned full-time to their laboratories.

In a revised effort in 1998 and 1999, the institute set up daughter firms to attempt once again to commercialize many of the same technologies. The difference is that the institute now retains some financial commitment to help ensure the success of the firms. While success may be difficult, the backing of the institute provides some financial and technical reinforcement for the efforts. (See Box 8.3 for a list of the technologies that are to be implanted in daughter firms.)

Meanwhile, the city administration has adopted an aggressive role in promoting the commercialization of technologies. It has several strong assets that have not been fully exploited in the search for commercialization opportunities. First, the city receives and retains payments of federal taxes of local firms, including Value Added Tax and property and profit taxes. The tax revenues are not remitted to Moscow. Therefore, Snezhinsk can entice firms to locate in the city by offering special tax breaks. Secondly, the city controls a Small Business

---

Box 8.3
Technologies of Interest to the Institute of
Technical Physics in Snezhinsk

Hydroabrasive cutting
Quartz fiber production
High pressure materials synthesis
X-ray computer-based tomography
Medical gamma sterilization
Packaging radioactive materials
Fast burst nuclear reactors
Ionization dosimeters
Electrical connectors
Pressure differential meters
Fluid flow regulators
Automobile wheel disks using new alloys
Gas-oxygen cutter
Antenna feeder systems

Note: These technologies are in addition to those mentioned in the text.

SOURCE: Provided by representatives of the Institute of Technical Physics at a meeting of U.S. and Russian technical specialists in Zarechny, Russia, March 1999.

Development Fund which receives funds from abroad without requirements to convert hard currency to rubles or to pay taxes except to the city. Thirdly, a federal customs office is located in Snezhinsk, greatly simplifying clearance of imported products.

At the same time, Snezhinsk has lost some of its previous attractiveness as a tax haven (a 50 percent tax savings plus the advantage of paying all taxes to a single organization) for Russian firms headquartered elsewhere. In order for a firm to be registered in the city, 90 percent of the property and 70 percent of the working capital of the firm must be retained there. Thus, in 1998-1999, the number of registered firms declined from 400 to 120.

The city administration is interested in promoting the commercialization of the institute's high-tech achievements, even though there may be conflicts with the institute in this area. Also the city facilitates establishment of other companies that will increase tax revenues and provide jobs (e.g., production of shoe polish, fabrics, perfumes). A number of companies that have been in place for years are also in a sense under the patronage of the city (e.g., producers of macaroni, sausages, beer, and lingerie, and providers of services such as civil engineering).

Snezhinsk is taking several steps to promote its commercialization agenda, which includes the following plans:

- *A business incubator for small entrepreneurs who have difficulties finding space, utilities, and communications services for new businesses.* The city plans to establish a facility outside its fence but within city limits so entrepreneurs can take advantage of special tax breaks accorded to firms located there. The planners have turned to funding agencies in Moscow that have interests in promoting high-tech activities.

- *A training center for small business entrepreneurs.* The training would concentrate on two specific themes: (a) preparation of persuasive proposals for potential funders of projects and (b) the administrative, legal, labor, and related aspects of establishing and managing a small business in Russia. European funders are interested in this plan.

- *A Moscow-based representation office.* This office would seek out potential investors, entice Russian and foreign organizations (particularly western companies already represented in Moscow) to establish offices in Snezhinsk, and provide information on potential cooperative projects that could draw on the capabilities of Snezhinsk specialists.[30]

Given the handicaps of geographic and physical isolation, both local entrepreneurs and institute specialists have difficulty knowing which aspects of their expertise have market potential outside the city. Even in areas of high promise, they may have difficulty cultivating customers for their products.

Certainly for the next decade, it will be impossible for residents to maintain even the current standard of living without substantial new income streams (beyond the reduced, but still assured, defense contracts) from Moscow and abroad. The small businesses operating in Snezhinsk do receive some income from outside, and certain Moscow ministries, such as those responsible for education and health, provide a little money for activities in the city. But overall, the most important source of funds will continue to be the institute's payroll, a payroll in increasing jeopardy as Russia reduces its commitment to new nuclear weapons.

Despite the discouraging economic outlook for a city accustomed to special treatment, Snezhinsk is not in as difficult straits as many other Russian cities. At the top of the list of Snezhinsk's advantages is a population that highly prizes the security on the streets, and suggestions for opening the city meet strong resistance. Also, the good medical facilities attract residents of nearby towns as well as local citizens. The dacha gardens have expanded, and the beauty of the surrounding landscape looms large in the lives of the residents.

The city's population is slowly growing. Russians long associated with the Soviet nuclear program who had lived outside Russia are resettling there. Also, extended family members of Snezhinsk residents, particularly elderly females, are returning to the city's security. This factor is so pronounced that, in 1999, the ratio of female to male adults over the age of 55 in the city was 2 to 1.[31]

Finally, as to the children who, at least by tradition, should be the next generation of scientists, the youth is increasingly attracted to excitement of larger cities. Some dream of lives abroad, particularly in England, which has sponsored a number of youth exchanges with Snezhinsk. Television remains far more popular than computer games. A startling statistic from a recent survey reflects a youth disenchanted with careers in science. Of 18 students enrolled in the undergraduate physics faculty of the Physical-Technical University who were queried in a recent poll, only one indicated an interest in a career in science. The others had their eyes on more profitable business careers.[32]

The residents of Snezhinsk will band together to withstand economic pressures. While a few will reach out in their commercial endeavors, most will remain a tightly knit community. They like the personal safety in the city in contrast to the crime elsewhere, and they are accustomed to the strict security governing nuclear secrets. They recognize the importance of retaining rights to apartments both for themselves and for their relatives. Some of the wealthiest residents nearing retirement age may follow their children to Moscow and other cities, while outsiders from Russia and from abroad will be a growing presence on the streets and in the laboratories. But, for at least the next decade, Snezhinsk will remain largely aloof from the mainstream of Russian life.

Outlook for the Three Cities

Looking at these three cities, the residents of Zarechny have the best chance of prospering in the near term, even under difficult economic conditions. With a small population, effective control of street crime, and international sources of income from several products, Zarechny scientists and engineers are in a good position to weather the storms seeded by economic turmoil. And, with nuclear power, rare gases, rare-earth metals, and gold reserves, it is unlikely that this town will fade away.

Obninsk, with a larger and younger population but with an aging scientific and industrial workforce, faces more difficult times. Only if the local entrepreneurs are successful in their regional outreach do they have a chance of contributing to a revitalization of the city. This outreach will have to encompass Moscow, and not just the immediate environs of Obninsk, even though the crime spillover from Moscow is already a significant force in Obninsk. As a few residents continue to prosper—some from international scientific grants and others from criminal activities—the gap between rich and poor will become even more evident.

Snezhinsk's scientists are engaged in many nuclear issues, and these issues are simply too important for Russia or western governments to permit the collapse of the city. But, commercially viable undertakings on a significant scale are not on the horizon. While small commercial projects may be possible in a few areas, the large projects that can revitalize life in the city have yet to be developed. One missed opportunity has been development of a customer base throughout the region, a customer base that considers products made in Snezhinsk to be comparable to products imported from Europe and Asia.

In all three nuclear cities, entrepreneurial successes are usually linked to government support of activities. The Russian market for nuclear technologies is small. International competition is severe. A few non-nuclear technologies have been of global interest, but an equally promising approach is import substitution (substituting locally made products for more expensive imports) in Russia and the other countries that were formerly part of the Soviet Union.

The attitudes and goals of the cities' young people is crucial to the cities' technology futures. These cities, with strong scientific heritages and capabilities, should be developing the next generation of technology entrepreneurs, but few signs point in that direction. The challenge is to convince youth that, in Russia as in other advanced countries, the potential for businesses that rest on success in technological innovation can in the long run be more rewarding, financially and professionally, than many of the get-rich-quick business schemes currently being pursued.

Notes

1.   M.V. Shubin, "Presentations at the Scientific Conference Commemorating the Fortieth Anniversary of Obninsk," City of Obninsk, 1997, pp. 1-4.

2. A.V. Zrodnikov and A.P. Sorokin, "Obninsk—Science City of XXI Century," unpublished manuscript, Institute of Physics and Power Engineering, Obninsk, September 1998.

3. Ibid.

4. An example is the planning in the East Bay region of California, which includes Lawrence Livermore National Laboratory.

5. "Organization of a Center for Training Specialists in the Field of Science and Technology Management," "Statute of the Obninsk Venture Fund," and "Interagency Program of Innovation from 1998-2000." These unpublished manuscripts were provided by the city administration in September 1998. There are other reports describing the initiatives included in the documents; but as noted in the text, implementation has been difficult.

6. Discussions in Obninsk with city administrators, July 1998.

7. David Hoffman, "Cure for Russia's Nuclear Headache Proves To Be Painful," *The Washington Post*, December 26, 1998, p. A1. For additional background see National Research Council, *Protecting Nuclear Weapons Material in Russia*, (Washington, D.C.: National Academy Press, 1999).

8. Zrodnikov and Sorokin, "Obninsk—Science City of XXI Century."

9. Discussions in Obninsk with city administrators, March 1999.

10. Information collected by Obninsk city administration, March 1999.

11. Ibid.

12. Visit to Beloyarsk nuclear plant, April 1993.

13. Meeting in Obninsk with the Minister of Atomic Energy, October 1998.

14. Visit to Beloyarsk nuclear plant, April 1993.

15. "Laser Diagnostics and Pure Technologies ENTEK," Technocenter MINATOM brochure, 1998.

16. Ibid.

17. Fedor Polezhaev, "Zarechny, the Little City that Can," *Business in Russia,* March 1996, pp. 4-5.

18. "Federal Program 'Creation of Technolopolis Zarechny,'" dated 1997, provided by Zarechny city administration, 1998. "Results of Fulfillment of Plan of Social-Economic Development, City of Zarechny, 1997," provided by Zarechny city administration, 1998.

19. Discussions in Zarechny, April 1999.

20. Ibid.

21. Ibid.

22. Ibid.

23. Discussions in Snezhinsk, October 1993.

24. B. Yemelyanov, *Opening the First Pages in the History of the City of Chelyabinsk 70 (Snezhinsk)*, Uralskiy Rabochiy, Yekaterinburg, 1997.

25. Discussion in Moscow with former director of program on use of nuclear explosions for peaceful purposes at the Institute for Technical Physics, September 1998. For another assessment that differs somewhat (although the general conclusions are the same) see Milo D. Nordyke, "The Soviet Program for Peaceful Uses of Nuclear Explosions," *Science and Global Security,* volume 7, 1998, pp. 1-117.

26.   Russian Federal Center—VNIITF Homepage, www.ch70.chel.su, February 1999.

27.   Ibid.

28.   Discussions in Washington, D.C. with VNIITF senior officials, January 1999.

29.   Russian Federal Center, Homepage.

30.   Discussions in Livermore, California, with the Mayor of Snezhinsk, November 1999.

31.   Discussions in Zarechny with Snezhinsk city administrators, March 1999.

32.   Discussions in Zarechny with the specialist from Snezhinsk who conducted the survey, March 1999.

9

U.S. Efforts to Contain Dangerous Technologies while Promoting Foreign Investments

Are you helping us or are we helping you?

Official of Russian Agency for Cooperation and Development, 1993

U.S. firms will seek 2 percent ownership of Russian companies for access to commercial information, but few will make large investments since the likelihood of profits is very low.

U.S. Chamber of Commerce, 1999

For more than five years, the U.S. Department of Energy (DOE) has been funding civilian-oriented projects that draw on the technical capabilities of Russian weapons scientists and engineers while providing them with new income streams. But, in addition to participating in these projects, some Russian specialists continue to work on the development of weapons of mass destruction in Russia's military program. Indeed, DOE doesn't know even the names, let alone the backgrounds, of many scientists involved in their projects. Is the United States financing the Russian weapons program under the mistaken belief that weaponeers are being directed to new careers? Also, the principal beneficiaries of DOE funding have not been the Russians carrying out the projects but U.S. collaborating laboratories, which have received over two-thirds of the funds. Of the remaining one-third sent to Russia for their researchers, most has ended up in the accounts of tax collectors, a corrupt Russian pension fund, and creditors of the institutes where the scientists work. These findings of the General Accounting Office (GAO) in February 1999 dealt a temporary setback to U.S. government programs designed to prevent proliferation of Russian technologies to rogue states and terrorist groups while at the same time promoting commercialization of Russian technologies for the civilian market.[1]

Does the GAO report mean that this DOE program and related efforts financed by the U.S. government should be abolished, an implied threat of Senator Jesse Helms (R-NC) who ordered the GAO audit? Absolutely not. The programs are of vital interest to the United States. We have seen signs of leakage of Russian weapons know-how to Middle Eastern and Asian states that can cause trouble for not only their neighbors but for large regions of the world. At the same time, there are examples of successful redirection of Russian technologies to civilian applications that should eventually help buttress an economic revival and bring greater stability to a country in turmoil.

Why doesn't the Russian government itself assume responsibility for preventing this leakage of Russian technology? The government is seized with many financial needs and will not give priority to preventing the flow across its borders of expertise and technologies that might end up in irresponsible hands. In the absence of aggressive U.S.-financed programs to provide civilian-oriented employment and economic opportunities for Russian weaponeers and defense-oriented institutes, the likelihood of diffusion of dangerous know-how would be much higher than at present.

As to developing technologies for peaceful purposes, the Russian government endorses such efforts. However, the payoff is long term, and the immediate demands for Russia's limited financial resources for other purposes are overwhelming. Therefore, technology-oriented programs by the U.S. government, often in partnership with the American private sector, can be timely and helpful.

Can the problems uncovered by GAO be fixed? Absolutely, and steps are already under way to retrofit the DOE program that was under attack. Russian specialists working on civilian programs at U.S. expense should not be involved in defense programs. DOE should insist on a list of participants for each project and an accounting of their activities during the course of their contractual commitments. Such information is provided by the same Russian institutes for other

U.S.-sponsored programs. The initial naivete of DOE officials—that they did not want to offend key Russian scientific leaders by asking for sensitive personnel information—should by now be dispelled.

As to how U.S. government funds are distributed, DOE is changing its past ways. A much larger share of the funds is now used in Russia in preference to New Mexico, the site of two DOE laboratories. As has been shown, fewer funds are diverted to Russian taxes and overhead, and more accurate accounting of expenditures is taking place.

While imperfections still cover some aspects of the program, projects are becoming more sharply focused, with greater promise of tangible results both in keeping weaponeers in place and in providing marketable goods and services. Most importantly, DOE recognizes that individual projects will be meaningful only if they lead to sustained activities over many years. While achieving sustainability will be difficult—and in many cases not possible—the establishment of this goal is changing the unrealistic short-term orientation of earlier efforts.

DOE's activities in Russia are far-reaching, but other U.S. government programs have a comparable if not greater impact on the use of advanced Russian technologies. They too redirect Russian expertise to peaceful purposes. And they help set the stage for more effective use of technologies in a market-oriented economy.

Specifically, the U.S. Department of Defense (DOD) implements the Nunn-Lugar program and has also sponsored a wide variety of other technology programs at Russian institutes and enterprises. The Nunn-Lugar program facilitates the downsizing of the Russian complex that supported the development and deployment of weapons of mass destruction. It draws on many Russian research, engineering, and construction organizations to destroy missile silos, dismantle nuclear weapons, and safeguard nuclear material. Other DOD programs are directed primarily at obtaining Russian technologies that can be helpful to U.S. military programs, and to this end hundreds of technology contracts have been signed between several dozen DOD organizations and many more Russian research institutes.

NASA manages a large array of U.S.-Russia technology programs. The centerpiece of NASA's activities is support of Russian participation in the International Space Station (ISS) which calls on Russian design bureaus and enterprises to provide modules for the ISS. The Russian enterprises involved have in turn successfully engaged western firms in joint efforts to produce engines for space launches and components for satellite communications systems.

The U.S. government supports a number of activities that directly promote the commercial interests of American firms. These include grants for feasibility studies of commercial opportunities, political risk insurance for private sector investments, and fast-track financing for American companies attempting to use Russian technologies for products that will sell either in Russia or in international markets. Also, almost all of the more than 500 American companies involved in Russia look to the U.S. government for support in pressuring the Russian government to reduce administrative hassles, legal uncertainties, and criminal threats that confront businesses. Figure 9.1 provides an historical background as to how private alliances have evolved in a high-risk environment.

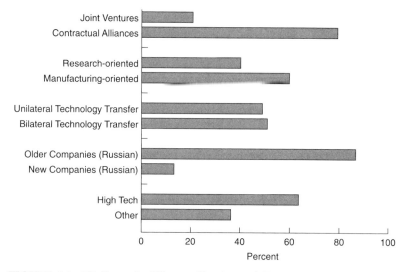

FIGURE 9.1   192 Strategic Alliances (Russian and Foreign Firms, 1988-1995). SOURCE: J. Hagedoorn and J. Sedaitis, *Research Note on Partnerships in Transition Economies: International Strategic Technology Alliances in Russia.* Center for Economic Policy Research: Stanford University. Nov. 1997.

Vice President Al Gore, in his interactions with counterparts on a long-standing Binational Commission, regularly intervenes on behalf of U.S. companies that run into roadblocks to their efforts to expand activities in Russia. In March 1998, for example, the vice president placed his imprimatur on several business ventures in Russia. These included a multibillion dollar oil production sharing project in the northern area of Russia involving Conoco and Lukoil; joint efforts of AGCO and the Chelyabinsk (region) to assemble agricultural equipment in Russia valued at $62.5 million; delivery of road construction equipment costing $55.5 million to the Federal Road Service by eight American companies; and a $1.3 million commitment by Corning to work with Samara Cable Company to produce fiber optic cable for the country's telecommunications infrastructure.[2]

Lessons learned from experiences in implementing U.S. government-financed technology programs and related commercial activities can help improve future approaches to bilateral cooperation.

DOE's Support of Technology Commercialization

The nonproliferation objective of the DOE program that came under GAO scrutiny—the Initiatives for Proliferation Prevention (IPP)—was certainly not the problem. Civilian employment opportunities for former weaponeers are critical. Unfortunately, the DOE specialists who set up the program had little background in Russian history, language, or culture and they had limited experience in carrying out projects in Russia. They did not understand Russian accounting systems, tax requirements, or labor and salary practices. They were insensitive to corrupt practices that date back decades, even centuries. They did not take time to learn from other U.S. programs that had been well managed. Therefore, blunders were inevitable. The GAO quickly found the mistakes.[3]

While GAO highlighted administrative problems, the program approach of DOE is critical. From the outset of the program, DOE officials underscored the importance of an "exit strategy" for each project—e.g., within three years of U.S. government funding someone else would take over, with the U.S. private sector being the primary

candidate to make the projects self-sustaining. To that end, a combination of American advisers and U.S. private investment was to be the
formula for success.[4]

Thus, much of the funding has supported advisers from DOE
laboratories who in turn were to stimulate interest among American
firms to become involved in projects, using U.S. government cost-sharing as an incentive. Such reliance on private firms that are reluctant to
risk their own funds in Russia without supplemental U.S. government
contributions should have raised warning flags as to the commitment
of those firms and the long-term viability of projects. But DOE was
under Congressional pressure to start projects as soon as possible, even
if they involved firms with marginal interests in Russia.

Many American participants in IPP projects believe U.S. experience in doing business in a market economy provides a good model for
Russia. They respect Russian technical competence but question Russian business acumen. Also, they believe that American investors
should play a key role in designing project details.

Russian counterparts have a different perspective. Most importantly, they want to design projects their own way. They recognize that
funders will review and perhaps modify their proposals. But Russian
organizations are seldom enthusiastic about American specialists who
proscribe detailed work plans. If access to the international market is
the contribution of western partners, the Russians are delighted. But
they are also aware of the Russian market, and they are suspicious of
motivations of American advisers who overlook this market as a low
payoff arena. They are impatient with seemingly endless consultations
involving Americans not attuned to the Russian scene. Finally, they
have been numbed by endless delays in Washington that may or may
not lead to promised projects. Their priority is financial support for
immediate action, not never-ending advisory services.[5]

Both DOE officials and Russian counterparts are correct. United
States experience can be helpful. Foreign investment can be important. But local initiatives and impatience must be respected. U.S. officials should listen carefully to Russian experts. Also, they should recognize that, at present, there are limited foreign investment

opportunities and that Russian institutions can make progress using their own resources.

In mid-1999, DOE reported it had supported 80 IPP projects that attracted the interest of U.S. industry. The private sector's matching contributions to the projects, including the direct and indirect costs incurred by the companies, were twice the size of DOE's contributions. Examples of projects included recovery of tungsten carbide from metal scrap, production of medical isotopes, manufacture of photovoltaic solar panels, and development of oil eating microbes.[6] A few months later, the U.S. Industry Coalition, set up to assist DOE, reported 18 projects were approaching market realization (see Appendix D).

Private sector interest in a project does not equate with market success. Not a single one of 79 projects that were examined by GAO in 1997 had resulted in sustained commercial activity. The outlook for the current list of 18 looks better. The matching contributions of the private sector reported in 1999 and an emphasis on sales as the measure of success suggest that DOE may now be on a more promising track.

As we have seen, considerable progress can be reported. The emphasis remains on supporting projects that have the dual objectives of assisting with nonproliferation and also contributing to an industrial base in Russia for energizing economic development. The concept of an exit strategy is alive, but with a more realistic perspective of the time needed to interest investors in new innovations and the difficulty in bringing products to market.

However, the cohort of former weapons scientists likely to undertake projects are set in many of their ways and lack business talent. Projects should also include, when necessary, innovative Russian entrepreneurs who were either too young to participate in Soviet defense programs or had little interest in such programs. An important criteria for selecting at least some of the key Russian participants in cooperative projects should be their capability to minimize costs while ensuring quality so that products will sell. Cost consciousness is not a trait of weaponeers.

Other DOE programs can also be important in stimulating technology efforts among Russian institutes and firms. For example, in its cooperative efforts to help safeguard uranium and plutonium in Russia, DOE is gradually switching from purchasing American equipment—physical barriers, detection sensors, and alarm systems—to purchasing comparable Russian products. An important objective of this procurement policy is to encourage evolution of stronger local manufacturing capabilities for such items so the Russians will be in a better position to sustain the effort after U.S. support ends. With a guaranteed DOE-financed start-up market for production of security-oriented technologies to be installed in nuclear facilities, the Russian firms that have won contracts are also looking more broadly at the demand by banks and industrial companies for security devices. This market demand is expanding dramatically in response to the growth in crime and threats of terrorism.[7]

Yet another DOE program, the Nuclear Cities Initiative, is intended to support a partial transformation of the 10 closed nuclear cities, including Snezhinsk which was a centerpiece of the previous chapter, to centers for the development of civilian technologies. The interrelated objectives are civilian jobs for weaponeers and new small firms in the cities.[8] In early 1998, DOE bannered the headline, "We're off to a fast start."[9]

But a key Russian official responsible for organizing field activities described progress during 1998 and 1999 as "a cold shower," He reported many unfulfilled promises regarding foreign investments that were supposed to be on the way.[10] DOE's rejoinder was that the U.S. Congress was the culprit in cutting back funding for the program. This carried little weight with Russians uninterested in Washington budget negotiations but concerned about yet new waves of American advisers.

What is different about this program? Job creation has long been the objective of other programs. The new dimension is the consideration of the needs of entire cities rather than the focus only on individual technology projects.[11] Of course, technology projects have been the lifeblood of the cities and will continue to play an important role in the search for new income streams. But, in the absence of reliable city services, social safety nets for displaced workers, and recreational and other activities for youth, continued tranquility in the cities is in serious question. These human requirements demand greater tax revenues for the cities—revenues primarily the result of new economic ventures, whether the businesses are high- or low-tech.

The initial activities supported by DOE—training in business skills, preparation of business plans, and establishment of business centers—are considered by some Russians well-worn approaches that have produced few new businesses in open cities, let alone in cities behind fences. Others think they are just what is needed. One past problem with such programs has been the emphasis on concepts rather than on actual business plans for projects and products.

A welcome recent addition to the financial aspects of training programs has been supplemental incomes provided by the U.S. program for workers displaced during downsizing of the Russian nuclear weapons complex. The workers can then undertake retraining activities to develop new skills without cutting classes to scrounge for funds simply to survive.[12]

Can the Nuclear Cities Initiative succeed with fences still inhibiting access by foreigners or Russians into them? More fundamentally, what is the measure of success? DOE plans to gauge success, at least for the initial $30 million expenditure, by the number of jobs created, with the target being a total of 500 in three cities. Since the layoff of 50,000-75,000 weaponeers is anticipated in the 10 cities during the next several years, 500 new jobs will be an important start only if they have a large multiplier effect.[13] The key is the types of new jobs.

Some will be short-term. Others will be long-term. Some jobs will benefit an entire city, such as jobs that upgrade telecommunication networks, while other jobs will have little impact on the lives of people other than the participants. Professional opportunities involving software development will attract former weaponeers. Other work will attract personnel who have had no direct connection with military programs owing to their age or recent arrival. Some jobs will have no multiplier effect. Other jobs can stimulate downstream employment, including development of technologies for use in a radioelectronics plant. In short, jobs should be weighted as well as counted.

Further complicating measurement of success is the fact that some new job holders would probably find jobs without the program. On the other hand, some may spin off from newly created jobs and form their own companies. They would thereby create additional work-places.

In any event, DOE should dig into the details of how the program influences not only the lives of the direct participants but also impacts on the social and economic viability of the cities, the regions, and in-deed the country. If a proposed project to find new ways to treat pros-tate cancer succeeds, the benefits from this single project could dwarf the costs of the entire program. If a project to develop affordable opti-cal fiber technology results in new communication links with remote areas of Russia, the payoff to the country could be substantial. If the program demonstrates even on a small scale that commercial profit can result from greater openness of closed cities, the program could be a pacesetter for new directions in how closed cities are governed.

In all of these DOE efforts, the metric for measuring progress cannot be sharp and crisp. Success should not be assessed simply on the basis of numbers of new jobs. On the other hand, if unemploy-ment is not significantly reduced, the programs are probably not very helpful.[14]

DOD's Programs to Redirect Russian Technologies

Under the Nunn-Lugar program initiated in 1991, DOD provides financial support for a variety of activities that draw on engineering skills of both American and Russian contractors in downsizing the Rus-sian military complex. The largest component of the program is di-rected at destroying missile silos, missiles, and bombers in accordance with international arms control agreements. Other activities include storing and protecting fissile material removed from nuclear warheads, converting nuclear reactor cores from reliance on weapons-usable nuclear material to use of other types of uranium, and destroying Russia's large chemical weapon inventory.[15]

Major engineering projects are required in all of these areas. For example, three Russian shipyards have received contracts to destroy over 500 submarine-based missile launchers during the next several years. This requires using heavy-duty cranes, metal cutting equipment, other industrial tools, and scrap handling equipment. Destroying almost 100 land based silos also requires heavy industrial equipment, while the destruction of several hundred missiles will be carried out in new oxidizer conversion facilities. As to the conversion of nuclear reactor cores, extensive design work is needed in order to modify existing facilities to meet new nuclear reactor specifications.[16]

While Russian engineers had the technical wherewithal to carry out these projects, the shipyards and other organizations involved needed to revamp their procedures for contracting so as to comply with American requirements. They worked on the basis of fixed price contracts, adjusting internal accounting procedures to accommodate new requirements for accountability. This experience has been a useful introduction to western ways of operating in a market economy, and the enterprises are now in much-improved positions to enter into contractual arrangements with other western organizations as opportunities arise.

Innovation has become the byword in the chemical destruction arena. After many months of attempting to convince Russia to use high-temperature destruction techniques developed in the United States, DOD finally agreed to Russia's use of innovative chemical detoxification techniques, at least at one major facility. Unfortunately, difficulties arose with environmental groups near the facility opposing the planned destruction. The program was further delayed due to backtracking by Russia on its matching contributions. Finally an impatient U.S. Congress withheld funding for the proposed Russian effort.[17]

As to DOD's non-Nunn-Lugar programs, two types of efforts stand out. First, many Pentagon units have simply purchased Russian know-how of interest. The two most widely publicized deals were the purchase of the Soviet SV 300 missile and the commissioning of 200 Russian weapons scientists to prepare technical histories of Russian nuclear weaponry. Also, hundreds of agreements have been inked for cooperation between Russian research institutes and about 40 DOD components ranging from the Cold Regions Research and Engineering Laboratory (Army) to the Arnold Engineering Development Center (Air Force) to the Undersea Warfare Center (Navy).[18]

Appendix E identifies many technology challenges confronting the

Russian government as a result of arms control agreements and developments related to downsizing the defense complex.

The International Space Station and the Aerospace Complex

For more than two decades, American and Russian astronauts and cosmonauts have flown together on missions directed at opening the frontiers of space. Since the mid-1990s, the Russian government has committed about one-half of its entire civilian research and development to the International Space Station (ISS). NASA, determined to meet an internationally agreed schedule, has also devoted considerable resources to help ensure that Russia is able to meet its commitments in a timely manner. NASA's total involvement with the Russian space program has required expenditures of more than $1 billion, with a significant portion for programs that reinforce Russia's funding commitment to the ISS.[19]

In order to concentrate a huge portion of Russia's skimpy budget on a single project, the Russian government has significantly reduced support for other areas of science and technology. Nevertheless, in upholding its commitment to the ISS, Russia can point to one area where its technological capabilities are surviving. Of course, the driving force for such a hefty commitment has been the political consequences at home and abroad if Russia were not to participate in this global endeavor. The expenditures have supported use of the Mir space station as a test bed for procedures to be employed in the ISS support, support that continued until Mir was abandoned in 1999 and construction began on two of the first ISS components, to be deployed in space at the end of 1999.

In the late 1980s, the Soviet government entered into several international agreements that provided the legal framework for the international effort. Then, with the founding of the new Russia, the government was faced with the decision of whether to participate with 15 other countries in the 15-year ISS program or whether to have a parallel Russian effort. Russia still had the option of taking another tack, since the project was not under way. Despite political sentiment in

Moscow for Russia to go it alone and apprehensions in the West over the reliability of Russian participation, financial reasons overwhelmed political considerations concerning Russia's role. The West would save billions of dollars, and Russia had no other choice but to sign on if it wanted to remain a serious participant in space exploration.

Russia committed its unmatched experience in manned space flight to the international effort. It was to spend $300 million annually to support the effort and would eventually own 38 percent of the station's facilities. Russian specialists assumed such a commitment would keep them on the forefront of international space technology efforts.

But, because the United States will shoulder the largest share of the total costs of the $90 billion project, Russia will not be a pivotal player in technology decisions. Indeed, Russia's participation could eventually be limited to "taxi driver" services. Under this scenario, Russia would transport crews and replacement vehicles into space, they would be responsible for rescue efforts during emergencies, and they would handle many repair services.[20]

It will be a day of mourning for the Russian space industry if Russia is relegated to support services rather than cutting-edge activities. But every time Russian financial shortfalls raise international doubts about Russian ability to meet its commitments, other participants press to remove Russia from the mainstream of the program. Then the taxi driver scenario approaches reality. What's more, Russia is selling some of its rights to use the station to other interested governments.[21]

The direct technological payoff for the Russian economy from this international effort will be limited. Several thousand Russian engineers and technicians will have jobs, assuming that the Russian government continues to finance the effort or, if not, that NASA somehow convinces the U.S. Congress to provide more supplemental funds for Russia.

Of course, Russian firms that are participating in the ISS program will also reap spinoff financial and technical benefits. Of special relevance is the participation of the Energia, Energomash, and Khrunichev firms. They participate both in the ISS program and in joint ventures to launch communication satellites and manufacture upgraded rocket engines for American space launches.[22]

One example of a U.S. company's efforts to use the wherewithal of such firms is Lockheed Martin's agreement to purchase in Russia up to 101 new RD-180 rocket engines valued at about $1 billion. The first 18 engines are to be delivered by 2001. For this undertaking, Lockheed Martin has teamed with AMROSS, a joint venture involving Energomash and Pratt & Whitney. The engines are being built in Khimky, Russia, for use on one of the U.S. Air Force's family of rockets (Evolved Expendable Launch Vehicle). RD-180 engines should reduce assembly time and improve operational capability while cutting costs.[23] Lockheed Martin may also use the same rocket technology for commercial launches, a step that might result in an additional $2 billion in orders for Energomash.[24]

The ISS and related commercial deals help keep the Russian space industry alive. Some Russian critics, however, feel that such deals could harm Russian interests by giving away technology at unrealistically low prices. The more common response has been, "We had a choice: either sell the engines to someone who will use them or let them rust in the factory while the technology goes to waste. We chose the first option."[25]

Promoting Interests of U.S. Companies

Since 1991, the U.S. government has provided financial incentives, advisory services, and political support for U.S. companies interested in trade and investment opportunities in Russia, including many aerospace and other engineering-based companies. An early emphasis was on encouraging U.S. investments in conversion activities within the Soviet defense industry, both to uncover marketable technologies and to facilitate the downsizing of the military-industrial complex. Since 1994, this orientation has broadened considerably to include American private sector interests in natural resources and many industrial fields. Vice President Gore, together with his appropriate Russian counterpart, has co-chaired almost a dozen meetings of a Binational Commission that encourages greater involvement of American firms in Russia.

In the early 1990s, the U.S. government established the Defense Enterprise Fund (DEF) to identify advanced technology opportunities and to link Russian enterprises with American partners. To that end, DEF took equity positions in a few Russian technology companies, including a manufacturer of submarine components that was shifting to producing excavation equipment, an enterprise seeking new applications of satellite tracking technology in the telecommunications industry, and a company installing fiber optic networks in remote areas of Russia. Buoyed by success in these efforts, DEF had planned to establish a related fund involving American private investors. When the Russian economy took a nosedive in August 1998, however, private investors lost interest at least temporarily, and the plan was shelved.[26]

Also, since 1995 the U.S.-Russia Investment Fund—which received $440 million in capitalization from the U.S. Agency for International Development—has invested in more than 30 Russian companies, including firms involved in telecommunications, pharmaceuticals, and forestry. It is the only investor offering long-term loan financing for working capital and equipment to Russia's small business sector. Despite concerns over corporate governance issues that have not been adequately addressed by the Russian government, it continues to consider new projects, holding a belief that crisis survivors can use capital efficiently.[27]

From the outset, the U.S. Department of Commerce was a focal point for promoting American private sector initiatives. The department tried to target privatized Russian firms, although such a classification is often misleading. Some privatized companies are simply appendages of state enterprises. Some are stand-alone companies that seem on the right track toward independence. But few large companies have been privatized to the extent that they are no longer responsive to governmental directives. Thus, in practice, the department became less concerned about the roots of Russian participants in its programs than in their potential to contribute to a market economy that would create a favorable environment for achieving U.S. trade and investment objectives.

The Department of Commerce has several programs. With American firms, it cost-shares business internships for Russians at those firms'

U.S. facilities. It also assesses changes in legal and regulatory frameworks and identifies opportunities for American firms to work with specific Russian enterprises and research institutes. A recent initiative supports health-industry partnerships with two-way trade missions on medical equipment, pharmaceuticals, and health services.[28]

The U.S. Trade and Development Agency (TDA), an independent U.S. agency, encourages investments in Russia by providing grants to American firms on the order of $300,000-500,000 for feasibility studies of potential projects. These studies often employ Russian specialists as consultants to the firms. Should a feasibility study lead to a project, the consultants are then well positioned to participate in the project. TDA has supported more than 150 studies at a cost of about $50 million. Priority areas of interest have included oil and gas, power plants and electrical networks, transportation infrastructure, health care, and electronics.[29]

Yet another U.S. agency, the Overseas Private Investment Corporation (OPIC), operates as an investment bank customizing complete financial packages for projects. It insures projects against loss owing to expropriation, political violence, or problems in converting rubles to dollars. It also sponsors trade missions. As one example, OPIC has supported a joint venture of Lockheed Martin with the Krunichev and Energia firms to build a sea-based launch platform for communication satellites.[30]

The U.S. government also supports projects of the World Bank and the European Bank for Reconstruction and Development. Of special interest in advancing Russia's innovative capabilities is the possibility for Russian firms to bid on contracts of these organizations for goods and services tied to specific large projects. However, Russian firms frequently have technical difficulties in the competitions. A request for bids may specify early delivery of items whereas the interested Russian enterprise may have dormant production lines that cannot be quickly re-started. Also, conformance to western technical specifications may be required, but Russian firms may have a legacy of conformance to outdated specifications of the Soviet era. Nevertheless, Russian firms often win the competitions for contracts.[31]

Thus, there are many private sector activities with U.S. government support. But the volume of foreign investment in Russia is small in comparison with investments in other transition countries, such as Hungary, and U.S.-Russian trade is limited.[32] Western analysts repeatedly underscore the lack—not of money to finance proposed projects—but of bankable business plans coming from Russian organizations, alone or in partnership with western firms, as a constraint to more rapid development of alliances involving western partners.[33] The weakness of many business plans is a direct reflection of the gap between the capabilities of Russian institutions to develop technologies and their wherewithal to take technologies to market and sustain that market. This follow-through capability is precisely what lending institutions are searching for to ensure they will be repaid.

Despite the focus of U.S. government policies on facilitating activities of American firms, the private sector view of government efforts is at times negative. For example, the U.S. Chamber of Commerce notes that the expansion of U.S. government programs in Russia may be giving the Russians a lesson in inefficiency and bureaucratic imposition. The Chamber of Commerce has been rightly concerned about U.S. nonproliferation programs that often target the same commercial opportunities as traditional trade and development activities funded by U.S. agencies.[34]

In 1996, the Binational Commission co-chaired by Vice President Gore, recognizing that the step from the laboratory to the market was large and that new thinking was needed in Russia, decided to supplement the traditional routes of cooperation with special attention to commercialization of technology as a generic topic. A special working group was assigned to see how American experience might help improve the process in Russia. Russian government officials pointed to a few successes among small entrepreneurs in finding Russian customers for their products and hoped to replicate this experience many times over.[35]

On the positive side, the Russian Ministry of Science and Technology has concluded that Russian government funds are stimulating technology commercialization on a limited but important scale. The ministry points to progress in linking hundreds of research institutes to the Internet. Also, Russian government showcasing of technologies at international exhibitions has paid off with lucrative contracts. And the ministry's expert advisory services on the intellectual property rights aspects of international deals have helped Russian firms, according to the ministry. Still, in comparison with commercialization efforts in the United States, Russian activities are minuscule.

The U.S. motivation for supporting the work group in finding new ways to improve on Russian processes to commercialize technology was twofold. First, a number of U.S.-financed nonproliferation programs had generated research products that were languishing in Russian laboratories with no buyers in sight. Second, there might be new opportunities for American firms to benefit from improving Russian capabilities of taking products successfully to the marketplace.

The well known impediments to commercialization were quickly cataloged (e.g., high taxes, murky intellectual property rights, shortage of management skills, lack of marketing experience, hesitancy of venture capitalists to provide funds). Agreement was reached to promote an Internet-based Russian-American information system. Case studies of Russian-American business alliances in the high-tech area were undertaken. Training programs for Russian legal specialists in relevant fields were expanded.[36]

In response to the high-level interest in both countries in this topic, several additional U.S. programs have targeted technology commercialization. The U.S. Civilian Research and Development Foundation supports several small projects believed to be on the road to the marketplace with funds for scaling-up activities.[37] (See Appendix F for the foundations's expanded program.) The Eurasia Foundation supports projects to provide advisory services to Russian entrepreneurs searching for a market niche.[38] The Peace Corps has deployed volunteers with business skills in the heavily industrialized region near Samara on the Volga River.[39] And the U.S. Agency for International Development has sponsored small projects to familiarize Russian specialists with American approaches to linking research and development activities with the realities of the marketplace.[40]

The studies of the Binational Commission highlighted an impressive example of an American company contributing to both economic and security objectives. United Technologies Corporation (UTC) has been a pioneer in drawing on the military and nonmilitary strengths of the former Soviet Union. It has built a strong customer base in Russia. The company's Russian workforce now numbers 9,000 UTC employees, with the majority employed by Otis Elevator (a UTC company).[41]

The company first became involved in Russia in the 1970s, simply selling parts and equipment to the Soviet Union. Otis Elevator sold elevators, and Pratt & Whitney (a UTC company) provided commercial engines for western-made aircraft the Soviets had purchased. However, as recently as 1993, UTC sales were limited and that year earned only $8.7 million in revenues.[42]

The company's second-stage strategy combined American and Russian technological capabilities, with a good example being a joint effort with the Ilyushin airplane manufacturer to supply engines for the IL-96M, Russia's intercontinental 350-passenger aircraft. Eventually the Russian government purchased 20 commercial aircraft for $850 million, with a substantial portion of the payments going for the engines. Meanwhile, Carrier (a UTC company) introduced air conditioning units in response to the demand for cool Moscow apartments in the winter—the only way to lower the high temperatures caused by central heating is to either open windows or turn on air conditioners.[43]

UTC's third stage is to manufacture new products in Russia, with an example being heating and air-conditioning systems for Russian and western aircraft. In this case, Hamilton Standard (a UTC company) provided funds, equipment, and manufacturing expertise; while the Russian firm, Nauka Scientific, provided design expertise, an existing facility, and entry into the Russian market. Also under this strategy, Pratt & Whitney has teamed with Perm Motors to improve Perm's PS-90A jet engine and to develop a related industrial gas turbine engine.

U.S. government-initiated programs usually support development of technologies to be followed by searches for markets. In contrast, American companies define the markets and then undertake searches for the best ways to provide relevant technologies. In both cases, Russian workforces that supported the Soviet military-industrial complex—whether located in Perm or in nuclear cities—may play important roles. But the job longevity associated with the private sector approach usually surpasses that resulting from government-designed programs, which are less likely to result in commercial products.

In 1999, the prospects in Russia for many American companies rebounded as demand revived for foreign equipment and services in the energy, telecommunications, mining, and construction sectors. Investment opportunities for import substitution became more attractive in food processing and consumer goods enterprises as the ruble's slippage in the value increased the costs of imports. But American firms considering investment have considerable difficulty judging the market. Russians themselves are uncertain as to whether to cling to national pride in opting for Russian products or to concede that the quality of domestic products often lags behind the quality of foreign imports.[44]

Whither Cooperation?

The importance of continued support for U.S. programs to help downsize the Russian military complex, to shore up containment of dangerous materials and technologies within Russia, and to encourage redirection of weapon scientists and engineers to peaceful pursuits should be obvious for Congress and the American public. When the programs encounter difficulties, they should be fixed, not abandoned. The near-term costs of heading off international security crises in distant parts of the world, crises that could have Russian roots, dwarf the longer-term costs of responding to such crises. We should be prepared to stay the course with these programs for at least a decade. Longer if necessary. If the United States does not lead in this nonproliferation effort, no one will.

Very few cooperative programs are designed explicitly to strengthen Russian capabilities to commercialize promising technologies. For the nonproliferation programs, bringing products to the marketplace is an important secondary objective, however. If former weaponeers are able to profit from their civilian achievements, they should no longer need support from nonproliferation programs.

Also, many projects of American firms depend on the commercial success of Russian-made products. But, the American companies will retain interest in an activity only as long as it derives a profit. As has been shown, in the aerospace arena, with the appropriate support from the two governments, some technology programs can prosper, even with relatively long lead times from inception to market profitability.

On a broader basis, U.S. policy has been designed to support the evolution of a healthy Russian economy, including an appropriate business and regulatory environment. Programs to that end should enhance the likelihood for commercial success of innovative technologies. Sustaining and enhancing Russian technological capabilities, however, have not been at the center of cooperative programs.

The new focus on technology commercialization at the Binational Commission's level is important. The emphasis should be on current and future marketplace demands and not simply on the use of available technology. The integration of consumer interests and research and development planning must begin early and continue until sales patterns are established. Such a long-term approach to innovating for profit may be beyond the scope of bilateral projects, but officials of the two governments should repeatedly emphasize this important point.[45]

That said, the two governments should articulate an overarching strategy for bilateral technology cooperation, taking into account that many relevant programs currently are under way. Such a strategy could help sharpen the focus of individual projects, even if their primary purpose is not commercial success for Russian participants. Of course, when a U.S. government agency identifies an opportunity to enhance its mission by involvement in a program in Russia, it will shape the program to meet its own needs. When a U.S. company sees a chance to turn a profit—either long-term or short-term—it will continue to make the necessary investment to maximize the likelihood of commercial success, drawing on U.S. government programs for both financial and political support when appropriate. At the same time, greater U.S. sensitivity from both government agencies and private sectors to how important Russia's innovation capacity is to its future is in the interest of both countries and should be encouraged.

Now that thousands of U.S.-Russia projects have been undertaken, a few lessons learned should be considered in future programs.

1. *Give priority to the details of implementation.* Many aspects of projects cannot be anticipated until they are in progress, and skill in handling details is no less important than skill in developing an overall approach. For short-term projects involving modest sums of money, official endorsements by both governments are usually not worth the effort if they can be avoided. But, for lengthier efforts, such approvals are valuable and often essential, even if they delay implementation for many months or even years. Also, while trust between Russian and American colleagues has increased in recent years, a signed document is more reliable than a handshake in confirming mutual agreements.

2. *Train managers for specific jobs.* Management training for Russians should be tailored to specific responsibilities the trainee will assume upon a course's conclusion. General management training for employment in mythical positions is seldom cost-effective. American managers also need training. Many fall short in carrying out their responsibilities in Russia simply because they do not take time to consider how Russian management practices and American approaches can be most usefully combined.

3. *Don't ignore the Russian infrastructure.* U.S. organizations balk at paying for heat, electricity, or equipment upgrades in Russian laboratories. They should therefore anticipate disruptions resulting from breakdowns in the research infrastructure. New joint efforts are needed to upgrade the infrastructure for projects of particular interest to both sides.

4. *Rely on Russian ability to develop proposals.* If given general guidelines and financial incentives, Russian specialists can develop well-framed proposals that are more appropriate to the Russian setting than those that can be developed by consultants or scientists from abroad. American participants should, of course, carefully review proposals and be sure there is full agreement on the details finally adopted.

An overarching principle is to have realistic expectations. For example, there are only a limited number of fields, such as space propulsion, nuclear transmutation, machine tools, and light-weight alloys, in which Russian technology is superior to technology in other countries.[46] Of course, superior technology is not needed for every project, but often it is.

Strategic alliances based on the overall business of the U.S. company, and particularly global marketing considerations, are often preferred to efforts linked exclusively to Russia. For example, joint efforts may be directed at producing components or subsystems in Russia that can be incorporated into existing products, rather than to developing new products. Also, an emphasis on software rather than hardware may be less expensive and less risky with faster entry to the international market.[47]

United States agencies and companies operating in Russia know that crime and corruption are omnipresent. Also, the legal and commercial infrastructure is incomplete—a reliable commercial banking system, appropriate rights of minority shareholders, and ownership of land and property, for example, are works in progress. Uncertainties are rampant in all of these areas.[48]

What *is* certain, however, is that U.S. departments and agencies, private firms, and research laboratories now have in place an unprecedented network of organizational and administrative arrangements for cooperation involving large cadres of specialists in both countries. There is unfinished business in Russia from both the public and private vantage points. Fine tuning of U.S. policies and programs is needed, but it would make no sense to reduce engagement with Russia in the research and development and commercial arenas.

Notes

1. *Nonproliferation, Concerns with DOE's Efforts To Reduce the Risks Posed by Russia's Unemployed Weapons Scientists* (Washington, D.C.: U.S. General Accounting Office, GAO/RCED-99-54, February 1999).

2. "U.S. Secretary Daley Witnesses Signings Between U.S. and Russian Companies," *Fact Sheet,* Department of Commerce, March 11, 1998.

3. Discussion in Washington D.C. with DOE officials, November 1998.

4. Ibid., January 1999.

5. Discussions in Moscow and St. Petersburg with Russian recipients of U.S. government grants, October and November 1998.

6. "Initiatives for Proliferation Prevention Fact Sheet," distributed by DOE, May 1999.

7.   Discussions in Washington, D.C., with DOE specialists, November 1998 and April 1999. For a review of this program see National Research Council, *Protecting Nuclear Weapons Materials in Russia* (Washington, D.C.: National Academy Press, 1999).

8.   Discussion in Moscow with DOE representatives, October 1998.

9.   Briefing in Washington, D.C., by DOE representatives, April 1998.

10.   Personal communication with Russian project leader for NCI program in one of the target cities, October 1999.

11.   For a more comprehensive discussion of the NCI program see Sig Heckert, Mark Mullen, and Jim Toevs, "Nuclear Cities Initiative," unpublished manuscript, Los Alamos National Laboratory, March 30, 1998.

12.   "Frequently Asked Questions, Nuclear Cities Initiative," *Fact Sheet,* DOE, October 1998.

13.   For background on the NCI program see Briefing at Public Meeting at DOE Headquarters, Washington, D.C., November 1998.

14.   Ibid.

15.   Remarks by General Thomas Kuenning, Monterey Institute for International Studies, Monterey, California, December 1999.

16.   Ibid.

17.   Discussion with U.S. expert on Russian chemical destruction techniques, May 1998; Kuenning, Remarks.

18.   Glenn E. Schweitzer, *Experiments in Cooperation, Assessing U.S. Programs in Science and Technology,* The Twentieth Century Fund, New York, 1997, p. 31.

19.   *Ibid.,* pp. 30-31.

20.   "Will Russia's Role in Space Project Alpha Become Eclipsed?" *The Russia Journal,* April 19-25, 1999, p. 11.

21.   *Ibid.*

22.   For an expanded discussion of the activities of key Russian firms in joint aerospace programs see David Bernstein, *Commercialization of Russian Technology in Cooperation with American Companies,* Center for International Security and Cooperation, Stanford University, June 1999.

23.   "Lockheed Martin To Buy 101 RD-180 Rocket Engines from Russian-American Joint Venture," Lockheed Martin Press Release, June 17, 1997.

24.   Sujato Rao, "Rocket Exports," *Russia Review,* August 25, 1997, p. 27.

25.   *Ibid.*

26.   *U.S. Government Assistance to and Cooperative Activities with the New Independent States of the Former Soviet Union, FY 1998 Annual Report,* January 1999, available from the U.S. Department of State, p. 101; Discussion in Richmond, Virginia, with DEF official, June 1999.

27.   Olga Ananina, "U.S.-Russia Investment Fund/Delta Capital Management," *BISNIS,* U.S. Foreiegn Commercial Service, Moscow, March 2000.

28.   "Commercial Overview of Russia," *BISNIS*, U.S. Department of Commerce, June 1998.

29.   "TDA in the New Independent States," U.S. Trade and Development Administration, June 1998.

30.   "OPIC Highlights, New Opportunities and a Growing OPIC Portfolio in Europe and the NIS," Overseas Private Investment Corporation, June 1998.

31.   Interviews in Moscow with deputy directors of two Russian enterprises, April 1997.

32.   For a review of U.S. government-funded activities see U.S. Department of State, *U.S. Government Assistance* .

33.   Discussions in Washington, D.C., with representatives of western financial institutions interested in financing projects in Russia, World Bank symposium, March 1997.

34.   "U.S. Commercial Relations with the Russian Federation," U.S. Chamber of Commerce, originally issued 1996 but re-issued May 1999, p. 1; Discussion in Washington, D.C., with representatives of the U.S. Chamber of Commerce, May 1999.

35.   "Report of the Meeting of the U.S.-Russian Technology Commercialization Working Group," *Fact Sheet,* U.S. Department of Commerce, distributed in October 1997.

36.   "Russian Technology Commercialization," *Fact Sheet,* U.S. Department of Commerce, distributed in March 1998; "Russian Ministry of Science and Technology Activities in Technology Commercialization," *Fact Sheet,* distributed in April 1998; "Joint Statement on Priority Directions of American-Russian Cooperation in the Area of Technology Commercialization," *Gore-Chernomyrdin Commission X, March 10-11, 1998,* Washington, D.C., press release from the Office of the Vice President of the United States.

37.   "CRDF Support of Research and Development Collaborations Involving Industry," *Fact Sheet,* U.S. Civilian Research and Development Foundation, Arlington, Virginia, released October 1998.

38.   Discussions in Washington, D.C., with Eurasia Foundation specialists, February 1999.

39.   Discussions in Moscow with U.S. Embassy officials, October 1998.

40.   Discussions in Moscow with USAID officials, October 1998.

41.   Ruth R. Harkin, Vice President of United Technologies Corporation, "Being There First," symposium presentation manuscript, U.S.-Russia Business Council, April 1, 1998.

42.   Ibid.

43.   Ibid.

44.   "Doing Business in Russia—An Overview, U.S. and Foreign Commercial Service," U.S. Embassy Moscow, October 1, 1999.

45.   National Research Council/Russian Academy of Sciences, *Technology Commerciailization, Russian Challenges, American Lessons* (Washington, D.C.: National Academy Press, 1998). See the presentation by A. MacLachlan, "An Industrial Perspective on Technology Commercialization in the 1990s and Beyond," pp. 24-32.

46.   David Bernstein (editor), "Executive Summary," *Cooperative Business Ventures between U.S. Companies and Russian Defense Enterprises,* Center for International Security and Arms Control, Stanford University, April 1997, p. x.

47.   *Ibid.*

48.   See for example Eugene K. Lawson, *Russia Business Watch,* U.S.-Russia Business Council, Washington, D.C., Summer 1999, p. 3.

10 The Revival of Russian Technology

The failure of the IMF, the U.S. Department of Treasury, the news media, and Russia experts to foresee the current economic crisis should chasten anyone bold enough to hazard a prediction as to the future of Russia.

The International Herald Tribune, 1999

The most promising firms are small, high-tech companies with products successful in Russia, potentially successful in world markets, and with access to capital and practical management training.

U.S. Embassy, Moscow, 1998

Why waste time with problems in Russia where the likelihood of indigenous technology benefiting the United States or contributing to economic development is low? Globalization of modern technology is taking place in Europe and Asia, and that is where we should concentrate attention. Even other 'transition' countries, such as Poland and Hungary, offer more promise than Russia as technology partners for the United States.

This was the view of a panel of "experts" on international cooperation in science and technology assembled in Washington, D.C., in the spring of 1999.[1]

The rejoinder is simple and persuasive. Russia is too important to ignore. The country is a vast repository of natural resources. It has more trained scientists and engineers than any other country in the world, and they have fulfilled some of the most difficult tasks to confront any nation. They conquered barren wastelands and harsh arctic regions, and they overcame logistical nightmares in building a modern industrial nation that covers one-seventh of the Earth's surface.

On the ominous side, Russia is home to 20,000 nuclear-laden missiles and bombs at the ready and to hundreds of tons of weapons-grade plutonium and uranium located in storage areas throughout the country. As the Chernobyl accident demonstrated, the Soviet-rooted environmental side effects of Russia's industrial growth are of concern to the entire world. In the absence of adequate health care programs, tuberculosis, hepatitis, AIDS, and other diseases threaten to move toward Russia's borders and beyond. Finally, international criminal groups with roots in Russia and access to modern armaments—from plastic explosives to rocket launchers—must be held in check around the world.

Despite Russia's long history of technical achievements, technology development is now in the doldrums. But the country has an uncanny knack of surprising even the best experts. We cannot rule out the likes of the technology pioneers who designed the first commercial nuclear power plant, launched the first space satellite, invented the hydrofoil, developed laser eye surgery, and built machine tools purchased by countries around the world. The experts responsible for these accomplishments have passed on much of their prowess to younger generations of specialists, who are still in place despite the brain drain. Nor can we forget the efforts of Stalin, Khrushchev, and their successors to use nuclear, space, and other advanced technologies in ways that changed the course of history for the entire world.

Many Russians are visionaries. Some Russian schemes, such as those mentioned above, seemed unrealistic at one time. But they have proved achievable. Now we ask whether the highly talented team of electrical engineers who, in near isolation from world science and technology, designed and built the early Soviet computers can really fulfill their ambition to produce a microchip that will compete with Intel's most advanced product?[2] Will efforts of the Ministry of Atomic Energy to privatize nuclear power plants and attract foreign investors lead to a new generation of large, fail-safe reactors that are affordable, efficient, and secure?[3] Can a new gas pipeline follow the deep contours of the Black Sea's bed and dramatically increase Russia's export earnings without posing environmental problems?[4] And, at the local level, will the plans of city administrators to ensure that Moscow has the most modern crematorium with the latest computer-driven technologies save enough energy to offset the costs?[5]

That said, it is far better for the United States to have its laboratories and companies involved in cooperative programs aimed at the revival of Russian technology for peaceful pursuits, however slow, than to be on the sidelines constantly guessing whether developments dangerous for Russia or for the world are just around the corner. Besides, the potential benefit of an improved Russian economy—with a huge untapped market—is in itself worth some degree of effort. We not only need to understand technological advances in this large country, but we should draw on widely respected American know-how in influencing transformations within the Russian industrial complex. Such transformations are taking place every day with immediate security and longer term economic implications for the United States.

If the politicians who control purse strings in Washington don't recognize the importance of aggressive U.S. engagement to influence Russian technological developments, they should reflect on the predictions of the U.S. National Intelligence Council about Russia's ambitious military research program. In the near term this particular program will upgrade a range of conventional weapons systems, and it will turn out new generations of sophisticated armaments by 2010. In general, arms exports will continue to be one of Russia's financial mainstays. Most worrisome, upgrading missile and nuclear capabilities, to be more accurate and more destructive, will continue apace.[6] The United States cannot afford to be only a spectator to these developments.

At the same time, foreigners will not play decisive roles in shaping the future of Russian technologies that are so dependent on the economic environment. Historians already underscore that the United States missed a one-time window of opportunity to influence Russian economic developments in a positive and sustained direction in the early 1990s. Russia reformers who put their faith in American textbook models are now bearing the brunt of the responsibility for Russia's economic mess—a 73 percent inflation rate in 1998, a 40 percent drop in gross domestic product from 1991 through 1998, and a loss of real money income of 40 percent from 1991 through 1998.[7] Against this perception that foreign advisers share much of the blame for the prolonged "transition depression," policies will only be effective if the Russian government and the public have a sense of ownership of the ideas and the approaches—a conviction that the policies are conceived in Russia for the benefit of Russians.

Foreign investments and collaborative programs promoted by western organizations can be important, particularly in the short term. However, unless these efforts are also viewed in Moscow, St. Petersburg, Novosibirsk, Vladivostok, and elsewhere as programs that have been shaped by Russians and that support Russian objectives, in the long term they will not be significant. They may even collapse in the short term.

Russian politicians regret the government's mistakes in turning over to western bargain hunters much technology that, in their view, should have secured the nation's economic future. They are frustrated that financially there was little choice, but they are still determined in their efforts to recover their lost leadership in the high-tech arena. In the words of the president of the Russian Academy of Sciences, echoing a doctrine that has repeatedly paid off in the United States and other western countries, "Technology must again become our engine of economic growth."[8]

Some western economists dismiss such statements as unrealistic bravado, arguing that Russia should forget about re-emerging as an industrial power. Russia should exploit its comparative advantage in raw materials while turning its highly skilled work force into a labor pool for foreign entrepreneurs. But this will not be the Russian way. Such a view is rightly considered in Moscow as western arrogance, and Russian leaders will not accept the notion that the country should become a repository of cheap labor while other countries derive the profits from processing energy, mineral, and timber resources extracted in Russia. They want Russia to be involved in many aspects of the value chain, from extraction to sales of finished products.

Thus, however bleak the economic horizon, leaders in Moscow and elsewhere will cling to their goal of Russia again becoming an industrial powerhouse, as the Russian people continue to believe in themselves, however bleak the economic horizon. One 1999 poll showed that 72 percent of the population wants foreign debts to be repaid using Russia's scarce internal resources rather than seeking more loans to reschedule the debts. To these responders, money is of course important, but national pride also means a lot.[9]

Despite the hopes of Russian leaders for stability and better times, shifting political and economic policies will continue to shackle technological progress. Innovation requires a long-term commitment. And, the more the uncertainty, the less the interest of potential investors. Even if there are consistent financial ground rules, industrial technologies that can become competitive on a large scale will only appear if the government jump starts the innovation process that extends from invention through modern manufacturing to marketing.

During the transition period, both greater protection of the Russian market from foreign competition and government assumption of some of the risk of innovation are needed. These measures can encourage skeptical domestic industries and individual consumers to turn to Russian products in their efforts to make ends meet. Then manufacturers will have to gradually show them that "made-in-Russia" guarantees both on-time delivery and acceptable quality.

Of course, corruption throughout the government and a decline in the health of Russian youth could be showstoppers to progress on any front. Researchers may devise better surveillance systems for monitoring bank transactions and develop more nutritious food offerings, but they will hardly solve the critical problems of rampant dishonesty and dietary deprivation aggravated by the rise of poverty. Only by joining forces with other forward-looking citizens and legislators who are appalled by corruption, the neglect of children, and other social ills will they be able to help force government into taking more responsible action on these crucial issues.

Western-sponsored programs will remain of considerable importance, especially in the national security arena. But international cooperation and foreign investment on the limited scale of the past will have but a minor impact on the Russian economy. More ambitious efforts, commensurate with the importance of Russia to the world and carefully designed to protect financial investments, can help move the country in directions that are truly rewarding for the Russian people and for other countries as well.

Political and Economic Challenges

Several trends and underlying currents in Russia have pivotal impacts on the future prospects for technological development.[10] For the first time in modern Russian history, there is no political ideology guiding the country. No one knows what is politically correct. Most adopt the philosophy, "We will do what we want if we can get away with it." Central planning, market economy, and regional autonomy have all become nebulous phrases interpreted in many different ways. Even the meaning of democracy lacks a consensus, and new political parties stir little interest outside Moscow. Intellectual disarray is the order of the day—a disarray that hardly provides confidence that long-term investments in research and technology will be secure.

Thus, the continuing turmoil over ownership of technological assets—past, present, and future—of the state is to be expected. Soviet-era facilities have been transferred to private parties in favored positions. They have taken them legally or illegally and are prepared to protect their acquisitions with guns and personal connections that—in the absence of a worthy legal framework—are more important than constitutional arguments.

Having seen this diversion of state assets, a large portion of the Russian population believe they too have a right to share in Soviet assets, even if this means taking property now belonging to the Russian state. Stealing from the state has never been considered real theft. During the Soviet era, the population felt like soldiers in an all-encompassing army; and in armies the world over, borrowing items from supply lockers or motor pools is seldom considered a real crime.

This attitude has fostered economic crime that is so pervasive it is more or less accepted as a way of life. Supported by a growing legion of participants in unseemly activities and genuinely abhorred by only a few of the particularly aggrieved, crime is considered a great nuisance but an inevitable daily occurrence. As if Russia's homegrown thieves were not enough, a worldwide criminal network has positioned itself to share in the spoils of a vulnerable Russian state. Russia's once-sealed borders have been thrown open, with controls on imports and exports of goods widely circumvented. Consequently, business transactions must include the costs of placating criminals and must be absorbed on company balance sheets—at least in the short term—before resources can be freed up for exploring new ways to make better technology-based products.

Obviously, for the foreseeable future the Russian economy will not mirror economies that function well in the West, and there is not even a pretense of equal opportunity for all investors. To be sure, the country has been cleansed of a communist-brand economy. The Russian version of capitalists, however, represents central control of a new type. They will resist by force, if necessary, the threat of losing their cash cows.

The cost of transition from communist to capitalist economics has been tremendous in terms of capital flight, evasion of taxes, lost production capabilities, and human suffering and disillusionment. In the end, misguided efforts have led to a total failure to achieve the widely sought objective of economic prosperity for the general population. Thus, policies are desperately needed that have economic prosperity as their primary objective. This means an improved standard of living, not just for a handful but throughout the country.

A market economy that provides this improved standard of living should continue to be the ultimate goal. If Russia is to be a significant participant in the global economy—and it should be—it must play by the international rules calling for economies driven by market forces. As demonstrated during the past decade, however, progress along the road to free markets will continue to be sporadic. With that reality in mind, the Russian government should make a stronger effort to ensure that social benefits flow to those who are not yet part of the new economy as well as those who don't need safety nets. Obviously, overall progress will be at a much slower pace than hoped for in the past.[11]

Indeed, an even more severe economic crisis may be waiting in the wings. A dark cloud hangs over near-term economic forecasts. Some experts warn of hyperinflation just over the horizon accompanied by a deepening recession that may cause the collapse of the government installed in 2000. If such a prediction comes true, they see a replacement regime that takes a firmer hold on the economy to restore disintegrating law and order, while raising the specter of violent confrontations and a return to repression.[12]

Another, more likely scenario in view of recent history is a slow but steady "Russification" of the concepts of a market economy, with an emphasis on avoiding violence. This new economy will also require more effective measures for law and order and more central control of economic assets and economic transactions. While there undoubtedly will continue to be suspicious incidents of instant wealth and expanding pockets of abject poverty, somehow the country will muddle through without resort to a political revolution.

Central to the functioning of a market economy is the flow of money among government agencies, enterprises, institutes, and individual consumers, with commercial banks being critical nodes of the system. After the Russian banking scandals of 1998 and 1999, barter and counter trade seemed more attractive; but they can take firms only so far. Serious efforts toward technological revival require safe and efficient mechanisms for money transactions. Western banks with expanded charters for operating in Russia offer the only way to restore confidence during the next few years among the large number of potential customers of the banking system who should be key participants in economic revitalization (see Box 10.1).

At the same time, the Russian government harbors a fundamental dislike for western banks operating in Russia, perhaps because so many officials have cozy relationships with Russian banks of their own choosing. Nevertheless, creditors in Russia and abroad should press hard for greater authority for the western banks. If given such authority, responsible financial institutions will likely expand their operations.

Returning to the clarion call of Russian leaders for technology to spur economic growth, the new market economy should be technology-friendly. Governmental measures must compensate for the handicaps of being located in Russia: the geography of Russia, the country's management traditions, and the experiences of the workforce reinforce separation of research, production, and marketing.

Box 10-1
Offshore Banks with Licenses to Operate in Russia

Bank of Austria (Austria)
ABN Amro (Netherlands)
Chase Manhattan (U.S.)
Citibank (U.S.)
Credit Lyonnais (France)
CS First Boston (U.S.)
Dialog Bank (U.S.)
Dresdner Bank (Germany)
ING Barings (Netherlands)
Republic National Bank of New York (U.S.)

SOURCE: *Commercial Overview of Russia, BISNIS.* U.S. Department of Commerce-International Trade Administration, September 1999, p. 22.

The inadequacies of the physical, legal, and financial infrastructures to support technology development also contrast sharply with the favorable business environments in other countries where technology has thrived. Without new policies and programs, few Russian organizations will be able to cross the bar and succeed in the global marketplace. If Russian organizations do not become players in the global economy, they will have an increasingly difficult time competing for sales of goods and services in Russia.

Thus, if the economy is to grow technology must be nourished. While western economists cringe at the words "protectionism," "subsidies," and "monopolies," these concepts are not necessarily bad if applied in moderation. If carefully limited, they can be crucial for technological revival. Defining and enforcing the limitations is the key and will require months of debate, years of false starts, and a decade or more of experience until a satisfactory approach is in place.

Implementing a Realistic Technology Policy

The Russian Ministry of Science and Technology often has analyzed the problems confronting Russian economic growth based on modern technologies. The ministry, with roots that date back four decades, has an understandable bias toward central control of technological assets. Also, the ministry emphasizes the supply side of technology rather than market demand. As a result, ministry leadership pushes the programs of the government institutes under its patronage that generate technologies. Nevertheless, ministry analysts do highlight key problems to be resolved and offer sensible suggestions for Russia to eventually regain its position as a prosperous industrial nation.[13]

In February 1998, the ministry developed an important framework for a technology policy. Surprisingly, other concerned ministries concurred with the proposed approach. These ministries are often reluctant to endorse policies developed by other organizations, particularly policies that overlap their responsibilities. The ministry's principles are bold and, if supported with modest financial resources, could be far-reaching.

- Higher tariffs should be levied during the transition period on imports of advanced technology items in order to give Russian firms a better chance at establishing themselves on the domestic market.
- Regional governments should increase their support for programs within the science cities and should assume greater responsibility for better telecommunication networks within the regions. Federal research institutes in the science cities and elsewhere that are oriented toward local problems should be transferred to the jurisdiction of the regional governments.
- Inventors should have greater shares of ownership in their discoveries and better protection of their rights. Also, the ownership of equipment made available by the government to research institutions should not be dictated by the government but should be decided by mutual agreement.
- Important research and development projects with potential commercial applications should, when necessary, be financed by the

government as well as by funding provided by the private sector. Government support for such research and development projects should be transparent to all stakeholders in the future of Russia.

• The government should provide repayment guarantees for bank loans to entrepreneurs for commercializing potentially important inventions and, when appropriate, should cover the interest charges for such loans. But the government should not directly finance commercialization activities. To further lower the risks inherent in innovation, the government should guarantee that well-conceived high-tech investments by entrepreneurs will be at least partially recovered even in cases of failures to penetrate the market. [14]

Some of these ideas have been around for a long time. However, the formal embrace of this sensible suite of proposals by the government is significant. If put into practice, the long-term prospects for technology commercialization would be much brighter than at present.

But what will be the source of the government funds for a significant program of cost-sharing of research and development and of covering costs of failed modernization and innovation efforts, as proposed in the last two principles of the ministry? The Ministry of Finance has so many demands on so few resources that it is an unlikely source. The private sector, both in Russia and abroad, might consider cost-sharing on specific projects but surely will not provide funds to cover the government's part of the bargain. Existing foreign assistance programs are already so committed to specific target areas that reorienting their efforts seems a remote possibility. Thus, the only realistic source is a new program of funds provided by foreign governments and international agencies, a program that is free of historical baggage and can be shaped with a view to the future not to the past.

For almost a decade, some experts in the West have called for a Marshall Plan for Russia.[15] At several summits of the heads of state of western countries, it seemed that assistance packages in the tens of billions of dollars might be forthcoming and constitute a new version of the highly successful program to revitalize Europe after World War II. However, most of the billions of dollars that became available soon came under the control of the IMF and other international financial organizations most concerned with promoting their version of economic reform while keeping the Russian debt at a manageable level.

At the same time, proposals for a Russian Marshall Plan always encounter a series of valid concerns from western Russia experts. The mafia would steal the money. The macro-economic framework is not in place to encourage the private sector to sustain the program when funding runs out. Russian management of large programs is always inept. There would not be many bankable business plans to consider.

In short, a Russian Marshall Plan is not realistic nor is it appropriate. The current situation in Russia is different from the military, political, and economic situation in western Europe 50 years ago. Still, the concept of a program to help jump start self-sustaining industries that was important for Europe then is important for Russia now.

Given financial and political realities, rebuilding Russian industries in a short period of time is not feasible. Rather, the dual focus for financing a technological revival suggested by the Ministry of Science and Technology—namely, government-industry funding of research and development projects and government assumption of some of the risks of innovation—is sound, recognizing that the payoff will be long term. But it also will take years for Russia to have an economic and legal framework in place for any program to have large-scale and sustained impact.

Thus, the objective of the first few years should not be to revitalize the economy on a major scale. The objective should be to put in place a few technology modules that successfully penetrate the marketplace and that could be replicated month-by-month and year-by-year. In parallel, the improvements needed in the banking sector, in tax collection, and in other critical areas that have been identified throughout this book must go forward.

As to deeply embedded western concerns over not wasting money in Russia, funds from abroad could be protected if the management of all financial transactions of say $1,000 or more were vested in a western accounting organization with strong integrity. With regard to skepticism over development of solid proposals, when provided financial incentives Russian specialists can develop the essential elements of proper proposals for research and development grants and business plans for commercial loans. As seen in smaller western-financed programs, they would rise quickly on the learning curve and soon convince skeptics that Russians can respond to market requirements.

Small Russian companies or semi-autonomous units within or outside the walls of enterprises and institutes should serve as research centers or profit centers for individual projects. They are rewarded for each success; and when failures mount, they are abandoned. Realistic rent and energy payments by the centers should be included in proposals, despite Russian tendencies to undervalue these services. Also, the proposals should reflect the need to pay for protective services against the mafia. But approved proposals should not call for funds to be spread over entire institutes or entire enterprises simply to keep workers employed. To this end, overhead rates should not exceed 50 percent, in contrast to the 500 percent that is often charged in order to keep oversized institutions alive.

How large should the projects be? What would be the criteria for selection? Who should decide which projects are supported? Russian and western organizations already have accumulated considerable experience in all of these areas during their activities in Russia.

First, with regard to research and development matching grants, the projects might range from $100,000 to $3,000,000 over periods of 1-3 years. One-quarter to one-half of the funds would be provided by the Russian company that intends to use the research results in a new or improved product or process. A provision could call for repayment of a grant if the research and development project leads to a commercial success.

Turning to loan guarantees for projects that introduce innovations into the marketplace and to the scheme for partial compensation of unsuccessful entrepreneurs for taking risks in innovation, the projects might range from $1,000,000 to $20,000,000. These projects would target major innovative activities requiring considerable start-up costs. Some projects might be scaled down to service small entrepreneurs, although there are already small programs in place for this purpose (as shown in Chapter 2).

The primary criterion for selecting research and development projects for funding should be long-term marketability potential. For

projects to introduce new industrial and consumer products and manufacturing processes, the criterion should also be marketability, but in
the short term. The cost-sharing between researchers and industry and
the relations between manufacturers and potential customers are important marketing catalysts.

The selection of projects must be Russian decisions that are documented in a clear way for the general public. For large projects, there
should be project assessments prepared by reputable western consulting firms. The review and selection procedure should inspire confidence in the program.

What would be the cost of such a program? The initial financial
commitment by foreign governments and international agencies should
be on the order of $100 million dollars per year climbing in five years
to an annual level of about one billion dollars. This level is large enough
to command attention and support at the highest levels of government
but not so large as to exceed the absorptive capacity of Russia nor the
limits of western financing capabilities.

The amount seems trivial in comparison with the trillions of dollars of investment required to modernize all Russian industries. But all
industries should not be modernized. Those areas where Russia has
either a comparative cost or quality advantage or at least near-parity
with the West probably deserve support. Also, in some areas lower-
quality, lower-cost goods might be appropriate for the Russian market
during the transition period.

A little money can go a long way if it targets technologies with
multiplier effects and is carefully guarded en route to its intended purpose. Perhaps 50 percent of the funds would be returned to the government in loan payments that could then be recycled. The other 50
percent may be eventually lost on projects that did not meet expectations. This would be an excellent record given all the risks in any program of innovating for profit.

The proposal, of course, conforms to the principles enunciated by
the Ministry of Science and Technology; and as long as it is funded by
the West the likelihood that the Russian government would embrace
the approach is high. Of special importance to the Russian government, the new resources would be focused on Russian institutes and

companies. The companies could involve western partners as suppliers, subcontractors, or marketing consultants if they so desired. But the use of all funds would be the responsibility of Russian research and profit centers operating under the watchful eye of the western accounting firm hired to monitor the flow of money.

A related initiative should be the adoption by the central government and by regional and local governments of a "Buy Russia" policy directly challenging the incestuous relationships that have developed between government procurement officials and foreign suppliers of goods and services. This policy would require that for any project involving Russian government funds—federal, regional, or local—a Russian company would receive the contract. Only if a Russian company were not available to produce acceptable goods or services in a timely manner could procurement from a foreign source be undertaken.

In time, such a policy would be a major change in the current way of doing business in Russia. It could provide a stimulus to the revival of technology-based production focused on the needs of specific Russian customers. In the near term, there would be fierce resistance by both politicians and bureaucrats to giving up their foreign connections. For example, during a trip to Russia in 1999, I encountered three German businessmen. One was selling computer software to the news agency, TASS. Another installed water pumps for the Moscow city government. The third had a contract for electrical connectors needed by Moscow housing authorities. The businessmen each readily acknowledged that Russian firms could easily underbid them with goods of comparable quality, but such firms could not offer business trips to the Bavarian Alps. Thus, establishing and enforcing ground rules concerning the definition of "local availability" of goods and services would not be easy, but would be crucial to having a useful program.

There are not many shortcuts to reviving Russia's slumping industry—an industry with much outdated equipment, with few reliable suppliers, and with even fewer dependable customers. Most enterprises and institutes are saddled with long-standing debts and oversized workforces. Still, Russians are skilled at finding technical solutions to problems, and they should be at home with new technological efforts. Such efforts, if targeting customers with access to funding, may be the only hope of Russian organizations moving from the red to the black column during the working days of much of the current labor force.

Adding to Russia's difficulties, the products resulting from some of the country's greatest technological strengths are on the security warning lists of the international community. Electronic control devices, high-strength plastics, chemical mixtures, and nuclear materials are becoming ever more entwined with both military applications and economic development around the world, and the uncertainties between appropriate and inappropriate markets are increasing. International cooperation both at the governmental level and through private sector alliances can help illuminate these growing ambiguities. Such clarification is an important first step in heading off diplomatic clashes that further complicate technology development in Russia.

Showstoppers: Increasing Corruption and Declining Health

Few Russians believe that corruption will ever disappear from the scene. "From time immemorial people have been bribing." "Corruption is in our nature. It's in us, in our mentality." "The rich do it because they always want more." "It's so big that it may lead to an uproar one day." These were interview responses of Russians to the question, "Is it possible to fight corruption?"[16] Foreigners are well aware that personal profit is a primary interest of policemen who flag down cars for minor traffic transgressions and bureaucrats who issue permits of all types. Table 10.1 estimates payoffs from certain types of services in Russia.

Thus, corruption takes many forms. In 1997, the Russian criminal code for the first time called for the punishment of bribery involving commercial organizations. Many other proposals to combat corruption have been offered by Russian and foreign experts. Of critical importance is a commitment, including action agendas, at the highest levels of government to fighting corruption; and the public must be convinced that the leaders of the nation are not diverting state resources to their own overseas bank accounts. High visibility prosecu-

TABLE 10.1 Buying Favors in Russia, 1996

Type of "Favor"	Cost of "Favor" (in dollars)	% of Firms that Participate
Enterprise registration	288	44
Visit by fire/health inspector	67	23
Visit by tax inspector	250	21
Phone line installation	1071	100
Lease for state-owned space (monthly fee per square foot)	26	39
Export registration	643	43
Import registration	133	50

SOURCE: Keith Henderson, informal presentation, U.S. Agency for International Development, March 1999.

tions of corrupt officials, particularly those in high positions, are important to show that the commitment is real.[17]

Other steps can be taken. Of central concern is the handling of government funds, and an emphasis on transparency of public transactions is the key. Appointing "inspectors general" within government agencies has been suggested, although they would certainly need bodyguards when they began investigating details of financial scandals. More aggressive reporting of corruption by the media and establishing nongovernmental anti-corruption advocacy groups have also been proposed.[18]

Westerners should become more sensitive to the boundary between personal favors, legitimate business dealings, and corruption. For example, to many Russians trips abroad are highly cherished, whatever the sponsors' motivation. If the trips are for Russian children searching for foreign scholarships, the sponsors will be long remembered and usually rewarded back in Russia. Western governments and foreign businesses seldom consider international visits that grease the skids for political dialogues or business deals in Russia as contributing to corruption. I am not suggesting cutting back on appropriate cultural exchanges or normal business dealings. I am suggesting greater diligence by western firms and governments in examining the real reasons for proposed trips.

Checking corruption is crucial if technology is to make a significant impact on the Russian economy. The amount of money that must be funneled to technological development is substantial. When financial stakes become large, corruption becomes the order of the day. What can the researchers do to help? The ethos of science—transparency, objectivity, merit-based review, competition among all comers—is in principle an antidote to corruption. Researchers should, by example, help spread these traits throughout society. While the impact will be indirect and slow in coming, it can nevertheless complement the more direct and more immediate action by the government to clean up its act.

A second barrier to developing a strong Russian economy is the declining health of the population, and particularly the endangered health of Russian youth. Recent reports suggest that 75 percent of pregnant women have a serious pathology during pregnancy due to malnutrition, endometriosis, or sexually transmitted diseases. The implications for newborns are ominous. Malnutrition during early childhood may also account for reduced height and weight as children develop.[19]

Persuasive evidence of the decline in the health of Russian youth is provided by the Russian army, which must reject large numbers of potential recruits due to health problems. Whether the disqualified recruits are mentally disturbed, infected with syphilis, or have smaller than normal chest measurements, the poor condition of the labor pool is causing alarm throughout the country. When the increased use of tobacco, alcohol, and narcotics are taken into account, the outlook for future generations is not bright.

The health of Russian children speaks directly to the future health of Russia. Regardless of the technologies that may be uncovered in the next decade, a sick nation will not be able to sustain economic viability. The Russian scientific community should be outraged by the situation. Modern drugs should be widely available in Russia, and the importance of good nutrition should not be a mystery. As for the U.S. foreign assistance program in Russia, a much stronger commitment than the current $9 million per year for the health sector is in order. A demonstrated concern over the well-being of ordinary people should resonate well with Congressional and other political leaders in Washington who want to be helpful but are reluctant to become entangled with the Russian government on more controversial issues.

Disproving the Hypotheses

Against a background of economic stagnation and industrial decay, do the following hypotheses foretell the role of technology in Russia's future?

• Because Russia's research and development expenditures are between 5 and 7 percent of U.S. expenditures, we should not expect competitive Russian products to find their way to the international marketplace.
• Because the contribution of Russia's small innovative firms to the gross domestic product is less than 1 percent, these incubators of new technologies will have little impact on the economic condition of the country.
• Given the pessimistic job outlook for talented young Russians, growing numbers of the best students will seek education and positions abroad.

If these assertions hold up over the long term, then Russia will surely remain in dire straits. But, while they seem appropriate for 2000, they do not have to be the predictors of Russia's future. Russia has both the economic incentive and the technical wherewithal to stop the downhill slide of its technology. And with unwavering political will and strong international support, within 10 years Russia can again be in a position to effectively use its large bank of technical talent as a basis for providing a decent standard of living for its population.

In particular, four approaches can make a difference between treading water in a shrinking pool of resources and making forward progress that benefits the Russian people.

• Build an economic framework that stimulates industrial activity, resting in large measure on the use of Russian technologies, and that distributes the benefits of industrial growth in a fair and equitable manner.

• Facilitate partnerships between Russian industry and universities that convince students innovation is intellectually challenging and can be financially rewarding.

• Establish export policies for sensitive items that provide western trading partners with confidence that Russia is living up to its international commitments and that a responsible government is in charge of the country.

• Encourage recognition by western governments of the importance of long-term stability in Russia, a recognition that receives comparable weight with traditional concerns over near-term avoidance of a hard-line coup, a civil war, or a nuclear accident.

In 1999 there were hopeful signs. Russian firms were penetrating the Russian consumer market, as the devaluation of the ruble made the costs of imports prohibitively expensive for many Russians. The Duma finally adopted legislation that enables foreign companies to participate, at least in a limited way, in developing Russia's oil reserves (production sharing agreements). Thirteen million Russians traveled abroad that year, suggesting that wealth is spreading more broadly than had been assumed.

Finally, no other country can profit more from the information revolution than Russia. Given its vast geography, its lack of worker mobility, and its many countrywide pockets of technical expertise, information technologies open all types of time-saving and money-saving opportunities. With millions of kilometers of decaying Soviet-era telephone lines, poor communications have repeatedly inhibited business deals both within Russia and with foreign customers. Electronic messages, while still heavily dependent on telephone lines, circumvent many trouble points, and internal and external communications have improved enormously in recent years. Meanwhile, in cities throughout the country, small shops increasingly customize computer equipment and programs to satisfy customer demands ranging from security systems to storing data files.

In addition to upgrading internal information capabilities, Russian computer scientists and programmers have for more than a decade been working on joint projects with western firms. In recent years, a handful of Russian software firms have successfully entered the international market without the necessity of strong ties to western partners. For example, the firm ABBYY Software House is known for its optical character recognition, ParaGraph is known for its handwriting recognition, Elvis for its encryption capabilities, and Dialog Nauka for its anti-virus programs.[20]

As in all things Russian, however, criminal elements have entered the Internet arena. In 1996, Russian hacker Vladimir Levin stole $2.8 million from Citibank's main computer, and in 1997 and 1998 America Online and CompuServ shut down their direct access numbers in Russia in response to cases of credit card fraud. Because of the phenomenal skills of Russians hackers, Russia will continue to be a locus of ingenious cyber scams.

International cooperation in a number of fields will remain important when payoff for the Russian economy is clear—in areas such as fisheries, aerospace, and computer software. There are a few technical areas in which Russia lags but could learn quickly from western experience, such as biotechnology.[21] Russia could also learn from central European approaches in integrating technological achievements into commercial activities, from efforts in South Korea and Singapore to catch up with world leaders in high-tech areas, and from success of Russian emigrees in setting up incubators in Israel linked to western European partners.[22]

The importance of the U.S.-Russian relationship, which spans many areas of technology, should not be underestimated. Few officials on either side are aware of the full extent of this relationship, which has involved thousands of attempts to focus Russian technological resources directly on market opportunities. Why have some projects worked while others have disappeared without leaving a footprint? Some answers have been provided in this book.

Now, Russian officials from the president, the leaders of the Duma, and the governors on down must recognize that technology is indeed a key to the future of the country. They must activate the political and economic switches to energize dormant Russian know-how and to stimulate new experts in solving problems facing the nation. Then, technology will command market shares that help ensure stability while promoting peace in Russia and throughout the world.

Notes

1. Meeting in Washington, D.C. at the National Research Council, March 1999.

2. Vladimir Merkushev, "Putting Its Chips on the Table," *The Russia Journal,* September 6-12, 1999, p. 14.

3. Matthew L. Wald, "Russian Nuclear Power Company Looks West for Bailout," *The New York Times,* April 12, 1999, p. A10.

4. Discussion in Moscow with Russian specialists involved in design of gas pipelines, October 1999.

5. "Computer for Cremation of Muscovites," *Moskovskiy Komsomolyets,* April 4, 1999, p. 1.

6. *Global Trends 2010,* National Intelligence Council, Washington, D.C., undated but released for the second time in December 1998.

7. "By the Numbers," *Russia Review,* January 1999, p. 9.

8. Yu.S. Osipov, "On the Basic Priorities of Scientific-Technical Development of Russia," unpublished manuscript, provided by Russian Academy of Sciences, Moscow, October 1998, and discussions with Osipov, June 1999.

9. "What They Are Saying," *Russia Review,* January 1999, p. 10.

10. For an elaboration on the political setting, see Rene Nyberg, Ministry of Foreign Affairs of Finland, "Russia and Europe," presentation to European Commission Representation, Bonn, January 20, 1999.

11. Ibid.

12. Michael R. Gordon, "Russia's Options: Muddle Through or Collapse," *International Herald Tribune,* January 5, 1999, p. 13.

13. "Russian Science Reform 1997-2000, The Concept," Ministry of Science and Technology, Moscow, November 1997, summarized by U.S. Embassy, Moscow, February 1998.

14. Ibid.

15. Among the most vocal advocates of a Marshall Plan for Russia at conferences and on television during 1998 was Professor Charles Weiss, School of Foreign Service, Georgetown University, Washington, D.C.

16. "RJ Street Poll: Is It Possible to Fight Corruption in Russia?" *The Russia Journal,* September 13-19, 1999, p. 24.

17. "An Anti-Corruption and Good Governance Strategy for the Twenty-first Century," presented at International Conference on Corruption at the U.S. Department of State, February 24, 1999. See also the Primakov anti-corruption plan in Judith Matloff, "Showing Russians Who's Boss," *The Christian Science Monitor,* February 11, 1998, p. 1.

18. Ibid.

19. Murray Feshbach, "A Sick and Shrinking Nation," *The Washington Post,* October 24, 1999, p. B07.

20. Karl Emerick Hanuska, "What's the Net Effect as Russia Gets Wired?" *Russia Review,* June 19, 1998, pp. 30-1.

21. Kirsten Vance, "Programming Success," *Russia Review,* June 19, 1998, pp. 32-4.

22. V.A. Vasin, L.E. Mindeli, *The Strategy of Competitiveness and Problems of Russia Science and Technology Policy,* Center for Science Research and Statistics, Moscow, 1994, pp. 40-55. See also the World Bank seminar on business incubators, World Bank, Washington, April 12, 1999.

Epilogue

As my flight approached Sheremetyevo Airport in the spring of 1999, I was depressed over the devastating reports about developments in Russia. Deaths were outpacing births, and the population was shrinking by 800,000 each year. Thirty-five percent of the population had incomes below the poverty level. Many science teachers who were supposed to receive $20 per month had not been paid for a year. The portion of the economy that was still operating on a monetary basis and not relying on barter and deferred credits was one-half the size of the Dutch economy. Exports had declined by 16 percent in 1998 and imports by 19 percent while Russian production of goods continued to tumble. And the fate of the most progressive voice in the Duma, Galina Staravoitova, who had been assassinated in St. Petersburgh a few months earlier, was a warning sign of a political U-turn in Russia's future.

A week in the Urals buoyed my spirits somewhat. Life didn't seem so bad there. Despite all the ominous predictions, Russia had survived the winter. Banks were slowly reopening. Paychecks were gradually reappearing. While the ruble had plummeted in value internationally, inflation was not as severe as predicted. To be sure, the prices of bread and milk had increased dramatically; but the costs of gasoline, housing, and clothing were only modestly higher than during the fall of

1998. Russian colleagues were not nearly as concerned about their future as I had anticipated. They have learned to adjust to economic shocks of all sizes.

Returning to Moscow, I began to sense that, over the long haul, the financial crisis in August 1998 was simply another bump in the road. While economists pointed to unpaid debts and to terrible economic indicators, four of my colleagues revived my optimism that Russian technology can again become a force in economic growth—but patience and persistence must replace any past illusions of near-term payoff from technological innovation.

The management of the new state enterprise, Russian Technologies, had put behind them the hundreds of failures of other organizations to market technologies developed for the Soviet military machine. The firm, selected by the Russian government as the focal point for promoting exports of dual-use technologies, had just claimed its first success in Europe and the United States—the marketing of a pilot ejection seat. Other products in the electronics field were being declassified and would soon also be available, according to the management. Why were they apparently succeeding when others had failed? The new leaders understand both Russian and western profit motivations. They price items at a sufficiently low level to capture buyers skeptical of items made in Russia but at a high enough level to ensure that the return to Russia will provide incentives for manufacturers to increase their interest in producing quality products. Also, they only promote technologies that have been approved for sale by government officials responsible for protecting Russian industrial secrets, thus heading off bureaucratic delays once customers indicate interest in possible purchases. They are attempting to demonstrate that, while Russia is open to all types of offers, the nation is no longer a technology flea market that bites you when you try to take items out of the country.

My next stop was the Innovation Agency, established in 1994. Its mission sounds similar to that of several other organizations—promoting small innovative businesses. But, in practice, its approach has two important differences. First, it does not rush the commercialization of technology since a few sustained successes that take several years to launch are better than many short-lived immediate successes. Second, small firms that feed technologies to large firms are the targets, with the important multiplier effect. Often the small firms are absorbed by large firms, and immediate multiplication based on larger workforces and new market opportunities may result.

Then, at the Ministry of Science and Technology, a small group of specialists was busily preparing reports on the state of innovation in Russia. While the national statistics indicate that the downward slide of Russian industry continues, there were two bright spots. These specialists could point to many examples—in the enterprises, in the research institutes, and in the small firms—of new Russian technologies finding paying customers at home and abroad. Secondly, the specialists clearly understand those factors that encourage innovation and those that hold back efforts to upgrade industrial performance. And their diagnoses provide an important point of departure for developing policies for economic revitalization.

Finally, even my concerns over the unchecked rampage of corruption were assuaged. A colleague from a Russian organization that was selected to receive a $50,000 grant from a western foundation asked me to help him have the money sent to an American institution that could administer the grant and keep tabs on expenditures. He was worried that, if the money came directly to him and his colleagues, the temptations to divert some of the funds would be very great. He simply did not want to be a party to misuse of funds.

These unanticipated encounters highlight the determination of some Russians to press for changes that will pave the way for another chance for technology. Of course, appropriate macroeconomic and security policies are critical to the promotion of technology. But, unless modern technology is available in the first place and is aimed in the right direction, even the best such policies will have little meaning.

In the 1930s, the Soviet Union organized its engineers to industrialize the country after the flirtation with free market economics fizzled. Now the engineers, the economists, and the security experts must work hand in glove in a new political environment if yet another industrial revolution in Russia is to become reality. And, as in the 1930s, foreign specialists can lend a helping hand.

Appendixes

A
Characterization and Sources of Russian Research and Development

A.1 Characterization of the 4,137 Russian R & D Institutions (1997)

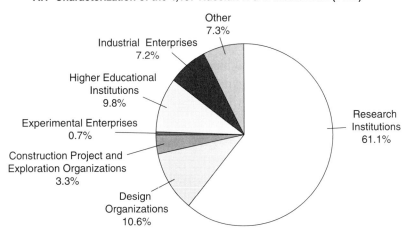

FIGURE A.1 Characterization of the 4137 Russian research and development institutions, 1997; SOURCE: *Russian Science and Technology at a Glance, 1998.* Center for Science Research and Statistics: Moscow, 1999, pp. 10, 47, 94, 96.

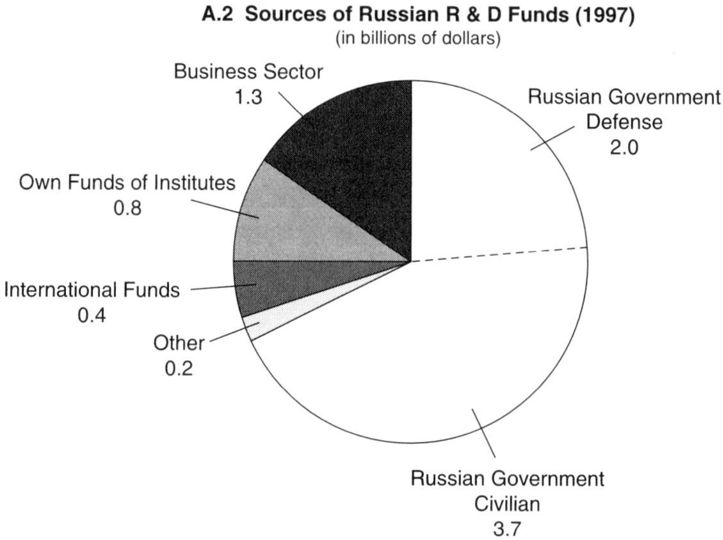

A.2 Sources of Russian R & D Funds (1997)
(in billions of dollars)

FIGURE A.2 Sources of Russian research and development funds, 1997 (in billions of dollars). SOURCE: *Russian Science and Technology at a Glance, 1998.* Center for Science Research and Statistics: Moscow, 1999, pp. 10, 47, 94, 96.

B

Scientific Organizations with the Status of State Scientific Centers of the Russian Federation

Central Aerohydrodynamics Institute (named after Professor N.E. Zhukovsky) of the Aviation-Space Agency (Zhukovsky)

Scientific-Research Physical-Chemistry Institute (named after L. Ya. Karpov) of the Ministry of Economics (Moscow)

Central Institute of Aviation Engines (named after P. I. Baranov) of the Aviation-Space Agency (Moscow)

Physics and Power Engineering Institute (named after Academician A. I. Leipunsky) of the Ministry of Atomic Energy (Obninsk)

All-Russian Scientific-Research Institute for Aviation Materials of the Aviation-Space Agency (Moscow)

State Scientific Center of Virology and Biotechnology "Vector" of the Ministry of Health (Koltsovo)

All-Russian Scientific-Research Institute of Inorganic Materials (named after Academician A. A. Bochvar) of the Ministry of Atomic Energy (Moscow)

All-Russian Electrotechnical Institute (named after V. I. Lenin) of the Ministry of Economics (Moscow)

State Scientific-Research Institute of Aviation Systems of the Aviation-Space Agency (Moscow)

State Scientific-Research Institute of Genetics and Selection of Industrial Microorganisms of the Ministry of Economics (Moscow)

Flight Research Institute (named after M. M. Gromov) of the Aviation-Space Agency (Zhukovsky)

Scientific Research Institute of Atomic Reactors of the Ministry of Atomic Energy (Dmitrograd)

Arctic and Antarctic Scientific-Research Institute of the Federal Service for Hydrometeorology and Monitoring of the Environment (St. Petersburg)

Institute of Biomedical Problems of the Russian Academy of Sciences (Moscow)

State Scientific-Research and Design Institute of Rare Metal Industry of the Ministry of Economics (Moscow)

State Scientific Center of Applied Microbiology of the Ministry of Health (Obolensk)

State Scientific-Research Institute of Thermal Power Instrument Making of the Ministry of Economics (Moscow)

Scientific-Research Institute of Organic Intermediates and Dyes of the Ministry of Economics (Moscow)

Central Scientific-Research and Experimental Design Institute of Robotics and Technical Cybernetics of the St. Petersburg State Technical University of the Ministry of Education (St. Petersburg)

Troisk Institute of Innovation and Fusion Research of the Ministry of Atomic Energy (Troisk)

Scientific-Production Complex "Technological Center" of the Moscow State Institute of Electronic Technologies of the Ministry of Education (Moscow)

Central Scientific-Research Institute (named after Akademician A. N. Krylov) of the Agency for Shipbuilding (St. Petersburg)

Central Scientific-Research Institute of Structural Materials "Prometey" of the Agency for Shipbuilding (St. Petersburg)

Acoustics Institute (named after Academician N. N. Andreyev) of the Russian Agency for Shipbuilding (Moscow)

Central Scientific-Research Institute "Gidropribor" of the Agency for Shipbuilding (St. Petersburg)

Central Scientific-Research Institute "Elektropribor" of the Agency for Shipbuilding (St. Petersburg)

Central Scientific-Research Institute for Technology of Shipbuilding of the Agency for Shipbuilding (St. Petersburg)

Obninsk Scientific Production Enterprise "Tekhnologia" of the Aviation-Space Agency (Obninsk)

Scientific-Production Association "Astrophysica" of the Agency for Conventional Armaments

Scientific-Production Association "Orion" of the Agency for Conventional Armaments (Moscow)

All-Russian Scientific Center "State Optical Institute (named after S. I. Vavilov)" of the Agency for Conventional Armaments (St. Petersburg)

Russian Scientific Center "Kurchatov Institute" (Moscow)

Central Scientific-Research Automobile and Automobile-Engine Institute of the Ministry of Economics (Moscow)

All-Russian Scientific-Research Institute of Metrology (named after D. I. Mendeleyev) of the State Committee for Standards and Metrology (St. Petersburg)

Scientific-Production Association for Machine-Building Technology of the Ministry of Economics (Moscow)

Institute of Immunology of the Federal Department of Biomedical and Extreme Problems of the Ministry of Health (Moscow)

State Scientific-Research Institute of the Chemistry and Technology of Organoelement Compounds of the Ministry of Economics (Moscow)

Central Scientific-Research Institute of Chemistry and Mechanics of the Agency for Military Supplies

State Scientific-Research Institute of Organic Chemistry and Technology of the Agency for Military Supplies

Russian Scientific Center "Applied Chemistry" of the Agency for Military Supplies (St. Petersburg)

Institute of High Energy Physics of the Ministry of Atomic Energy (Protvino)

Institute of Theoretical and Experimental Physics of the Ministry of Atomic Energy (Moscow)

All-Russian Scientific-Research Institute of Legumes and Groat Crops of the Academy of Agricultural Sciences (Streletskoye)

State Scientific-Research Institute of Non-Ferrous Metals of the Ministry of Economics (Moscow)

Joint-Stock Holding Company "All-Russian Scientific-Research and Design-Construction Institute of Metallurgical Machine-Building (named after A. I. Tselikov)" (Moscow)

All-Russian Scientific-Research Institute of Geological, Geophysical, and Geochemical Systems of the Ministry of Natural Resources (Moscow)

Complex Scientific-Research and Construction-Technological Institute of Water Supply, Sewage Systems, Hydraulic Engineering Structures, and Engineering Hydrogeology of the State Committee for Construction and Housing-Communal Complexes (Moscow)

Hydrometeorological Scientific-Research Center of the Federal Service for Hydrometeorology and Monitoring of the Environment (Moscow)

Scientific Research Center "Construction" of the State Committee for Construction and Housing-Communal Complexes (Moscow)

All-Russian Scientific-Research Institute of the Plant Industry (named after I. I. Vavilov) of the Academy of Agricultural Sciences (St. Petersburg)

Institute of Biophysics of the Federal Department of Biomedical and Extreme Problems of the Ministry of Health (Moscow)

State Scientific-Research Institute of Physical Problems (named after V. F. Lukin) of the Agency for Systems Management (Moscow)

All-Russian Scientific-Research Institute of Physical-Technical and Radiotechnical Measurement of the State Committee for Standards and Metrology (Mendeleyevo)

Central Scientific-Research Institute of Ferrous Metals (named after I. P. Bardin) of the Ministry of Economics (Moscow)

State Scientific-Research Institute of Biological Instruments of the Ministry of Health (Moscow)

State Scientific-Research Institute of Ultra-Pure Biopreparations of the Ministry of Health (St. Petersburg)

Urals Institute of Metals (Yekaterinburg)

Source: Supplement to the Order of the Government of the Russian Federation, January 29, 2000, No. 159-r (in Russian).

Science Cities
of Russia

Cities (48)

Balashika-1, Moscow Region
Biysk, Altai District
Dimitrovgrad, Ulyanov Region
Dimitrov-7, Moscow Region
Dolgoprudny, Moscow Region
Dubna, Moscow Region
Dzerzhinsk, Nizhnygorod Region
Dzerzhinsky, Moscow Region
Fryazino, Moscow Region
Istra, Moscow Region
Khimki, Moscow Region
Klimovsk, Moscow Region
Korolev (Kaliningrad), Moscow Region
Krasnoarmeysk, Moscow Region
Krasnodar-59, Krasnodar District
Krasnoznamensk (Golitsino-2), Moscow Region

---

*Closed Nuclear Cities

Lesnoi (Sverdlovsk-45) Sverdlovsk Region*
Lytkarino, Moscow Region
Miass, Chelyabinsk Region
Nizhnaya Salda, Sverdlovsk Region
Novosibirsk-49, Novosibirsk Region
Novouralsk (Sverdlovsk-44), Sverdlovsk Region*
Obninsk, Kaluga Region
Omsk-5, Omsk Region
Ostashkov-3, Tver Region
Ozersk (Chelyabinsk-65, Chelyabinsk-40), Chelyabinsk Region*
Perm-6, Perm Region
Prabdinsk, Nizhnygorod Region
Primorsk, Leningrad Region
Protvino, Moscow Region
Pushchino, Moscow Region
Raduzhny, Vladimir Region
Redkino, Tver Region
Reutov, Moscow Region
Sarov (Kremlev, Arzamas-16), Nizhnygorod Region*
Seversk (Tomsk-7), Tomsk Region*
Snezhinsk (Chelyabinsk-70), Chelyabinsk Region*
Sosnovy Bor, Leningrad Region
Trekhgorny (Zlatoust-36), Chelyabinsk Region*
Troitsk, Moscow Region
Ust-Katav, Chelyabinsk Region
Yubileyny (Bolshevo-2), Moscow Region
Zarechny (Penza-19) Penza Region*
Zarechny, Sverdlovsk Region
Zelenogorsk (Krasnoyarsk 45), Krasnoyarsk District*
Zheleznogorsk (Krasnoyarsk-26), Krasnoyarsk District*
Zheleznodorozhny, Moscow Region
Zhukovsky, Moscow Region

Separated Districts of Cities (5)

Akademgorodok, Irkutsk Scientific Center of the Russian Academy
of Sciences
Akademgorodok, Krasnoyarsk Scientific Center of the Russian
Academy of Sciences
Akademgorodok, Novosibirsk Science Center of the Russian
Academy of Sciences
Akademgorodok, Tomsk Scientific Center of the Russian Academy
of Sciences
Zelenograd-Moscow (on the territory of the Moscow Region)

Towns (12)

Beloozersky, Moscow Region
Borok, Yaroslav Region
Chernogolovska, Moscow Region
Koltsovo, Novosibirsk Region
Krasnoobsk, Novosibirsk Region
Melenky, Vladimir Region
Mendeleyevo, Moscow Region
Novostroika, Moscow Region
Obolensk, Moscow Region
Orevo, Moscow Region
Remmash, Moscow Region
Star City, Moscow Region

Source: Russian Ministry of Science and Technology, November 1999.
(in Russian)

Commercialized Technologies at Russian Institutions

Technology Type	Projected/Current Sales
Positron Emission Tomography	$755,000
Nanophase Metal Powders	$5,000,000 in annual revenue
Tc-99m Radiopharmaceutical	$65,000
Gas Chromatograph	$200 million
Recycling of Co-mingled Metals	$1.2 million
Smart Video	$35 million
High Energy Ion Technology of Interfacial Thin Film Coatings	$2.5 million
High Performance Sealed Source Phantoms for Nuclear Medicine	$2 million
Acoustic Nozzle	$19 million
Powder-based Synthesis of Nanocrystalline Material Components for Structural Applications	$2 million
Computer-Aided Discovery and Development of Crop Protection and Human Health Agents	$100-150 million per year

Recombinant Luciferase and Related Reagents for Portable Photometric Detectors	$25 million (years 1-4)
Geophysical Diagnostic Imaging for Oil Recovery	$760 million per year
Russian Neutron Irradiated Gallium Arsenide	$5 million
Shallow Water Imaging Sonar for Environmental Surveying	$2 million
Parallel Mathematical Libraries	$5-7 million
Electronic Knee Protheses	$5 million
Field-Portable CdZnTe Radiation Detector	$10 million in first two years

Source: Commercialized Technologies, United States Industry Coalition, October 1999, funded through the Initiatives for Proliferation Prevention Program (IPP) of U.S. Department of Energy.

Author's Note: This document was distributed on Capitol Hill during the fall of 1999 in support of the IPP program. While the document presents an impressive display of Russian technological strengths, staff members of the Department of Energy stated that they believe the sales projections are optimistic and that only five or six of the technologies are likely to succeed in the marketplace on a significant scale in the near term. Nevertheless, the focus on commercial sales is an important departure from past practices of emphasizing technologies without regard to marketing.

E

Technology-Intensive Projects of Priority Interest to the Russian Ministry of Foreign Affairs

- Missile fuels and oxidizer reprocessing infrastructure
- Solid-fuel missile engine destruction infrastructure
- Infrastructure for unloading, transportation, and temporary storage of nuclear submarine spent fuel
- Infrastructure for reprocessing, storage, and disposal of radioactive waste, including nuclear submarine reactor units
- Elimination of 410 solid-fuel inter-continental ballistic missile from nuclear submarines
- Dismantlement of 30 strategic nuclear submarines and 120 multi-purpose nuclear submarines
- Destruction of coastal storage facilities for spent fuel and radioactive waste of the Navy in the northern and far east regions
- Chemical weapons destruction facilities in Gorny and Schuchye
- Demilitarization of former chemical weapons production facilities
- Disposal of the casings of missile engines and launch containers
- New jobs for former defense program specialists, particularly in closed cities
- Alternative thermal and electricity generating capacities in Zheleznogorsk and Seversk in place of plutonium production reactors

- Manufacturing of inserts to package fissile material resulting from nuclear weapons destruction
- Enhancement of protection, control, and accounting systems for nuclear materials and nuclear installations
- Disposal of plutonium no longer required for defense purposes through use in MOX fuels

Source: "ETRI and Future Funding Issues, Russian Perspective," Presented at the Monterey Institute for International Studies by Spokesman for Ministry of Foreign Affairs, December 12, 1999.

F

Next Steps to the Market Program of the U.S. Civilian Research and Development Foundation

Background

The program is intended to support projects to facilitate commercial utilization of research results. It involves collaborations between scientists and engineers in Russia and U.S. companies. The foundation's investment in each project will average $75,000 for a period of two years. The U.S. companies must make matching contributions.

Types of Activities Supported

Russian applicants may request grants for individual financial support, equipment and supplies, and travel as well as for business development activities such as:

• Training in technology commercialization, including management and intellectual property issues.
• Assistance in preparing a business plan, conducting a patent search, or locating professional counsel in the U.S. and in Russia on intellectual property matters.

(Extract from program announcement of March 13, 2000)

- Participation in technical meetings, trade shows, etc., to present or demonstrate potentially marketable technologies.
- Developmental follow-on to research in progress or already carried out necessary to demonstrate technologies to potential entrepreneurs or investors.
- Development plans for the use of the new technology.
- Management consulting services.

Business Issues that Should Be Addressed

- What technical/market problem is being solved?
- How does the proposed technology address this market need?
- What is the market for this technology and who are the customers?
- What market research has been done to date including market size, competition, etc.?
- What is the status of intellectual property related to this technology?
- What is the commercialization plan for the technology, including production, financing, marketing, and distribution issues?
- What resources will be required to carry out the business plan?

Criteria for Evaluating Proposals

- Technical merit
- Potential for commercialization
- Project feasibility analysis and potential implementation risks
- Level of U.S company's financial commitment
- Strength of business discussion

Author's comment: Given the small size of the grants and the requirement that a U.S. company (not a Russian company) must make a matching contribution in cash or in kind limits the potential of the program to make a major impact on technology commercialization activities. Nevertheless, it should demonstrate interesting approaches and serve as a pilot program for larger Russian-oriented efforts should they develop.

Index

A

Abu Dabai arms bazaar, 65-66
Abu Dabai bazaar for selling, 65
    Chinese purchases of, 61
    customers for purchases of, 64
    decline in Russian sales of, 64-65, 83
    excess Russian inventory of, 69
    Indian purchases of, 64
    North Korean purchases of, 72
    Promexport, exporter of, 67
    Rosvooruzhenye, exporter of, 67
    purchases by cocaine dealers of, 65
Aerospace firms
    exodus of Russian scientists from, 144
    joint venture of Pratt-Whitney and Energomash, 43, 236
    participation in International Space Station by, 73
    redesign of aircraft for defense conversion by, 78
    rocket engine purchases by Lockheed Martin from, 43, 236
    unemployment in, 73

AFK Sistema holding company (Moscow), 19
Agrobank, closure of, 7
Akademgorodok (Novosibirsk)
    aspirations of city founder for, 172
    Decline of research activities in, 173
    early emphasis on economic payoff from research conducted in, 170
    education opportunities in, 173
    information technology, priority of, 173
    skepticism over payoff from investments in, 172
    success in attracting specialists to, 170
Akrikhin (Russian pharmaceutical company)
    Bristol-Myers Squibb, cooperation with, 3
    business difficulties of, 1-3
    USAID investments in, 2
Anthrax, Russian research capabilities concerning, 142
Armaments
Arzamas 16 (*See* Sarov)

Atomic Energy
    international conferences on, 72
    Iranian purchase of nuclear power
        plant, 71-72
    leakage of technical information
        from Minatom complex, 144
    military applications of, 72
Avtovaz, increased sales of, 23

B

Banking system
    Central Bank diversions of funds
        within, 105
    effects of 1998 financial collapse
        on, 104
    expanded charters for western
        bank participation in, 256-257
    financial monitoring of, 87
    openness of Konversbank to
        western audits within, 104
    profitable banks in, 105
    role in capital flight of, 106
    Russian mistrust of western bank
        participation in, 256
    Soviet antecedents to fraud in, 256
Barter
    avoiding tax through, 134
    examples of, 12-15
    growth of, 4
Basic research
    decline of, 23
    dual-use dimensions of, 73
    intellectual property rights and,
        73-74
Beloyarsk nuclear power station
    (Zarechny), 205-206
Berezovsky coal mine, tax payments in
    noncash form by, 13
Biopreparat
    former biological weapons
        activities of, 189-190
    research institutes of, 189
    sales of pharmaceutical products
        by, 190

Brain drain
    characteristics and impact of, 140-
        166
    decline in research staffs due to,
        153
    destinations of scientists who leave
        weapons complex, 143
    emigration from Physical-Technical
        Institute (Moscow), 157
    employment opportunities for
        Russian scientists in Moslem
        countries, 142
    foreign laboratory of Institute of
        Microbiology as alternative to,
        158
    foreign sabbaticals of Landau
        Institute of Physics as
        alternative to, 158
    international flows of expertise
        from, 154-155
    international grants as counter to,
        158
    military significance of engineering
        skills, 145
    number of Russian specialists of
        proliferation concern, 144-145
    proliferation aspects of official trips
        abroad, 147-148
    proliferation of weapons
        knowledge, xv
    recruitment of former weaponeers
        by Sunshine Industrial
        Company, 147
    recruitment of retired scientists
    rogue state interest in hands-on
        weapons experience, 146
    temporary employment abroad,
        149, 156
    western program as counter to, 142
Bristol-Myers Squibb, cooperation
    with Akrikhin company, 3
Bush, George, as adviser on economic
    reform, 8

C

Capital flight
approaches to reduction of, 107
customs control of travelers and, 98
European havens for, 106
impact on availability of investment
capital caused by, 107
money laundering dimension of, 106
Careers in science and technology
decline in working conditions for,
158, 166
education as critical springboard
for, 164
loss of prestige of, 158
reasons for failure in, 159
reasons for success in, 158
western programs for
encouragement of, 166
Center for Nuclear Research (CERN)
as customer for inert gases from
Zarechny, 207
Central Aerohydrodynamics Institute
(Zhukovsky)
competition from western
researchers for international
customers of, 180
termination of military contracts of,
180
wind tunnels of, 180
Central Bank, diversion of funds by,
105
Chernogolovka (science city in
Moscow region)
investigations of anti-missile
systems, 182
research on industrial explosions,
182
research on rocket fuels, 182
China
armament production agreement
with Russia, 62
armaments purchases from Russia
by, 61, 64
biology contracts with Russian
institute, 54

impact of military alliances with
Russia, 62
purchases of Russian nuclear
accelerators by, 175
Chubais, Anatoly, misrepresentation to
IMF, 4
Closed cities
activities of Ministry of Defense in,
191-192
nuclear cities designated as, 191
special privileges for, 191
Commercialization of Russian
technologies
business alliances of U.S. firms
interested in, 226
projects of Russian organizations
with potential for, 165
U.S. government support of
feasibility studies of, 226
Construction industry
asphalt quality improvement in
small segment of, 43
office building innovations in, 44
Corruption
apathy of public toward, 264
bribes paid by small firms as a
result of, 17, 50
costs to businesses from, 265
diversion of funds of IMF as result
of, 110-111
economic impact of, 8
forms of, 264-265
high-visibility prosecutions as
warning against, 265
researchers resistance to, 253
technology-intensive firms as
victims of, 266
transparency of financial
transactions as a counter to, 110
whistleblowers to help counter, 110
Customs procedures
capital flight control by, 98
clearance of goods through, 133
economic importance of duties
collected through, 133
Cyprus, as tax haven, 87

D

Dappi (village in Far Eastern region),
  decline of, 22
Debt burden of Russia
  magnitude of, 7
  relief from, 26
Defense conversion
  aircraft redesign through, 78
  alternative strategies for, 78-79
  cost limitations of, 63, 83
  definition of, 76
  examples of technologies
    appropriate for, 74-75
  failures in, 76
  funds of Russian government for,
    76
  inappropriate military facilities for,
    76, 83
  lack of business skills for, 76, 83
  maximizing immediate income as
    strategy for, 78
  myths about, 82-83
  need for new approaches to, 83
  western involvement in, 83-84
  western skepticism over, 77
Defense Enterprise Fund, investments
  of, 237
Department of Commerce (U.S.)
  business internships for Russian
    specialists offered by, 237-238
  health-industry partnerships
    supported by, 238
Department of Defense (U.S.)
  acquisition of Russian technologies
    by, 225, 233
  contracting procedure upgrading
    in Russian firms due to, 233
  Nunn-Lugar program of, 225
Department of Energy (U.S.)
  capabilities of program managers
    of, 227
  Initiatives for Proliferation
    Prevention program of, 223-224
  Intellectual Property Rights policy
    of, 123

  Nuclear Cities Initiative program
    of, 230
  Use of Russian equipment in
    cooperative programs of, 230
Dual-use technologies
  achievements by nuclear cities in
    development of, 187
  ambiguities in end use associated
    with sales of, 264
  business success based on, 82
  developing country interest in, 70
  export control regime for, 63
  international sales competitions of,
    70
  repositories in Russia of, 70
  research programs for development
    of, 73
  Russian Technologies, exporting
    firm of, 67, 273
  sales by Russia of, 63
Dzerzhinsky (science city in Moscow
  region), 178-179

E

Economic crime
  criminal code that deals with, 109
  contract killings related to, 108
  cocaine-for-arms aspect of, 65
  economic reform and, 109
  enforcement capabilities to combat,
    109
  history of, 108
  privatization as it relates to, 102, 107
Economic decline in Russia
  crash of 1998 and impact on, 1-2,
    33-35
  shock therapy as failed strategy and
    contributor to, 8
  social instability due to, 25
  successes in spite of, 37, 39
Economic environment
  corruption and business aspects of,
    135
  enforcement of regulations as
    necessity for, 135

general conditions, xiv-xv
western prescriptions for, 4-5
Economic model for Russia
aspirations for improvement of, xii-xiv
costs of transition to, 255
innovation incentives as component of, 268
Made-in-Russia label as symbol of poor quality, xviii, 33, 41, 253
standard of living improvement needed for viability of, 255
technology as multiplier of benefits from, xvii
unique requirements for, 29
Electrotechnical Institute incubator (Moscow), 50
Energomash
Iraq overtures for missile components, 68
Pratt-Whitney joint venture with, 43
Entrepreneur-Physicists at Moscow State University, ix
Eurasia Foundation, advisory services for entrepreneurs by, 240
European Union, grants to Russians scientists by, 34
Export control requirements
enterprise reluctance to comply fully with, 80-81
illegal export seizures, 81
information flow and, 150
international regimes for, 63, 80
Iran nuclear sales as dispute over, 81
laws of Russia concerning, 81
Soviet influence on Russia's approach to, 80
trading partners' anxiety over nonconformance of Russia with, 268
U.S.-Russian cooperation in implementing, 79-80
U.S. sanctions on Russian institutes for noncompliance with, 82

F

Far East region
economic opportunities in, 20-23
isolation of population of, 22
Federal Securities Commission (Russian), role of, 87, 103
Financial transactions
banking system avoidance in conducting, 89-90
cash transfers, 95
dollar-ruble conversion requirements of, 90
government garnishments of, 89-90
International Science Foundation (Soros) system for, 96
International Science and Technology Center system for, 95
offshore schemes for, 87-89
overhead payments in, 96
paper trail of, 95
payments to scientists, 96
time delays in, 98
Financing of innovation
foreign company investments for, 93
foreign government funds for, 93
Fund for Development of Small Firms in the Scientific and Technical Sphere and, 91
Fund for Technology Development (Russian) related to, 92
Funds of Ministry of Economics related to, 92
regional funds for, 92
Russian government funds for, 91-94
St. Petersburg Technology Fund for, 93
Foreign investments, xii
Fryazino (Science city in Moscow region), 184-185
Fyodorov, Boris, 6

G

Gates, Bill, visit to Moscow of, 164
Gazprom
    barter transactions of, 14
    Caspian Sea interest of, 35
    environmental monitoring priority
        of, 35
    gas-ruble payments scheme of, 15
    innovation support by, 142
Globalization of technology, 249
Goldman, Sachs, and Co., role during
        financial crisis of, 8-9
Gore, Al, role in binational
        commission, 227, 236, 239
Gorky Automobile Plant, noncash tax
        payments of, 13
Gromov Flight Research Institute
        (Zhukovsky) test facilities, 180
Gubkin Oil and Gas Academy,
        linkages with industry, 162

H

Health of Russian Youth
    decline in, 266
    impact on military recruitment of,
        266
    USAID programs directed to, 267
Human Resources
    active researchers, decline in, 39,
        153, 155
    aging of workforce,151-152
    salaries of scientists, 165

I

Import substitution
    bureaucratic resistance to changing
        policies related to, 263
    general strategy for, xiii, 3
    technological opportunities related
        to, 263
India, purchase of Russian armaments,
        64

Inflation in Russia, control of, 5
Information revolution
    computer hackers and, 269
    opportunities for Russia from, 268,
        269
    software capabilities of Russia
        related to, 269
Initiatives for Proliferation Prevention
        program
    activities of, 223-224
    commercialized technology of,
        286-287
    "exit strategy" of, 227
    relevance of U.S. experience to, 227
    Russian interest in, 228
    U.S. Industry Coalition in support
        of, 229
Innovation
    dimensions of, xiv
    economic impact of xi-xii
    environment for, 10
    factors inhibiting, 41
    Gazprom programs for, 42
    government support for, 253
    impact on businesses of, ix
    long-term commitment for, 253
    macroeconomic framework for, 9
    microeconomic framework for, 9
    profiting from, xiii
    Russian capabilities for, xi
    Russian enterprise interest in, 41
Institute of Atomic Energy (*see*
        Kurchatov Institute)
Institute of Aviation (Moscow), U.S.
        sanctions for Iranian contacts,
        163
Institute of Catalysis (Boreskov)
    contracts with western firms of, 174
    recruitment of university graduates
        by, 174-175
    retention of aging scientists by , 175
    spinoff firms from, 174
Institute of Chemical Technology
        (Mendeleyev), U.S. sanctions
        for Iranian contacts, 163

Institute of Hydrodynamics
(Novosibirsk), water jet
technology of, 172-173
Institute of Immunological
Engineering (Lyubchany), land
rental income of, 52-53
Institute of Light Weight Alloys
(Moscow), development of
titanium golf clubs by, 74-75
Institute of Machine Building
(Kaliningrad)
meteorite destruction system
developed by, 181
oil fire extinguishing device
invented by, 181
synthetic diamond manufacturing
at, 181-182
toxic waste incinerator of, 181-182
Institute of Microbiology, foreign
laboratory of, 158
Institute of Nuclear Physics (Budker)
accelerator sales to China by, 175
basic research budgetary shortfalls
of, 176
emigrant network for contract
facilitation for, 175
radiation of timber products using
equipment built at, 175-176
Institute of Physical Chemistry
(Karpov), 199
Institute of Physics (Landau), foreign
laboratory of, 158
Institute of Physics and Power
Engineering (Obninsk), 203
Institute of Power Engineering
(Moscow)
recruitment of university graduates
by, 164
Zarechny branch of, 207
Institute of Radioelectronics and
Radioengineering (Fryazino)
German affiliate of, 185
medical diagnostic equipment of,
185
spinoff firms from, 185

Intellectual property rights
author's certificates as claims of,
120
background technology claims of, x
basic research and, 73-74
commission to resolve conflicting
claims of, 121
conformity to WTO standards for,
118
Department of Energy policy on,
123
distribution among partners in
international projects of, 113-
114, 115, 123, 126
enforcement problems of claims of,
117-118
government-funded projects and,
118-123
hybrid of new and old technologies
with respect to, 121
institutes' priorities for, 122
international recognition of Russian
patents and claims of,115-116
International Science and
Technology Center's model for,
114, 124
interpretations of Russian law
concerning, 114
patent filings for, x
patent infringements and, xv
piracy of computer software
relative to, 116
piracy of video cassettes relative to,
116
privatization and complication of,
121
reverse engineering in violation of,
113
strategic technologies protected as,
120
western-funded projects and
practices concerning, 116, 125
western use of Russia discoveries
not protected as, 118

International cooperation
    downsizing Russian military
        complex through, 242
    dual-use technologies and, 73
    expectations of results from,
        244-245
    investment opportunities for U.S.
        companies with regard to, 242
    lessons learned from, 244
    measures of success of, 229
    need for strategy for, 243
    network of organizational linkages
        for, 245
    Russian initiatives for, 244
    Russian Ministry of Foreign Affairs
        interest in, 288-289
    science and technology programs
        and, xiii
    U.S. involvement in Russia in, xiii,
        242
    U.S. nonproliferation programs
        based on, xvi
International Monetary Fund
    criticisms of policies of, 6
    greater accountability by, 110-111
    policies of, 3-4
    role in 1998 crash of, 5-6
    U.S. government support of, 6
International Science and Technology
        Center
    intellectual property rights model
        of, 114, 124
    Snezhinsk involvement in activities
        of, 213
International Space Station
    aerospace firms involvement in, 73,
        151-152, 225-226, 234-235
    financial problems of Russia in
        support of, 234-235
    Russia's future role in, 235
Investment capital
    importance for innovation of, xvii
    joint-venture difficulties and, 134
    oil company reluctance to support
        research with, 10-11

Iran
    biological weapons and interest of,
        140-141
    International Atomic Energy
        Agency inspections in, 71
    nuclear power station purchase by,
        71
    training of nuclear specialists in
        Russia from, 71
    U.S. suspicions about activities of,
        141
Iraq
    Energomash contract with, 68
    Mars Rotor Company contract
        with, 68
    missile component purchases by,
        67-69
    Research and Testing Institute of
        Chemical and Construction
        Equipment contract with, 68

J

Japan
    model of government-industry
        cooperation of, 27
    post-war recovery experience of, 27
    skepticism of Russian economic
        reform of, 26
    trade with Russian Far East by, 22
Johnson and Johnson (U.S. company)
    tax problems in Russia of, 132

K

Kalinin, Yuri, director of Biopreparat,
        189-191
Kaliningrad (science city in Moscow
        region), 181
Kamchatka
    economic decline in, 22
    fisheries in, 21
Karachai Lake (in Urals), nuclear
        accident, 213

Karpov report on tax collection, 13
Kazan incubator successes, 56, 91
Khabarovsk, exports from, 21
Koltsovo (science city in Novosibirsk
    region), 189
Konversbank, open to western audits,
    104
Krisha (*see* "roof")
Kurchatov Institute of Atomic
    Energy
    barter transactions of, 14
    concept of State Scientific Centers
        developed by, 46
    counter-proliferation capabilities
        of, 46

L

Lavrentyev, Mikhail, founder of
    Akademgorodok (Novosibirsk),
    172
Lebedev, Yuri, proposed revisions of
    patent laws, 158
Lockheed-Martin Company, purchase
    of rocket engines, 43
Lubertskoe Production Association
    (Dzerhzhinsky)
    forest fire suppression technologies
        of, 179
    gas technology research by, 179
    workforce reduction at, 179
Luzhkov, Yuri, accomplishments as
    mayor of Moscow, 18-20

M

Marketing
    importance of, x
    lack of skills of Russian
        entrepreneurs in, 229
    opportunities following crash of
        1998 to test skills in, 55
Mars Rotor Company, contract with
    Iraq, 68

Marshall Plan
    financial sources for variant of, 260
    jump starting technology-oriented
        enterprises through variant of,
        259
    revised concept of, xvi, 259
McKinsey Global Institute (Moscow),
    industrial analysis, 25
Metal Park Company, production of
    titanium golf clubs, 164
Ministry of Defense
    closed city activities of, 191-192
    science city interests of, 177
Ministry of Economics, funds for
    improved products, 92
Ministry of Finance
    delays in salary payments due to,
        33
    neglect of research and
        development budgets by, 11
Ministry of Science and Technology
    analytical capabilities of, 274
    innovation support by, 91
    Internet support by, 239
    research support by, 11
    schools of science concept of, 153
    State Scientific Centers program of,
        47-48
    technology policy proposed by,
        258-159
Moscow
    financial success of city
        administration of, 18-20
    foreign debt of, 20
    privatization policy of, 19
    rental of city property of, 19
    research support by, 20
    residency policy of, 19
Moscow Institute of Technology
    (Bauman), linkages with
    industry, 162
Moscow State Institute of Electronic
    Technology (Zelenograd),
    linkages with industry, 163
Moscow State University, physicist-
    entrepreneurs, ix

N

NASA
cooperative programs for
International Space Station of,
152, 225-226
young Russian scientists in need of
support by, 152
National Academy of Engineering,
view on innovation, ix
Natural resources
aluminum industry tax exemption
as example for, 129
value added to, xii-xiii
Nesterenko, Lyudmila, computer
software entrepreneur, 54
Nestle company, import substitution,
24
Nonproliferation programs
alternative income streams
provided by, 148
channel for information through, 15
European community involvement
in, 150
Initiatives for Proliferation
Prevention as, 223-224
Nunn-Lugar program and, 225
sustainability of, 148, 224
Nuclear cities
access to, 196
aging of populations of, 219-220
characteristics of, 186
downsizing weapons complex in 196
dual-use technology achievements
of, 187
examples of, 197-219
international cooperation interests
of west in, 220
proliferation vulnerability of, 187
security conditions in, 187, 196
studies of social and economic
conditions in, 188, 195-220
technological pedigrees of, 196
unique problems in, 197
western programs to prevent
turmoil in, 187

Nuclear Cities Initiative, program of
Department of Energy
activities of, 231
development of, 230-232
objectives and priorities of,
230-232
measures of success of, 230-232
support of social infrastructure
through, 230
North Korea, acquisition of Russian
missile technology, 72
Nunn-Lugar program
chemical weapons destruction
through, 233
importance of, 225, 232

O

Obninsk (science city in Kaluga
region)
business advantages of, 205
business plan of, 200
developments in, 197-205
Experimental Science City
designation of, 202
Fast Critical Facility in, 203-204
history of, 198
innovation center in, 5
Institute of Physical Chemistry
(Karpov) in, 199
Institute of Physics and Power
Engineering in, 203
local control of federal facilities in,
201
mafia influx into, 202
nuclear material stocks in, 203-204
open city aspects of, 204
private business in, 195
prosperity of some scientific
leaders of, 205
reactor research in, 198
Research and Production
Enterprise Tekhnologia in, 204
small firms in, 201
state research organizations in, 200

tax payments in goods and services to, 202

underemployment of scientists in, 204

university-level institutions in, 202

Obolensk (science city in Moscow region), 189

Oil industry
Sakhalin production-sharing agreements of, 26
Sakhalin prosperity due to, 21
support of research by, 42-43

Overseas Private Investment Corporation, financial services of, 238

P

Patents (*see* Intellectual Property Rights)

Pharmaceutical industry, outlook for Russian companies, 3

Physical-Technical Institute (Moscow), emigration from, 157

Physical-Technical University (Snezhinsk) 219

Political trends
crime and democracy, 254-255
democracy Russian-style, 254-255
lingering Soviet mentality, 254

Pratt-Whitney, joint venture with Energomash, 43

Primakov, Yevgeny, 1

Privatization of enterprises
economic crimes related to, 102
enforcement of regulation weaknesses during, 102-103
minority shareholder rights during and after, 103
schemes for, 102
theft in natural resources industry during, 103
voucher system relative to, 102

Promexport state company, armament exports by , 67

Propiska (residency permit for Moscow), 19

Prostitution, in Far East, 22

Pushchino (science city in Moscow region)
biomedical research in, 184
housing conditions in, 184
living conditions in, 184
potato research in, 183
university-institute linkages in, 184

R

Radon (Moscow city radiological cleanup firm), 20

Relcom (Russian company), Internet provider, 52

Research and development infrastructure
administrative overhead increases in, 154
aging facilities of, 40
characterization of, 278
equipment obsolescence in, 40
funding decline in, xv, 36, 88
importance of, xiii
scope of, 36

Research and Production Enterprise Tekhnologia, Obninsk, 204

Research and Testing Institute of Chemical and Construction Equipment, contract with Iraq of, 68

"Roof"
costs of, 99-101
definition of, 90
services provided by, 99-101
western company interests in, 101

Rosasfalt (Russian company), roadbuilding technology of, 44

Rosshelf (Russian company), exploration of undersea oil and gas resources by, 52

Rosvooruzhenye (Russian company), export of armaments by, 67

Russian Anti-piracy Organization, protection of video cassettes by, 116

Russian Innovation Agency, promotion of small innovative firms, by, 273-274

Russian Technologies (Russian state company), sales of dual-use technologies by, 62, 67, 273

Russian technology
    contribution to economic growth of, 252, 256
    engineering contributions to, 251
    environmental side effects of, 250
    examples of achievements of, 250
    legal infrastructure to facilitate development of, 257
    military potential of, 251
    opportunities for, 250
    prestige linked to, 252
    U.S. related to, 251

S

Sachs, Jeffrey, 8

Saint Petersburg State Mining Institute, linkages with industry, 163

Saint Petersburg Technology Fund, 93

Sakhalin
    oil development on, 21, 26
    oil production sharing agreements and, 26

Salaries
    delayed payments for scientists of, 11, 33
    foreign contracts as supplement to, 89
    on-time payments in 1998 of, 88

Samara Region
    higher education in, 24
    innovative firms in, 24
    relative prosperity of, 24

resources of, 23-25

Sanctions, imposed on Russian institutions by U.S. government for inappropriate transfers of technology to Middle East states, 163

Sarov (science city in Nizhnygorod region), incubation of software firm in, 54

Science cities
    basic research in, 169
    budget shortfalls of, 176-7
    criteria for designation of, 191
    defense interests in, 171, 177
    economic decline in, 171
    educational opportunities in, 192
    enclaves in Moscow region for, 176
    intellectual boredom in, 185
    land rental activities in, 177
    list of, 283-285
    organized crime interests in, 177
    regional significance of, 192
    reluctance to abandon facilities in, 192
    revival of, 192-193
    special status of, 192
    tax benefits for, 178
    technological capabilities of, xvi
    transparency of biological research in, 190-191
    western interests in, 192-193

Small business
    advisory services to support, 49
    crime avoidance by, 50
    entrepreneurship and, 16
    financial support for, 49
    innovative firms as, 4, 15-17, 35-66
    locations—including technoparks and incubators—for, 48-49
    low technology in, 15-17
    market opportunities for, 17
    problems faced by, 17
    Samara innovative firms in, 24
    Snezhinsk training center for 217
    success stories of, 49-50

tax holidays for, 128
unregistered firms operating as,16
Zarechny failures of, 208
Snezhinsk (science city in Chelyabinsk
   region)
   business incubator in, 217
   commercialization failures in, 215
   developments in, 211-219
   environmental survey of radiation
      levels in, 214
   export control analytical center in,
      215
   history of, 212
   Institute of Technical Physics, 219
   intelligence activity suspicions of
      security forces in, 213
   ISTC projects in, 213
   peaceful uses of nuclear explosions
      program developed in, 212
   population growth in, 218
   safety on the streets of, 218
   salary delays in, 213
   small business development fund
      in, 217
   tax exemptions for, 216
   tax haven for Russian firms in, 216
   training program for small business
      in, 217
   test site (proposed) for detecting
      nuclear tests to be located in,
      214
Soros, George, International Science
   Foundation of, 96
Soviet Union
   decline of favored positions of
      defense scientists of, 37-38
   engineering skills in
      industrialization of, 274
   old-line managers of, 57
   technology legacy of, xvii, 37-38
State Research Centers (*see* State
   Scientific Centers)
State Scientific Centers
   concept of, 45-46
   debt growth in, 47
   debt swapping by, 47

decline in resources for, 36-37
establishment of, 45-48
financial support by Ministry of
   Science and Technology for,
   47-48
Kurchatov Institute as initiator of
   concept of, 46
list of, 279-282
programs of, xv
special privileges of, 48
technological potential of, 48
Subsidies for research and
   development, importance of, 57
Sun Shine Industrial Company (Hong
   Kong) as recruiter of weapon
   scientists, 147

T

Tax evasion
   barter as mechanism for, 134
   bribery as method of, 130
   collection of unpaid taxes due to,
      129
   Cyprus as haven for, 87
   Johnson and Johnson as target for,
      132
   research institute approaches to,
      87-88
   scope of, 130
Tax policy
   changes proposed in, 94
   complaints over, xv
   definition of research institute for
      tax purposes, 127
   different types of taxes, 127
   enforcement laxities on taxation of
      imports, 17
   tax benefits for businesses in
      Snezhinsk, 216
   tax code ambiguities, 116
   tax exemptions for aluminum
      industry, 128
   tax exemptions for research, 99,
      127

tax exemptions for science cities, 178

tax exemptions for technical assistance, 97, 117, 132

tax havens for nuclear cities, 128

tax holiday for emerging businesses, 128

taxes on foreign residents in Russia, 131

tax on sales below costs, 136

tax rate reduction, 128

Technical universities
alumni assistance in finding contracts for, 160
avoidance of military draft by enrollment in, 160
career switching of graduates of, 161
deterioration of capabilities of, 160
enrollment increase in graduate engineering courses of, 161
income stream searches by, 159
linkages to military organizations of, 159
training of cadres for industry by, 160
two-track tuition system of, 160

Technology (*see also* dual-use technologies and intellectual property rights)
import of, xi
ownership of, xi

Technology hunters in Russia, ix

Technology policy
financial shortfalls for, 259
Ministry of Science and Technology proposal for, 258
protecting financial resources allocated for, 261-262
targetting selected technologies as component of, 262-263
technology fund (proposed) related to, 260-261
western support for Russian efforts to develop a, 259

Tetra (Russian firm), ix-xii

Titanium
golf clubs constructed from, 74-75
shovels constructed from, 24
value added through processing of ingots from, 61, 75

Topol M missile, 69

Trade and Development Agency, feasibility studies of technology investments, 238

U

United Technology Corporation (a corporation including Pratt-Whitney, Carrier, Hamilton Standard, and Otis Elevator)
cooperative research projects of, 241
joint ventures of, 241
product sales of, 241
technology sharing by, 241

U.S. Agency for International Development (USAID), support of activities of small businesses, 240

U.S. Chamber of Commerce, criticism of government programs by, 239

U.S. Civilian Research and Development Foundation, 240, 290-291

U.S. Industry Coalition
commercialized technologies of, 286-287
support of Initiatives for Proliferation Prevention program by, 229

U.S.-Russia Investment Fund, 237

V

Vector (Koltsovo)
contracts with foreign countries of, 54

openness of facilities of, 53
production of pharmaceutical
products by, 53-54
Velikhov, Yevgeny
Relcom Internet company
established by, 52
Rosshelf oil exploration company
led by, 52
State Scientific Center concept
developed by, 46
Venture capital, international sources
of, 94
Verkhne Saldinsky Manufacturing
Products Organization,
titanium ingot production, 75
Virtual economy of Russia, 13-14
Vyshinsky, Viktor, engineer-
entrepreneur, 56

W

World Trade Organization, Russian
accession to, 118

Y

Yarigin, Gennady, scientist-
entrepreneur, 33-35

Z

Zarechny (science city in Sverdlovsk
region)
access to, 209
autonomy of, 195
Beloyarsk nuclear power station in,
205-206
developments in, 205-211
exchanges of high school students
from, 210
gold discovery in, 28
inert gas production in, 207
Institute of Power Engineering
affiliate in, 207
law and order in, 210
noncash payments for budget of
city of, 13
nuclear power capability expansion
in, 206
production (proposed) of rare
earth metals, 209
region-wide development plans
developed in, 208-209
social services in, 210
small firm failures in, 208
youth disinterest in science in, 211
technopolis concept of, 208
Zhukovsky (science city in Moscow
region), 179